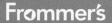

Montreal
day BY day®

4th Edition

by Leslie Brokaw and Erin Trahan

FrommerMedia LLC

Contents

Published by:

Frommer Media LLC

Copyright © 2020 FrommerMedia LLC, New York, NY. All rights
reserved. No part of this publication may be reproduced, stored in a
retrieval system or transmitted in any form or by any means, electronic,
mechanical, photocopying, recording, scanning or otherwise, except
as permitted under Sections 107 or 108 of the 1976 United States
Copyright Act, without the prior written permission of the Publisher.
Requests to the Publisher for permission should be addressed to
Support@FrommerMedia.com.

ISBN: 978-1-628-87491-4 (paper); 978-1-628-87492-1 (ebk)

Editorial Director: Pauline Frommer
Development Editor: Alexis Lipsitz Flippin
Production Editor: Kelly Dobbs Henthorne
Photo Editor: Meghan Lamb
Assistant Photo Editor: Phil Vinke
Photo Intern: Henry Lin-David
Cartographer: Liz Puhl
Indexer: Kelly Dobbs Henthorne

Front cover photos, left to right: Streets in Old Montréal. ProDesign
studio. Fresh bagels. Elena Elisseeva. Montréal Fine Arts Museum.
Benoit Daoust / Shutterstock.com.

Back cover photo: Basilique Notre-Dame de Montréal. Wangkun Jia.

For information on our other products and services, please go to
Frommers.com.

Frommer's also publishes its books in a variety of electronic formats.
Some content that appears in print may not be available in electronic
formats.

Manufactured in China

5 4 3 2 1

About This Guide

Organizing your time. That's what this guide is all about.

Other guides give you long lists of things to see and do and then expect you to fit the pieces together. The Day by Day guides are different. These guides tell you the best of everything, and then they show you how to see it *in the smartest, most time-efficient way*. Our authors have designed detailed itineraries organized by time, neighborhood, or special interest. And each tour comes with a bulleted map that takes you from stop to stop.

Hoping to see the sun set from the city's giant Ferris wheel, listen to live jazz with the locals in a Montréal jazz club, or twirl under the winter stars on an ice rink in Vieux-Montréal? Planning to spend time exploring Montréal's historic architecture, discovering new neighborhoods, visiting world-class museums, and joining the city at play in its green parks and on the quays of Vieux-Port? Whatever your interest or schedule, the Day by Day guides give you the smartest routes to follow. Not only do we take you to the top attractions, hotels, and restaurants, but we also help you access those special moments that locals get to experience—those "finds" that turn tourists into travelers.

The Day by Days are also your top choice if you're looking for one complete guide for all your travel needs. The best hotels and restaurants for every budget, the greatest shopping values, the wildest nightlife—it's all here.

Why should you trust our judgment? Because our authors personally visit each place they write about. They're an independent lot who say what they think and would never include places they wouldn't recommend to their best friends. They're also open to suggestions from readers. If you'd like to contact them, please send your comments our way at feedback@frommers.com, and we'll pass them on.

Enjoy your Day by Day guide—the most helpful travel companion you can buy. And have the trip of a lifetime.

About the Authors

Leslie Brokaw has co-authored Frommer's guides since 2006, including the newest *Frommer's Montréal Day by Day*, *Frommer's Boston Day by Day*, and *Frommer's New England*. She is a contributing editor for *MIT Sloan Management Review* and teaches at Emerson College, in Boston. She resides in the Boston metropolitan area.

Erin Trahan is an arts reporter, critic, and educator specializing in independent film. She has been a regular contributor to WBUR (Boston's NPR news station) and the ARTery since 2013 and has also written for *The Boston Globe*, *MovieMaker Magazine*, *Women's Review of Books*, and *The Independent*, where she served as editor from 2009 to 2016. As faculty at Emerson College, she teaches a course on film and TV journalism. She has co-authored nine Frommer's guides (on Montréal, Quebec City, Boston, and their surrounds) and has created adult education classes that travel to film festivals, including to Montréal. As a keen believer in public dialogue, she often moderates post-film panels and leads on-stage interviews with directors. On her more literary days, she writes essays and poems and for many years read poetry submissions for AGNI. She earned a BA from the University of Notre Dame and an MFA in poetry from Bennington College. She lives with her family on Boston's North Shore. If you run into her one day, she'll show you where she grew up in Michigan by pointing to the back of her hand.

An Additional Note

Please be advised that travel information is subject to change at any time—and this is especially true of prices. We therefore suggest that you write or call ahead for confirmation when making your travel plans. The authors, editors, and publisher cannot be held responsible for the experiences of readers while traveling. Your safety is important to us, however, so we encourage you to stay alert and be aware of your surroundings.

Star Ratings, Icons & Abbreviations

Every hotel, restaurant, and attraction listing in this guide has been ranked for quality, value, service, amenities, and special features using a **star-rating system.** Hotels, restaurants, attractions, shopping, and nightlife are rated on a scale of zero stars (recommended) to three stars (exceptional). In addition to the star-rating system, we use a **kids icon** to point out the best bets for families. Within each tour, we recommend cafes, bars, or restaurants where you can take a break. Each of these stops appears in a shaded box marked with a coffee-cup-shaped bullet ☕.

A Note on Prices

In the "Take a Break" and "Best Bets" sections of this book, we have used a system of dollar signs to show a range of costs for 1 night in a hotel (the price of a double-occupancy room) or the cost of an entree at a restaurant. Use the following table to decipher the dollar signs:

Cost	Hotels	Restaurants
$	under $100	under $10
$$	$100–$200	$10–$200
$$$	$200–$300	$20–$30
$$$	$300–$400	$30–$40
$$$$	over $400	over $40

Frommers.com

Now that you have this guidebook to help you plan a great trip, visit our website at **www.frommers.com** for additional travel information on more than 3,600 destinations. We update features regularly to give you instant access to the most current trip-planning information available. At Frommers.com, you'll find scoops on the best airfares, lodging rates, and car rental bargains. You can even book your travel online through our reliable travel booking partners. Other popular features include:

- Online updates of our most popular guidebooks
- Vacation sweepstakes and contest giveaways
- Newsletters highlighting the hottest travel trends
- Online travel message boards with featured travel discussions

An Invitation to the Reader

In researching this book, we discovered many wonderful places—hotels, restaurants, shops, and more. We're sure you'll find others. Please tell us about them, so we can share the information with your fellow travelers in upcoming editions. If you were disappointed with a recommendation, we'd love to know that, too. Please write to: Support@FrommerMedia.com.

14 Favorite
Moments

14 Favorite **Moments**

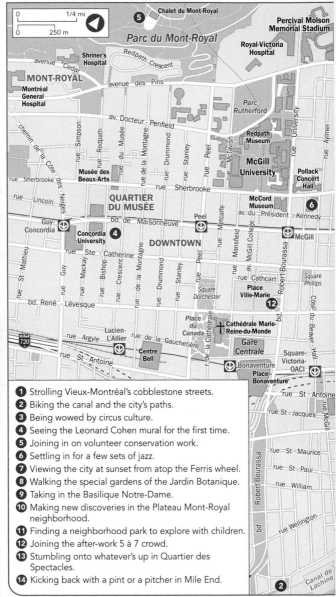

1 Strolling Vieux-Montréal's cobblestone streets.
2 Biking the canal and the city's paths.
3 Being wowed by circus culture.
4 Seeing the Leonard Cohen mural for the first time.
5 Joining in on volunteer conservation work.
6 Settling in for a few sets of jazz.
7 Viewing the city at sunset from atop the Ferris wheel.
8 Walking the special gardens of the Jardin Botanique.
9 Taking in the Basilique Notre-Dame.
10 Making new discoveries in the Plateau Mont-Royal neighborhood.
11 Finding a neighborhood park to explore with children.
12 Joining the after-work 5 à 7 crowd.
13 Stumbling onto whatever's up in Quartier des Spectacles.
14 Kicking back with a pint or a pitcher in Mile End.

Previous page: Rue Saint-Paul and rue Saint-Vincent in Vieux-Montreal.

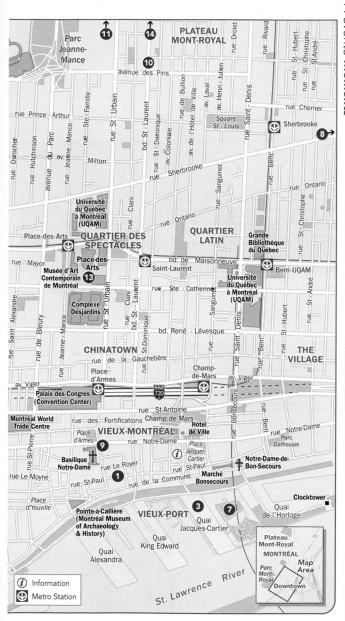

An enormous joie de vivre pervades Montréal. It's the largest city of the Québec province and the most French region of North America. Modern in every regard, Montréal has a beautifully preserved historic district dating back to its founding in 1642, skyscrapers in unexpected shapes and colors, and sprawling neighborhoods of artists' lofts, boutiques, and cafes. Snowy and cold a good 8 months of the year, the city has a calendar packed with festivals and other events that bring out natives and guests in every season. Here are 14 favorite moments in taking in this humming, bilingual metropolis.

Montréal's main square, Place Jacques-Cartier, by night.

❶ Strolling Vieux-Montréal's cobblestone streets. Beautifully preserved squares and repurposed warehouse buildings in this oldest section of the city transport visitors to the 18th century. (*Vieux-Montréal* translates to Old Montréal, and we use both phrases interchangeably.) In summer, find a cafe table on the Place Jacques-Cartier, the main square. In winter, lace up rental ice skates and twirl while the snow gently falls. Vieux-Montréal gloriously blends its old-world feel with creative modernity. *See p 78.*

❷ Biking the canal and the city's paths. Lachine Canal was inaugurated in 1824 so that ships could bypass the Lachine Rapids on the way to the Great Lakes. Redevelopment of the canal banks and environmental reclamation to clean up heavy industrial contamination created a popular spot for boating and biking. Bike paths on both sides pass 19th-century industrial buildings

that now house high-end apartments. Meanwhile, the city boasts an expanding network of more than 645km (400 miles) of bike paths for commuting and relaxing. Bikes are available at rental shops and from the BIXI short-term rental kiosks around the city. *See p 38 and p 164.*

❸ Being wowed by circus culture. The home base of the world-famous Cirque du Soleil is in Montréal, and the troupe usually sets up tents each spring on the quays (piers) of

Riding across the Lachine Canal.

An outdoor event at the popular Cirque Festival.

Vieux-Port, the Old Port district. Don't pass up the chance to see Cirque's magical, mysterious show, or to take in other circus events on the calendar around the city. *See p 121.*

❹ **Seeing the Leonard Cohen mural for the first time.** Montréal revels in public art, from street-level sculptures to lighting projections on buildings. Murals have become synonymous with this city, too, and can be found at nearly every turn. But this particular one, of the debonair musician towering over rue Crescent, 15 stories tall, takes our breath away. *See p 27.*

❺ **Joining in on volunteer conservation work.** Saturday mornings atop Mont Royal, the group Les amis de la montagne (Friends of the Mountain) invites all comers to help with environmental stewardship. Activities include inventorying the eggs of Monarch butterflies. *See p 57.*

❻ **Settling in for a few sets of jazz.** New Orleans may be the birthplace of jazz, but the music style in all its forms is widely embraced in Montréal. The monster Festival International de Jazz de Montréal celebrated its 40th year in 2019 and is an annual highlight for 11 days in June and July. Finding good jazz is easy year-round, too, at venues such as Maison du Jazz. *See p 117 and p 118.*

❼ **Viewing the city at sunset from atop the Ferris wheel.** The enormous Grande Roue de Montréal Ferris wheel now dominates the city's skyline in Vieux-Port. It's a pricey ticket, but hard to resist at sunset. If you're especially lucky, as

Throngs of fans descend upon Montréal for July's Festival International de Jazz.

The city's marvelous Jardin Botanique.

we were, you can hear music from the adjacent Cirque du Soleil tents and the whizz of the nearby MTL Zipline during your ride—making it an especially Montréal-specific experience. *See p 44.*

8 Walking the special gardens of the Jardin Botanique. The city's marvelous botanical garden spreads across 75 hectares (185 acres) and is a fragrant oasis 12 months a year. In spring, it's abloom in lilacs, tulips, and glorious crabapple trees. Year-round greenhouses are home to orchids, vanilla plants, and rainforest flora, while specialty areas such as the wooded First Nations Garden provide private spots to tuck away. *See p 53.*

9 Taking in the Basilique Notre-Dame. So ornate and breathtaking is this basilica that the church's Protestant architect converted to Catholicism. An evening light show, "Aura," drapes the space in a new persona, and is by turns bombastic, apocalyptic, night-clubby, and beautiful. *See p 9.*

10 Making new discoveries in the Plateau Mont-Royal neighborhood. Whether you hope to track down one of the city's great restaurants (obscured by scruffy surroundings as often as not) or stumble onto an exhibition of young Québécois artists,

you'll want to head to the city's main drags of boulevard St-Laurent (known to all as "the Main") and rue St-Denis. This is where you'll find the city at play—so join in. A directory of events and shops, from thrift stores and fashion boutiques to bakeries, nightclubs, and galleries, is online at www.boulevardsaintlaurent.com. *See p 80.*

11 Finding a neighborhood park to explore with children. Montréal's residential neighborhoods, such as the Plateau, Mile End, and Outremont, west of Mile End, all have well-maintained parks. Many have playgrounds that provide a bilingual oasis for children who are maxed out from sightseeing. *See p 36.*

12 Joining the after-work 5 à 7 crowd. After-work get-togethers are called cinq à sept (say "sank ah set," French for "five to seven"), and many bars have bargain drinks and appetizers. *See p 109.*

13 Stumbling onto whatever's up in Quartier des Spectacles. The city's former red-light district now hums with a different kind of cultural activity. There's a ton going on inside the grand buildings that host world-class museums, orchestras, and dance companies, but things are busy outside on the sidewalks, too. Depending on the time of year, you may find singing swings, chess boards with pieces the size of toddlers, or the international jazz festival in joyous full throttle. *See p 78.*

14 Kicking back with a pint or a pitcher in Mile End. There are dozens of places to sample craft beer in the city, but Dieu du Ciel is a longtime favorite. It's had the corner on local microbrews since 1998 (literally, it's on the corner of Ave. Laurier ouest and rue Clark), so grab a patio seat, then order up a pale ale along with shareable snacks like charcuterie or pretzels and let an afternoon or evening float by. *See p 111.* ●

1 The Best Full-Day Tours

The Best in One Day

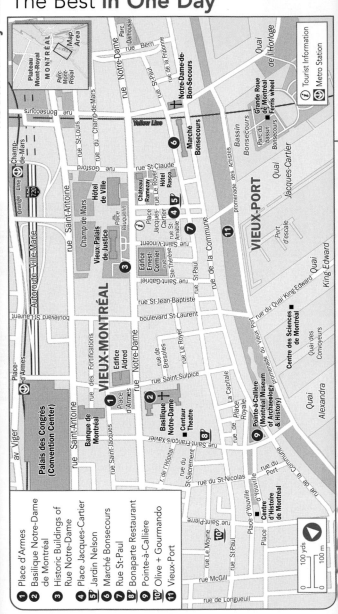

Place Mont-Royal
MONTRÉAL
Parc Mont-Royal

Map Area

ⓘ Tourist Information
Ⓜ Metro Station

1 Place d'Armes
2 Basilique Notre-Dame de Montréal
3 Historic Buildings of Rue Notre-Dame
4 Place Jacques-Cartier
5 Jardin Nelson
6 Marché Bonsecours
7 Rue St-Paul
8 Bonaparte Restaurant
9 Pointe-à-Callière
10 Olive + Gourmando
11 Vieux-Port

Previous page: Grand Roue de Montréal Ferris wheel.

Center your first day in cobblestoned Vieux-Montréal (Old Montréal) around the sites and atmosphere of the oldest and most historic part of the city. Montréal was born here in 1642, at Pointe-à-Callière by the St. Lawrence River, and this neighborhood's architectural heritage has been substantially preserved. Restored 18th- and 19th-century structures now hold shops, boutique hotels, galleries, cafes, bars, and apartments. The area's southern boundary is Vieux-Port (Old Port), a waterfront promenade that provides welcome breathing room for walkers, cyclists, and picnickers. Vieux-Montréal extends north to rue St-Antoine, once the "Wall Street" of Québec. START: **Take the Métro to the Place-d'Armes station.**

Montréal's lovely pedestrian plaza, Place d'Armes, is surrounded by architecture spanning 4 centuries.

❶ Place d'Armes. Much of the foot traffic of Vieux-Montréal passes through this small, handsome plaza. At its center is a monument to city founder Paul de Chomedey, Sieur de Maisonneuve (1612–76). It marks the spot where settlers defeated Iroquois warriors in bloody hand-to-hand fighting, with de Maisonneuve himself locked in combat with the Iroquois chief. De Maisonneuve won and lived here another 23 years. The buildings that surround the plaza are representative of Montréal's architectural growth over the years: at the far southwestern corner is a **Sulpician residence** of the 17th century; at the northern and southern ends are the **Banque de Montréal** (p 71) and **Basilique Notre-Dame** of the 19th century (**❷**, below); and on the east side is the Art Deco **Edifice Aldred** of the 20th century. The 23-story Aldred was built in 1931 and clearly resembles New York's Empire State Building, which was completed the same year. *Intersection of rues Notre-Dame and St-Sulpice.*

❷ ★★★ Basilique Notre-Dame de Montréal. This magnificent structure was designed in 1824 by James O'Donnell, an Irish-American Protestant architect who was so profoundly moved by the experience that he converted to Catholicism. The impact is understandable. Of Montréal's hundreds of churches, Notre-Dame has the most stunning

The stunning Basilique Notre-Dame de Montréal.

interior, with a wealth of exquisite details, including carved rare woods that have been delicately gilded and painted, a vaulted ceiling (studded with 24k gold stars), a 12-ton bell (among the largest in North America), and Limoges stained-glass windows (depicting moments from the city's history). O'Donnell bucked a trend toward neoclassicism when he designed this Gothic Revival masterpiece, whose exterior is reminiscent of Notre-Dame in Paris. Consider coming back at night for the **light show, "Aura"** (p 6), which gives the space a wild new look. Twenty-minute guided tours of the basilica are included with the entrance fee; a more expansive 60-minute tour is also available. ⏱ *30 min. 110 rue Notre-Dame ouest. www.basilique nddm.org.* ☎ *514/842-2925. Basilica admission C$8 adults, C$5 children 7–17, free for 6 and under and for those attending services. Daily at least 8am–4pm. Aura light show Mon–Sat, 1–3 shows a night; check website for times, which vary by month. Aura admission C$25 adults, with discounts for seniors, students, children, and families, free for children 5 and under. Métro: Place-d'Armes.*

❸ Historic Buildings of Rue Notre-Dame. Walk east on rue Notre-Dame, one of the grand streets of the old city and home to the Montréal government. (**Important navigational note:** Street numbers will get lower as you approach boulevard St-Laurent, which is the north-south thoroughfare that divides Montréal into its east and west halves. Numbers will start to rise again as you move onto the eastern side of rue Notre-Dame.) One block after Place d'Armes is **Palais de Justice,** on your left at 1 Notre-Dame est. The courthouse was built in the 1970s and took over operations from the **Vieux Palais de Justice** two

The impressive Hôtel de Ville, Montréal's old City Hall, with a restored copper roof.

blocks farther east, at 155 rue Notre-Dame est. That courthouse was completed in 1856, with the dome and the top floor added in 1891. (You'll be able to spot the differences.) The next building, at 275 rue Notre-Dame est, is the turreted **Hôtel de Ville** (City Hall). This ornate building has been Montréal's official City Hall since 1878. It was here, in 1967, that French president Charles de Gaulle delighted Québec separatists by shouting from the balcony, "Vive le Québec libre!" (Long live free Québec!) Renovations begun here in spring 2019 will close the building to the public until projected completion in summer 2021. Across the street, at 280 rue Notre-Dame est, is **Château Ramezay**, built in 1705 as a grand home to the city's royal French governors. It's now a museum (p 71). A more modern landmark will come into view, too: Looking farther east on rue Notre-Dame, you'll see the Molson beer factory in the distance. *Rue Notre-Dame from Place d'Armes to rue Bonsecours.*

④ ★★ Place Jacques-Cartier. The old city's main pedestrian plaza first opened in 1804 as a marketplace, and today it's a shopping and eating magnet for visitors year-round. In summer, performers fill the air with music and outdoor cafes serve as perches for people-watching. The 17th-century houses that line the wide promenade have

Re-enacting the New France period in Old Montréal.

A stroll along Place Jacques-Cartier in Vieux-Montréal.

steeply pitched roofs designed to shed heavy winter snows and small windows with double casements that let in light while keeping out wintry breezes. *If you're traveling with kids*, you may want to head straight from here to the attractions of the Old Port ([#11]), at the southern end of this plaza. *Btw. rues Notre-Dame and de la Commune.*

Right in Place Jacques-Cartier is **⑤ Jardin Nelson.** It has a porch adjacent to the plaza, but the special spot is its appealing tree-shaded garden court. Here, live jazz is presented every afternoon and evening. A gigantic 24-page menu runs from tacos and tartares to crepes and pizzas. Jardin Nelson is open mid-April through October and closed the rest of the year, and on busy nights it keeps things going until 1am. *407 Place Jacques-Cartier. www.jardin nelson.com.* ☎ *514/861-5731. $$.*

⑥ ★ Marché Bonsecours. Built in 1847 and first used as the Parliament of United Canada, Bonsecours is now home to restaurants, art galleries, and boutiques featuring Québécois products. Its massive dome served as a landmark for seafarers sailing into the harbor. Today the dome is lit at night. *350 rue St-Paul est (at the foot of rue St-Claude). www.marchebonsecours.qc.ca.* ☎ *514/872-7730. Free admission. Daily 10am–6pm, with extended hours in summer. Métro: Champ-de-Mars.*

Marché Bonsecours and the turreted Hôtel de Ville by night.

⑦ ★★★ kids Rue St-Paul. Stroll and take in this main walking street of Vieux-Montréal, lined on both sides with shops, bistros, and bars. Many decent art galleries have sprung up alongside the loud souvenir shops, and some recommended restaurants are here, too (see chapter 5). If you're done walking, head south a few blocks to the sights of the Old Port ⑫. ⓘ *1 hr. Métro: Champ-de-Mars.*

Looking to treat yourself? At the elegant **⑧ Bonaparte Restaurant,** adroit service pairs with high-style French cuisine. Highlights include Dover sole filet with meunière herbs and pine nuts. The two-course-plus-coffee business lunch (C$17–C$29) offers the best deal. The restaurant is inside the 30-room Hôtel Bonaparte, (p 132). *447 rue St-François-Xavier. www.restaurantbonaparte.com.* ☎ *514/844-4368. $$.*

⑨ ★★★ kids Pointe-à-Callière. A first visit to Montréal should include a stop at this continually modernized Archaeology and History Complex. Evidence of the area's many inhabitants—from Québec's earliest native tribes to French trappers to Scottish merchants—was unearthed during archaeological digs here, the site of Montréal's original colony. Visitors tour the exposed ruins of the earlier city by winding through a subterranean complex. ⓘ *1½ hr. 350 Place Royale. www.pacmuseum.qc.ca.* ☎ *514/872-9150. Admission C$22 adults, with discounts for seniors, students, children, and families, free for children 4 and under. June to mid-Oct daily 10am–6pm weekdays, 11am–6pm weekends; mid-Oct to May Tues–Fri 10am–5pm, Sat–Sun 11am–5pm. Métro: Place-d'Armes.*

Canada Day celebration at Vieux-Port.

Montréal's historic rue St-Paul is home to galleries, shops, restaurants, and bars.

Extremely popular, the earthy bakery/café **10** Olive + Gourmando is the real deal: It offers up croissants, scones, and hearty fare such as Cuban sandwiches and its Cha-Cha-Chia bowl with berry chia pudding, quinoa, and nut butter muesli. *351 rue St-Paul ouest.* ☎ *514/350-1083. www.oliveetgourmando.com. $.*

11 ★★★ **kids** Vieux-Port. Montréal's Old Port has been central to its commercial and economic status over the last 200 years. Now the converted waterfront and its piers (*quays* in French) are a playground year-round. The gigantic **Grande Roue de Montréal Ferris wheel** was installed here in 2017 and operates year-round. From June to September, **a miniature electric train** scoots around the area (board near the Ferris wheel). The **urban zipline** circuit is Canada's first. **Cruise companies** offer daytime trips from here along the St. Lawrence (p 143, bullet 10). **Centre des Sciences de Montréal**, the popular children's science museum, includes an onsite IMAX Telus theater (p 45, bullet 3). In cold months, a spacious **ice skating rink** becomes the focal point. ⏱ *1 hr. or more. www.oldportofmontreal. com.* ☎ *800/971-7678 or 514/496-7678. La Grande Roue C$25 adults, C$20 kids 3–17 and seniors, C$63 family of four. Mini train rides C$5. Zipline $C20. Ice skating C$7 adults, C$5 children 6–12, free 5 and under; skate rentals available. Métro: Champ-de-Mars, Place-d'Armes, or Square-Victoria-OACI.*

Archaeology Adventure in Pointe-à-Calliére.

The Best **in Two Days**

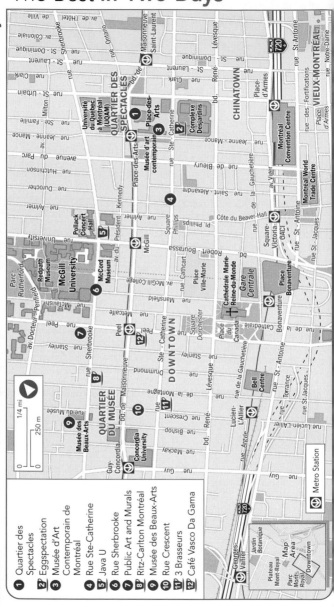

1 Quartier des Spectacles
2 Eggspectation
3 Musée d'Art Contemporain de Montréal
4 Rue Ste-Catherine
5 Java U
6 Rue Sherbrooke
7 Public Art and Murals
8 Ritz-Carlton Montréal
9 Musée des Beaux-Arts
10 Rue Crescent
11 3 Brasseurs
12 Café Vasco Da Gama

Metro Station

Spend day two in Montréal's arts and business districts, after soaking in the sights and tastes of the oldest section of the city on day one. The core of downtown Montréal isn't as densely packed as those of other major cities in North America, and it's deceptively large. Here you'll find the bustle and energy of a city at work and some of Montréal's grand promenades and cultural offerings. START: **Place des Arts station, and walk north 2 blocks on rue University to rue Sherbrooke.**

Inside the Place des Arts—Canada's top cultural complex.

① ★★ Quartier des Spectacles. This newly vibrant neighborhood (*quartier*) is home to the **Place des Arts** (p 121) plaza, site of the city's large concert halls, restaurants, and the **Musée d'Art Contemporain de Montréal (②)**. It's the city's cultural heart—where people flock for music concerts, opera, and many of Montréal's popular outdoor festivals. In April and May, an interactive installation of swings, called 21 Balançoires (21 Swings), lights up and plays music, delighting visitors of all ages. In the warm months also look for life-size chess boards and fountains of dancing waters. Facing the plaza on its southern side is one of the city's glitziest malls, **Complexe Desjardins**, at 150 rue Ste-Catherine ouest. Peek in to see one of the central access points to Montréal's Underground City of connected hallways, malls, and subway

entrances. 🕐 *15 min. 175 rue Ste-Catherine ouest. www.quartierdes spectacles.com. Métro: Place des Arts.*

② Eggspectation Don't be put off by the goofy name. The breakfast-centric restaurant, part of small chain, delivers. Maybe a breakfast poutine? Or one of the nine versions of eggs Benedict? *190 rue Ste-Catherine ouest.* 📞 *514/288-6448. www.eggspectation.com. $.*

③ ★★ Musée d'Art Contemporain de Montréal. The city's contemporary art museum, which goes by the acronym MAC, revels in the eclectic. Exhibitions include video installations, digital robotic arts, and studio glass creations. A major C$44-million expansion and renovation is in the offing, which will double the exhibition space and create a glamorous new facade. It's set for completion in 2021. 🕐 *1 hr.*

"L'Œil et l'Esprit" exhibit from the Musée d'Art Contemporain de Montréal.

Rue Ste-Catherine is one of the Montré-al's prime thoroughfares for shopping.

185 rue Ste-Catherine ouest. www. macm.org. ☎ *514/847-6226. Admission C$15 adults, with discounts for students and seniors; free for children 12 and under; half-price admission Wed 5–9pm. Tues 11am–6pm; Wed–Fri 11am–9pm; Sat–Sun 10am–6pm (check website for holiday schedules). Métro: Place des Arts.*

❹ ★ **Rue Ste-Catherine.** This is one of the city's big shopping streets, a mix of Canadian department stores, international brands, and local businesses. From Place des Arts, stroll 5 minutes west to 585 rue Ste-Catherine ouest, across from the small green park called

Square Phillips. Here you'll find **La Baie**—"the Bay"—successor to the famous fur-trapping firm Hudson's Bay Co., founded in the 17th century. Also abutting the park is **Henry Birks et Fils**, a preeminent jeweler since 1879. It opened an adjoining hotel in 2018, and its **Brasserie Henri** (p 53) is a posh stop for a bite. Note that a large section of Ste-Catherine is under construction until at least the end of 2020, in a project that will ultimately widen the sidewalks. Also note that Ste-Catherine has a smattering of adult strip clubs and sex shops right alongside the family-friendly fare; the street's mixed use is a Montréal signature. Just past Square Phillips, take a look at **Cathédrale Christ Church**, at 635 rue Ste-Catherine ouest (www. montrealcathedral.ca; ☎ 514/843-6577). Built from 1856 to 1859, this neo-Gothic building stands in glorious contrast to the city's downtown skyscrapers. It is the seat of the Anglican bishop of Montréal, and has a garden modeled on a medieval European cloister. It offers a Sunday 10am Sung Eucharist and 4pm Choral Evensong and a Saturday 4:30pm concert series, as well as active outreach to young adults

The neo-Gothic Cathédrale Christ Church.

and the LGBTQ+ community. ⏱ *15 min. for walking and a quick visit to the church. From here, turn north onto boulevard Robert-Bourassa to rue Sherbrooke. Metro: McGill.*

At the corner of rues Union and Sherbrooke, an outpost of the cheery **5** **Java U,** a local food chain, serves breakfast sandwiches, wraps, pastries, and, of course, coffee. *626 rue Sherbrooke. www.java-u.com.* ☎ *514/286-1991. $.*

6 ★★ kids **Rue Sherbrooke**

The broad boulevard of rue Sherbrooke is the main artery of what's known as Montréal's "Golden Square Mile." This is where the city's most luxurious residences of the 19th and early 20th centuries were located, and where the vast majority of the country's wealthiest citizens made their home—for a period of time, 79 families who lived in this neighborhood controlled 80% of Canada's wealth. Today, it's the city's grand promenade, still thick with former mansions, ritzy hotels, high-end boutiques, and special museums. The main campus of Canada's most

Canada's prestigious McGill University.

prestigious school, **McGill University**, is here, on the north side of Sherbrooke. (It has an expanse of lawn that's excellent for kids who want to run around.) Also in this section of the street, at 690 rue Sherbrooke ouest, is **Musée McCord,** a museum of Canadian history that has a contemporary, playful zest. Its edgy special exhibits make it especially appealing. There's an excellent **museum boutique** with books, toys, and made-in-Montréal crafts, and a lunchtime **bistro**. Outside is a larger-than-life Inukshuk stone figure by Jusipi Nalukturuk—the Inuit statues are icons of Canada. See p 91 for more details. Farther along the street, as you approach the **Musée des Beaux-Arts (9)**, look for #1195, Maison Louis-Joseph Forget. This former residence was completed in 1884 and features a cut-stone facade and mansard roof. It's now a historic monument. ⏱ *30 min. for Musée McCord. www.musee-mccord.qc.ca.* ☎ *514/861-6701. Admission C$19 adults, with discounts for seniors, students, and families; free for children 12 and under and to everyone on Wed after 5pm and first*

Palatial buildings abound along rue Sherbrooke—many were once residences of Montréal's wealthiest citizens.

Sun of the month. Tues, Thurs, Fri 10am–6pm; Wed 10am–9pm, Sat–Sun 10am–5pm. Métro: McGill.

❼ ★★★ Public Art and Murals. A block and a half south of Sherbrooke on McGill is the large permanent sculpture *The Illuminated Crowd*, by Raymond Mason. It captures the faces of a life-size crowd of figures in an array of feeling: hope, irritation, fear. It's worth taking a short detour for. At the corner of rues Sherbrooke and Peel, find Paul Lancz's white marble sculpture of a mother and child. You'll see other examples of art-work right on the streets all throughout the city, including Jim Dine's 1999 *Twin 6' Hearts* of painted bronze at the entrance **Musée des Beaux-Arts ❾**.

Feeling peckish? Dressed nicely? Consider taking afternoon tea at the **❽ Ritz-Carlton Montréal.** There are seatings at 12:30pm and 3:30 every day. Price is C$36 per person, with options for cham-pagne add-ons. ⏱ 1½ hr. 1228 rue Sherbrooke ouest. www.ritzmontreal. com. ☎ 514/842-4212.

❾ ★★★ kids Musée des Beaux-Arts. Montréal's grand Museum of Fine Arts, the city's most prominent museum, has a spectacu-lar permanent collection, including works by prominent French-Cana-dian landscape watercolorist Marc-Aurèle Fortin (1888–1970) and, in the ultramodern Jean-Noël Desmarais Pavilion, works by Old European masters and modern paintings by Picasso and Miró. But many visitors come for the temporary exhibitions, which can be dazzling. Past high-lights have included the glassworks of Dale Chihuly and the treasures of Catherine the Great, including her spectacular coronation coach. Enter through the modern annex on the

The Musée des Beaux-Arts is known for its European and Canadian paintings.

south side of rue Sherbrooke. It is connected by an underground tun-nel (which doubles as a gallery) to the original stately Beaux Arts building (1912) on the north side of the street, which was Canada's first building designed specifically for the visual arts. The adjacent church is a 2011 addition to the museum, and the nave of the church, which has Tiffany windows, has been con-verted into a concert space, Bour-gie Hall. Another new wing, the modern Michal and Renata Horn-stein Pavilion for Peace, opened in 2016 and has its own front door at 2075 rue Bishop, around the corner. ⏱ 2 hr. 1380 rue Sherbrooke ouest. www.mmfa.qc.ca. ☎ 514/285-2000 or ☎ 800/899-6873. Admission C$24 adults 31 and over, C$16 ages 21–30, free for everyone under 21. Wed 5–9pm C$12 for major exhibit only. Tues–Sun 10am–5pm plus Wed until 9pm. Also open Mon 10am–5pm July-Aug. Métro: Guy-Concordia.

❿ ★ Rue Crescent. This the often-raucous party street of down-town. A magnificent mural of favor-ite son Leonard Cohen—singer, poet, author—was inaugurated in 2017 and now overlooks the pro-ceedings. Crescent's most northern end has a few boutiques and jewel-ers, but its three blocks are best known for their gumbo of terraced bars and dance clubs and inexpen-sive pizza and falafel joints. **Sir**

Popular rue Crescent, home to shops and restaurants, is a central part of downtown Montréal's nightlife.

Winston Churchill Pub (no. 1459) and **Thursday's** (no. 1449) are among the venues that draw hundreds on warm days and nights, many with seasonal alfresco decks on the street. Festivities spill over onto nearby streets, with both **Maison du Jazz** (2060 rue Aylmer; www.houseofjazz.ca; ☎ 514/842-8656) and **Upstairs Jazz Bar & Grill** (1254 rue Mackay; www.upstairsjazz.com; ☎ 514/931-6808) presenting great music options. ⓧ *At least 30 min. See chapter 6 for bar and music venue details. Métro: Peel.*

If you have to eat right now, the dependable chain ⑪ **3 Brasseurs** has a location at the corner of rues Crescent and Ste-Catherine. It features burgers, flammekueche

pizzas, and such, and is open daily from 11am to at least midnight. Downtown offers lots of other options both fancy and casual, and right in between a few blocks from Crescent is ⑫ **Café Vasco Da Gama,** a sleek, high-ceilinged eatery with a Portuguese feel—the owners also run the esteemed Ferreira Café (p 104) on the same block. It's a great place for big breakfasts, sandwiches to go, and late-afternoon tapas. In this stretch of rue Peel, restaurants spill out into the street in warm months, taking over parking spots with outdoor cafes. *3 Brasseurs: 1356 rue Ste-Catherine ouest www.les3brasseurs. ca.* ☎ *514/788-9788. $$. Café Vasco Da Gama: 1472 rue Peel. www.vascodagama.ca.* ☎ *514/286-2688. $.*

Sir Winston Churchill Pub.

The Best **in Three Days**

MONTRÉAL
Longueuil
Lachine
Lasalle
La Prairie

MILE END ②

Parc Père-Marquette

Rosemont ⑤B

Parc Sir-Wilfrid-Laurier

av. Laurier
bd. St - Joseph

PLATEAU MONT-ROYAL ①

av. du

Laurier

Mont - Royal
Mont-Royal

Parc du Mont-Royal

Parc Jeanne-Mance

rue Rachel

av. Duluth

Parc La Fontaine

Croix du Mont-Royal

av. des Pins

Sherbrooke
Sherbrooke

av. des Pins

QUARTIER LATIN

Ontario

THE VILLAGE

McGill University
McCord Museum

Place-des-Arts

Bern-UQAM

bd. de Maisonneuve

Papineau

Peel
McGill

QUARTIER DES SPECTACLES

St-Laurent

DOWNTOWN

Ste - Catherine
CHINATOWN

Beaudry

INTERNATIONAL QUARTER

Champ-de-Mars

bd. René - Lévesque

Bonaventure

Square-Victoria
OACI

Place-d'Armes

rue St - Antoine

rue Notre - Dame

VIEUX-MONTRÉAL

⑤A

VIEUX-PORT

Palais des Congrès (Convention Center)

Île Sainte-Hélène

Parc Jean-Drapeau

Pont de la Concorde

La Biosphère

Jean-Drapeau

Île Notre-Dame

0   1/4 mi
0   250 m

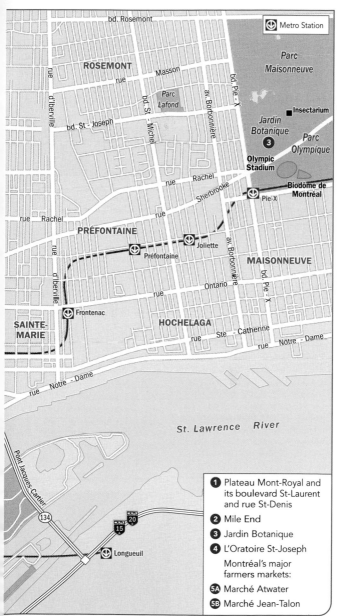

1 Plateau Mont-Royal and its boulevard St-Laurent and rue St-Denis
2 Mile End
3 Jardin Botanique
4 L'Oratoire St-Joseph
Montréal's major farmers markets:
5A Marché Atwater
5B Marché Jean-Talon

Pick and choose some of Montréal's other highlights on your third day. People-watching and soaking up the outdoors are rewarding ways to take up this rich metropolis, especially after 2 days of exploring relatively compact neighborhoods on foot.

Art murals line the streets of Montréal, especially along Boulevard Saint-Laurent.

❶ ★★ Plateau Mont-Royal and its boulevard St-Laurent and rue St-Denis. This is a pulsing area of the city. Although many of the young creatives who lived here in recent years have been priced out by "bobos"—bourgeois bohemians— and moved to Mile End and the neighborhoods beyond (Rosemont, Verdun, Villeray), there's still a lot to explore here. Boulevard St-Laurent, also known as "the Main," hums with offbeat boutiques, bars, and restaurants, attracting shoppers, students, and sightseers. Spend some time snacking and people-watching your way along the boulevard, perhaps starting at rue Sherbrooke and heading north. Keep an eye out for the proliferating public art, including colorful murals, that pepper this part of the city (see p 60). Parallel to boulevard St-Laurent and eight short blocks to the east, rue St-Denis also runs the length of the Plateau. Here, shopkeepers and people on the street are more likely to speak just French. Rue St-Denis extends from the Quartier Latin straight north, with some of the most interesting shopping blocks between rue Sherbrooke and av. du Mont-Royal. *Note that St-Laurent is the dividing line of the city: Addresses to its left are all on* the west side, and to the right all on the east, with the numbers ascending in both directions. ① *At least 1½ hr. Bd. St-Laurent, north of rue Sherbrooke to av. du Mont-Royal. Métro: St-Laurent. Rue St-Denis, north of rue Sherbrooke to av. du Mont-Royal. Métro: Sherbrooke.*

❷ ★★ Mile End. The artsy, multicultural, less busy Mile End starts at the northern end of the Plateau. It's a little hipper than the Plateau in spots, and a little fancier in others. One place to start is rue Bernard, going west from boulevard St-Laurent, which has quirky commerce and cafes. Another destination is avenue Laurier, west of the Main, which is prime for a stroll and upscale window shopping. Here the sidewalks are wide and the shops are fancy. You'll

Rue St-Denis is busy night and day.

find high fashion, imported gourmet fare, and food boutiques like **Juliette et Chocolate** (377 av. Laurier ouest; see p 60)—a local chain, but an extra-nice one. We offer a neighborhood tour of Mile End on p 60. *Mile End is bounded more or less by avenue Van Horne to the north, avenue du Mont-Royal to the south, rue Hutchison to the west, and rue St-Denis to the east. Métro: Laurier.*

❸ ★★★ Jardin Botanique.

Montréal's sprawling 75-hectare (185-acre) botanical garden is home to 10 themed exhibition greenhouses. One houses orchids; another has tropical food and spice plants, including coffee, cashews, and vanilla; another features rainforest flora. Spring is when things really kick in: lilacs, tulips, and blooming crabapple trees in May, lilies in June, and roses from mid-June until the first frost. From late February through April, butterflies flutter among the nectar-bearing plants in the main exhibition greenhouse, occasionally landing on visitors. Favorites among the 23 thematic gardens are the serene **Japanese Garden,** which has tea ceremonies and a stunning bonsai collection with miniature trees as

Montréal's botanical gardens are among the largest and most beautiful in the world.

old as 350 years; the wooded **First Nations Garden,** which highlights Native knowledge of plants and the agricultural focus on the "three sisters" of corn, beans, and squash; and the **Chinese Garden,** which evokes the 14th- to 17th-century era of the Ming Dynasty and was built according to the landscape principles of yin and yang. If you're visiting in September or October, consider tickets to the magical **Gardens of Light,** an evening event with colored lanterns lighting the paths of the three gardens mentioned here. The **Insectarium,** which was built especially for kids, is closed for renovations until summer 2021. ◷ *At least 2 hr. 4101 rue Sherbrooke est (opposite Olympic*

City of Festivals

Few cities in North America can rival Montréal when it comes to celebrations. Throughout the year, the city is home to some of the biggest and most heralded festivals in the world. Among the options to plan around: **Go Bike Montréal Festival,** which includes a nocturnal bike ride (Tour la Nuit) and the grueling Tour de l'Île, a 52km (32-mile) race around the island's rim (May); **Les FrancoFolies de Montréal,** featuring French-language pop, hip-hop, electronic, and world beat music (June); and the city's signature event, the **Festival International de Jazz,** which hosts major acts and free outdoor performances, many right on downtown's streets and plazas (July). Book a hotel room well in advance if you're visiting during these big parties. For details and more options, see "Festivals & Special Events" on p 162.

Kids love the playground in the Garden Botanique.

Stadium). www.espacepourlavie.ca/en/botanical-garden. ☎ 514/868-3000. Admission C$21 adults, with discounts for seniors, students, children, and families; free for children 4 and under. Check website for hours, which change seasonally. Admission includes access to the Insectarium (closed for renovations until summer 2021). No bicycles or dogs. Métro: Pie-IX.

❹ ★★ L'Oratoire St-Joseph.

This enormous copper-domed basilica is an icon of Montréal, although to see it in person you'll need to trek to the northern side of Mont-Royal (the small mountain that rises above downtown, and from which the city derives its name). The church has a seating capacity of 2,028 and the inner dome a diameter of 26m (85 ft.). It came into being through the efforts of Brother André, a lay brother in the Holy Cross order who earned a reputation as a healer. By the time he had built a small wooden chapel here in 1904, he was said to have performed hundreds of cures. He continued his work until his death in 1937. In 1982, he was beatified by the pope—a status one step below sainthood—and in 2010 he earned the distinction of sainthood. Many visitors come in the hopes of a miracle, sometimes climbing the 99 steps on their knees. Others come to hear the 56-bell carillon, which plays Wednesday to Friday at noon and 3pm, Saturday at noon and 2:30pm, and Sunday at 12:15 and 2:30pm. A

new visitor's center is expected to be completed by the end of 2020 and a new observation tower by 2022. 🕐 *1 hr. 3800 chemin Queen Mary (north slope of Mont-Royal). www.saint-joseph.org.* ☎ *877/672-8647 or 514/733-8211. Free admission to most sights, donations requested; guided tours C$6; oratory museum C$4 adults, C$2 children 6–17. Open daily 10am–4:30pm and weekends July–Aug until 5:30pm. Métro: Côte-des-Neiges.*

❺ ★★★ Montréal's major farmers markets.

A public market as a sightseeing destination? *Mais oui!* Montréal's indoor/outdoor farmers markets—❺ⓐ **Atwater,** west of Vieux-Montréal, and ❺ⓑ **Jean-Talon,** north of Mile End in Little Italy—are some of the best you'll find in North America. The city is surrounded by farmland and imbued with a strong commitment to local and organic produce. Both markets are grocery destinations for locals doing their shopping for vegetables, fruit, meats, fish, and baked goods, but the markets also sell treats that visitors can take home and have food counters for quick meals. Atwater is easy to get to from Vieux-Montréal by walking on rue St.-Paul or bike-riding along the picturesque Lachine Canal, and if the weather is good, there's no better way to take in the charms of the city and its rich visual character than by passing through it on foot or by pedal-power. 🕐 *1 hr. See p 93.* ●

Religious pilgrims flock to the L'Oratoire St-Joseph in search of miraculous healing.

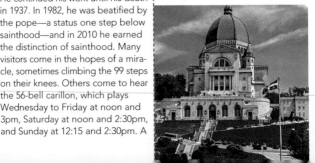

Design Montréal

Public art:

1A *La Tendress*

1B *The Illuminated Crowd*

1C Murals

Avant-garde architecture:

2A PVM

2B Habitat 67

3 Palais des Congrès

Creative reuse of industrial buildings:

4A Boris Bistro

4B Hôtel ÉPIK Montréal

4C Hôtel Gault

5 Darling Foundry visual arts venue

High design jewelry and accessories:

6A Conseil des Metiers d'Art du Québec

6B Harricana Par Mariouche

7 Deville Dinerbar

Previous page: Lanterns in the Chinese Gardens of the Jardin Botanique.

Montréal is one of North America's most stylish cities. The municipality works hard to capitalize on that appeal, enticing artists to live and create there and art-minded travelers to visit. (Even its subway poles are clever, umbrella-ing out into narrow mini poles for more people to grab hold of.) It is the first North American city to be appointed a UNESCO City of Design, celebrated for using creativity as a strategic factor for sustainable development.
START: **Métro: Laurier.**

❶ **Public art.** In recent years, Montréal has become awash in multimedia public art. The city has always delighted in putting sculptures right out on sidewalks—Paul Lancz's white marble ❶Ⓐ **"La Tendress,"** of a woman kissing the head of a child, is one sweet example, at the corner of rues Sherbrooke and Peel, while three blocks west, near the intersection of avenue McGill College and avenue du President Kennedy, Raymond Mason's large permanent sculpture ❶Ⓑ *The Illuminated Crowd,* an eggnog-colored work from 1985 in polyester resin, is a more intense work. It shows a life-size crowd of figures and "the flow of man's

emotion through space" as it says on the descriptive plaque. But the city has moved beyond sculpture. It has catapulted into the 21st century and now boasts an unusually large number of elaborate murals, light installations, and photo projections onto buildings around the city. An 11-day **mural festival** (www.mural festival.com) is held every June, celebrating urban art with music, artist talks, and the creation of collaborative visual art. **Art Public Montréal** (https://artpublicmontreal.ca) offers a rich database of where to find what—it has filters for location, medium, and date—and offers a downloadable mini-tour of eight murals in Plateau Mont-Royal. As

Leonard Cohen mural on rue Crescent.

Guided Tours by Land and by Sea

Square Dorchester is one of downtown's central locations and a gathering point for an initial tour. Montréal's central tourist office, open daily, is at the northern end of the square, at 1255 rue Peel. Bilingual attendants can help arrange tour tickets. (**Fun fact:** Looking south from this square, the blue-hued skyscraper with the triangle-shaped roof is 1000 de La Gauchetière, the tallest building in the city.)

Gray Line Montréal (www.grayline.com; ☎ 514/398-9769) offers 3½ hour guided tours in air-conditioned motorcoach buses daily year-round. Gray Line also offers a 2-hour "Hop-On, Hop-Off" tour on double-decker buses, and tickets can be used over a 48-hour period. **Amphi-Bus** (www.montreal-amphibus-tour.com; ☎ 514/849-5181) is something a little different: It tours Vieux-Montréal much like any other bus until it waddles into the St. Lawrence River for a dramatic finish. For a tour completely on the city's waterways, **Le Bateau-Mouche** (www.bateaumouche.ca; ☎ 800/361-9952 or 514/849-9952) is a glass-enclosed vessel reminiscent of those of the same name on the Seine in Paris. It plies the St. Lawrence River from mid-May to mid-October, taking passengers on a route inaccessible by traditional vessels and providing sweeping views of the skyline.

well, tour company **Fitz & Follwell** (https://montreal.fitz.tours/tour/the-montreal-street-art-tour) offers a 2½-hr. street-art walking tour that covers a lot of territory in the Plateau. To meander on your own, start at rue Sherbrooke and head north on ⑩ **boulevard St-Laurent,**

The city's main tourist office is at the north end of downtown's Square Dorchester.

Five years later, Montréal hosted the 1967 World's Fair, called Expo 67. It was hugely successful—62 nations participated and over 50 million people visited—and overnight, Montréal was a star. The city became a prototype for a 20th-century metropolis. One of the most exhilarating projects built for the event was **2B Habitat 67**, a 158-unit housing complex on the St. Lawrence River facing Vieux-Montréal. Designed by Montréal architect Moshe Safdie, it looks like a collection of module concrete blocks, piled together and interconnected. The vision was to demonstrate what affordable community housing could look like. Today it's higher-end housing and not open to the public. But it can be seen from the western end of Vieux-Port, and photos can be found at Safdie's website (www.msafdie.com). ① *View Habitat 67 from corner of rue St-Pierre and rue de la Commune.*

Place Ville-Marie, designed by I. M. Pei, is one of downtown's most important architectural landmarks.

which has perhaps the city's largest concentration of murals and graffiti.

❷ Avant-garde architecture. Keep in mind as you're touring Montréal that the French word *place*, meaning square or plaza, sometimes means an outdoor space, such as Place d'Armes in Vieux-Montréal. Other times it refers to a building or complex that includes stores and offices. **2A Place Ville-Marie** is in that category. When it was built, in 1962, the crucifix-shaped office building was extremely cutting-edge. Designed by I. M. Pei to cover an unsightly railway trench, the now-famous skyscraper at the corner of boulevards René-Lévesque and Robert-Bourassa, known locally as PVM, became home to the city's first subterranean shopping mall and a cornerstone of the new Underground City.

Built for the 1967 World's Fair, the modern Habitat 67 is now a private residence.

An interior view of the Palais des Congrès's patchwork glass walls.

❸ **Palais des Congrès.** A convention center as design triumph? As unlikely as that seems, yes. The center's transparent glass exterior walls are a crazy quilt of pink, yellow, blue, green, red, and purple rectangles. Step into the inside hallway for the full effect—when the sun streams in, it's like being inside a huge kaleidoscope. The walls went up from 2000 to 2002 as part of renovation and extension of the center and are the vision of Montréal architect Mario Saia. ⏱ *10 min. 1001 Place Jean-Paul-Riopelle. www.congresmtl.com.* ☎ *514/871-8122. Métro: Place d'Armes.*

❹ **Creative reuse of industrial buildings.** Much of Montréal's rich character derives from the careful reuse of industrial buildings. It's on display at the ❹Ⓐ **Boris Bistro** patio, where diners are seated in a street-facing courtyard behind the window-less facade of a stone building. And it's seen in hotels throughout the older part of the city, such as ❹Ⓑ **Hôtel ÉPIK Montréal**, in a converted 1723 building (p 133) and ❹Ⓒ **Hôtel Gault** (p 133). The Gault's designers and architects left the monumental concrete walls of a 19th-century textile warehouse raw and added brushed-steel work surfaces for a contemporary feel. The sleek lobby, with graceful arched windows, also functions as a public bar/cafe. ⏱ *20 min. All three venues are in Vieux-Montréal, at rue 465 McGill, 171 rue St-Paul ouest, and 449 rue Ste-Hélène. Métro: Square-Victoria-OACI.*

❺ **Darling Foundry visual arts venue.** Artists and high-tech businesses have been remaking the loft-and-factory district west of avenue McGill, at the edge of Vieux-Montréal, for the past 20 years. Among the pioneers is the Darling Foundry, an avant-garde exhibition space in a vast, raw former foundry. It showcases modern art and hosts performance evenings of "collective creation" in the summer months. ⏱ *30 min. 745 rue*

Montréal's Annual Fashion Fête

Fashion simmers in this city, where innovative locals are making international names for themselves. **Montréal's Festival Mode & Design** (www.festivalmodedesign.com), held in August, is a great way to survey it all. There are runway shows, pop-up stores, and music events throughout the Quartier des Spectacles. As well, important design personalities of Montréal are highlighted at www.designmontreal.com/en/news.

The City's New Champlain Bridge

Traversing the Saint Lawrence River, the massive new Champlain Bridge opened in 2019, replacing what's now called the old Champlain alongside it. It's epic in proportion and scale: 2 miles (3.4km) long with a 168m (551 ft.) concrete tower and stay cables on either side. Built in just 4 years, the spectacular bridge was dubbed the city's own "NASA moon launch" by the *Montréal Gazette*. As the main gateway to Montréal from the south, it will undoubtedly become iconic to the city. Read about it at www. newchamplain.ca/project/engineering/.

Ottawa. www.fonderiedarling.org. ☎ 514/392-1554. *Métro: Square-Victoria-OACI.*

❻ High-design jewelry and accessories. Our favorite Montréal jeweler is **J.R. Franco**, whose chic earrings and necklaces are made of brushed aluminum. His work is for sale at **❻A Conseil des Metiers d'Art du Québec** in Vieux-Montréal. Other signature Québec looks come from clothing designer Mariouche Gagné, who was born on Île d'Orléans near Québec City. She riffs on the city's rich history with the fur trade by recycling old fur into new garments, such as coyote earmuffs and fox stoles. Her shop, **❻B Harricana Par Mariouche,** is also in Vieux-Montréal. ⓛ *30 min. See p 91 and p 95.*

If you're in the mood for something splashy, check out **❼ Deville Dinerbar** downtown. It claims to take its cue from American diners, but that only goes as far as its use of booths for some of the seating and its enormous portions—you'd be hard-pressed to find an American diner with a marble bar or LolliPop Lamb Chops starters for C$27 (yes, prices are steep). Salads, sandwiches, burgers, and pastas share the huge menu with specialties such as bone-in veal parmigiana, beignets served with Nutella chocolate mousse, and gigantic goblets of cocktails for two—often as colorful as the pink neon signs around them. *1425 Stanley St. www. devilledinerbar.com.* ☎ *514/281-6556. Lunch and dinner daily. Métro: Peel. $$$*

Gastronomic Montréal

1 Vieux-Montréal food tour
2 Little Italy
3A Fairmont Bagels
3B St-Viateur Bagels
4 A smoked meat sandwich at Schwartz's
5 Food festivals
6 Brewpub tour
7 Marché Atwater

Certainly, the prevalence of French and American influences on the local cuisine looms large. But the city's international flavor permeates the kitchens of its restaurants, the shelves of its gourmet groceries and markets, and the food trucks that pop up in the summer months. Use every opportunity to sample the treats you find—go in with the idea that if you haven't tried it before, the time is now. START: **Métro: Jean-Talon**

❶ Vieux-Montréal food tour.

Walking is your best way to see the city, and adding in food makes it even more fun. You could design your own tour, but this one covers good ground and gets you right into the restaurants. The tastings include French onion soup from **Modavie** restaurant (p 105) and poutine and beer at a brewpub. The 3-hour tour covers 2.3km (1.4 miles). ⏱ *3 hrs. Starts at Crew Collective & Café, at 360 rue St. Jacques. www.localfoodtours.com/montreal/tours/old-montreal-food-tour/.* ☎ *438/600-0501. C$65 food only, C$72 food and alcohol. Check the website for days and times. Métro: Square-Victoria-OACI.*

❷ Little Italy.

Real-deal espresso and some of the city's best hand-made pasta and pizza can be found in this enclave influenced by a wave of Italian immigration during the early 20th century. What's more, it's home to one of the city's most vibrant year-round markets, **Jean-Talon.** ⏱ *2 hrs. www.mtl.org/en/experience/welcome-little-italy. See p 94. Métro:Jean-Talon.*

❸ Fairmont Bagels & St-Viateur Bagels.

Bagels? Yes! This is a city of bagel connoisseurs, and the unique texture and honey-tinged flavor of Montréal bagels warrant this entry. Bagels are serious business in this city, and ❸A Fairmont and ❸B St-Viateur are the giants who battle it out every year for the title of Best Bagel. St-Viateur uses wood-burning ovens and old-fashioned baking

Montréal's bagels are justifiably famous.

techniques brought from Eastern Europe by founder Myer Lewkowicz. The location listed here is a cafe with additional food options. Fairmont offers greater variety and is open 24 hours 7 days a week. Compare a classic sesame and be the ultimate arbiter yourself. *St-Viateur, 1127 av. du Mont-Royal est. www.stviateurbagel.com.* ☎ *514/528-6361. $. Fairmount, see p 104.*

❹ A smoked-meat sandwich at Schwartz's.

French-first language laws insist on the exterior sign SCHWARZ CHARCUTERIE HEBRAIQUE DE MONTRÉAL, but everyone just calls this old-time Jewish delicatessen Schwartz's. Housed in a long, narrow storefront, with a lunch counter and simple tables and chairs crammed impossibly close to each other, this is as nondescript a culinary landmark as you'll find. The deli might appear unassuming, but

The legendary Schwartz's delicatessen, renowned for its smoked meat.

it serves the smoked meat against which all other smoked meats are measured. ⏱ *1 hr. See p 108.*

5 Food festivals. For over 20 years, Montréal has celebrated winter in a style that is distinctly its own: with an indoor-outdoor festival in February of food and wine tastings along with music, dance, and circus theater. It's called **Montréal en Lumière** (Montréal in Light), and many of the city's top chefs participate. But that's just winter! In summer, festivals include **Oysterfest, A Taste of the Caribbean**, and the **International Kombucha Festival**. A citywide restaurant week (**MTLàTABLE**) takes place every November. *Details at www.montreal enlumiere.com; www.mtl.org/en/ experience/food-events; and https:// mtlatable.mtl.org.*

6 Brewpub tour. The same company that puts on the Vieux-Montréal food tour (**2**, above), and the Mile End food tour (p 60) also produces a craft beer walking tour. It takes guests through the Quartier Latin and Quartier des Spectacles. You'll probably want to have salad for breakfast and a vegan dinner after for counterbalance: The tour travels to three brewpubs, offers six tastings, and pairs the drinks with poutine, meats, cheese, nachos, and chocolate. ⏱ *3 hrs. Starts at Le Saint-Bock, at 1749 rue St. Denis in the Latin Quarter. https://localfood tours.com/montreal/tours/montreal-brewpub-experience-special/.* ☎ *438/600-0501. C$65. Check the website for days and times. Métro: Berri-UQAM.*

Many of Montréal's chefs participate in the Montréal en Lumière festival.

❼ ★★ Marché Atwater. Like Jean-Talon in Little Italy, the Atwater market, west of Vieux-Montréal, is an indoor-outdoor farmer's market that's open daily year-round. Deeply French, it features *boulangeries* and *fromageries*, fresh fruits, vegetables, chocolates, and flowers, as well as shops with food to go. **Première Moisson** (p 107) offers jewel-like pastries, artisan breads, and sublime terrines and a small seating area at which to nibble baguettes or sip a bowl of café au lait. **Chocolats Geneviève Grandbois** (☎ 514/933-1331) makes its own high-end chocolates and special treats such as Fleur de sel Caramel Spread—a salted caramel spread made in Montréal—and sells them from a small second floor kiosk. In the warm months, when the outdoor patio opens, **Satay Brothers** (☎ 514/933-3507), a Singaporean food stall, draws

Marché Atwater, one of Montréal's premier public markets, sells a mouthwatering array of fresh produce and other delicacies.

crowds. ⏱ 1 hr. 138 rue Atwater. Open daily. Métro: Lionel-Groulx.

Poutine: A Tasty Mess

It's the national comfort food: French fries with gravy and cheese on top. But not just any cheese. Québécois say the beauty of their beloved poutine lies in cheese curds that don't melt completely. Legend has it that the dish's name originated in 1957 when restaurateur Fernand LaChance received a request from a customer for French fries and cheese in a bag. He responded, *Ca va faire une maudite poutine!* Roughly translated, it means, "That's going to make a damn mess!" True, but it also made a bona fide culinary hit, which became even more popular when gravy was added to the mix a few years later.

So cherished is the dish that the fast-food chain Valentine started a petition for a poutine emoji, hoping to rectify the fact that, "Sadly, the people of Canada cannot virtually express their love for poutine." Consider it a must-try. It's available from both fast-food venues (including the good St-Hubert chain, which specializes in chicken) and high-end restaurants, where it's often dolled up with bacon, hot peppers, and even foie gras. In between is **La Banquise,** at the northwest corner of Parc La Fontaine, which offers some 30 variations (including vegan) to feed your need. *See p 102.*

Montréal's **Parks**

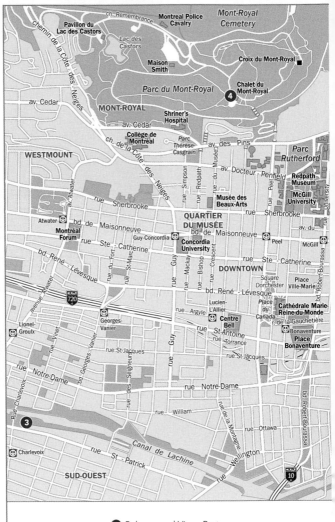

ch. Remembrance
Pavillon du Lac des Castors
Chemin de la Côte-des-Neiges
Montreal Police Cavalry
Mont-Royal Cemetery
Lac des Castors
Maison Smith
Croix du Mont-Royal ■
Parc du Mont-Royal ❹
Chalet du Mont-Royal
av. Cedar
MONT-ROYAL
Shriner's Hospital
av. Cedar
ch. de la Côte-des-Neiges
Collège de Montréal
Parc Thérèse-Casgrain
av. des Pins
Parc Rutherford
WESTMOUNT
av. Docteur-Penfield
Redpath Museum
rue du Musée
rue Simpson
rue Redpath
Musée des Beaux-Arts
McGill University
av. Atwater
rue Sherbrooke
rue Sherbrooke
QUARTIER DU MUSÉE
Atwater ⊕
bd. de Maisonneuve
bd. de Maisonneuve
Peel ⊕
av. du
McGill ⊕
Montréal Forum
rue Ste-Catherine
Guy-Concordia ⊕
Concordia University
rue Guy
rue Mackay
rue Bishop
rue Crescent
rue Ste-Catherine
rue du Fort
rue St-Marc
DOWNTOWN
bd. René-Lévesque
bd. René-Lévesque
Square Dorchester
Place Ville-Marie
bd. Robert-Bourassa
720
avenue Atwater
rue Vinet
Lucien-L'Allier ⊕
Place du Canada
Cathédrale Marie-Reine-du-Monde
r. de la Gauchetière
Lionel-Groulx ⊕
Georges-Vanier ⊕
rue Argyle
Centre Bell
rue St-Antoine
Bonaventure ⊕
Place Bonaventure
bd. Georges-Vanier
rue des Seigneurs
rue Guy
rue St-Antoine
rue Torrance
rue St-Jacques
rue St-Jacques
rue Notre-Dame
Rue Charlevoix
rue Notre-Dame
rue William
rue de la Montagne
bd. Robert-Bourassa
❸
rue Ottawa
Canal de Lachine
⊕ Charlevoix
rue St-Patrick
rue Wellington
10
SUD-OUEST

❶ Poke around Vieux-Port

❷ Bike the Lachine Canal

❸ Don't just look at the water—get in

❹ Take in the view from the top of the mountain

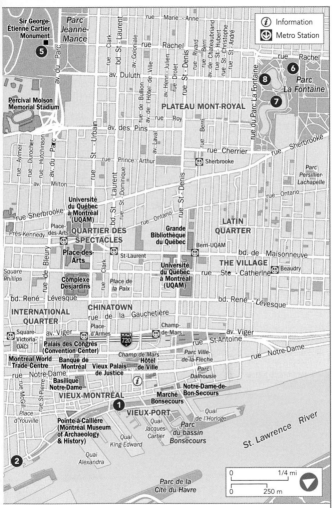

5 Drum with the Tam Tams

6 Enjoy some leisure time in pristine landscaping

7 Relax at a waterside café

8 Plan a night at Théâtre de Verdure

When you're looking to simply hang out in some green space, get into the water, or go for a bike ride, make like a Montréaler. (You need to work off all that eating and drinking, right?) Here are three great parks and some popular ways to take them in.

Vieux-Port & Lachine Canal

Montréal's Old Port—called Vieux-Port in French—is at the southern end of Vieux-Montréal and is the most easily accessed park for many visitors. There's a strip of green lawn along bike paths here, stretching along the waterfront parallel to rue de la Commune. The Lachine Canal bike path starts at the western edge, at rue McGill.

❶ Poke around Vieux-Port. The port area isn't that big—2km (1¼ miles) long, and 53 hectares (131 acres) in all. A fun summer option is to rent a **quadricycle** bike-buggy that can hold two to six people. The rental booth is at Quai Jacques-Cartier and the cost is C$26 for a three-seater and C$52 for a six-seater. Also at the port's far eastern end, in the last of the old warehouses, the 1922 clock tower, **La Tour de l'Horloge,** can

be climbed for free June through August. It has 192 steps that lead past exposed clockworks to observation decks overlooking the St. Lawrence River. ⏱ *1 hr. Waterfront along rue de la Commune, between rue McGill to the west and rue Bonsecours to the east. www.oldportof-montreal.com and www.ecorecreo.ca. See p 44 bullet 1 for other options. Métro: Place d'Armes.*

❷ Bike the Lachine Canal. The peaceful Lachine Canal is a nearly flat 11km (6.8-mile) waterway that begins at the western end of Vieux-Port. Well-used bike paths along most of both sides travel alongside locks and over small bridges. The path is open year-round and is maintained by Parks Canada from mid-April to mid-November. To rent a bike, stop by ÇaRoule/**Montréal on Wheels** (27 rue de la Commune est; www.caroulemontreal.com;

Strolling along Vieux-Port.

the *boulangerie* and *fromagerie* or any of the prepared food shops.

Parc du Mont-Royal

This mountain park within the city is popular with daytime strollers. We offer a **suggested walk of the park** on p 80, which provides a basic route for getting into and around the 200-hectare (494-acre) green space. Here are some favorite ways to enjoy the wooded park and its environs.

❹ ★★ **Take in the view from the top of the mountain.**
Renowned landscape architect Frederick Law Olmsted (1822–1903), left his mark on Montréal in Parc du Mont-Royal (Royal Mountain Park). The 232m (761-ft.) peak (Mont Royal) for which the city is named has miles of paths snaking through it. The terrace at the **Chalet du Mont-Royal** at the crest of the hill offers expansive views of the city below. It can be accessed by walking up the mountain, driving up, or taking the #11 bus that travels across the mountain. Parking is at the nearby **Maison Smith** (1260

Cycling the Lachine Canal Bike Path is one of Montréal's best outdoor experiences.

☎ 877/866-0633 or 514/866-0633). It rents bicycles with helmets from March to mid-December. Rentals are C$32 to C$50 for 2 hours, C$75 for the day. The staff sets customers up with maps (also downloadable from their website) and also offers organized bike rides of the canal for C$26 per participant, which includes the bike rental and a ride leader.

❸ **Don't just look at the water—get in.** Pedal boats are available for rental right in the heart of the Old Port. **Écorécréo** (www. ecorecreo.ca; ☎ 514/465-0594) charges C$26 for a half-hour and C$39 for an hour, and operates daily June to August and weekends September to October. About 4km (2½ miles) down the canal, kayaks, canoes, pedal boats, and small electric boats are available for rent at the Lachine Canal Nautical Centre from **H2O Adventures** (www. h2oadventures.com; ☎ 514/842-1306). If you don't want to bike or walk there, take the Métro to Lionel-Groulx and head south to the canal, passing the **Marché Atwater** where you can pick up food from

The view from Parc du Mont-Royal is one of the best in the city.

Enjoy the Outdoors, Come Snow or Come Shine

Montréal residents get outside at every possible opportunity, and there's plenty to do even when snow covers the ground. In winter, outdoor skating rinks are set up in Vieux-Port and at the Pavilion at Lac des Castors (Beaver Lake) in Parc Mont-Royal, with skate rentals available at both locales. Cross-country skiers take advantage of the extensive course at Parc Mont-Royal.

In warm weather, people pour outside. Biking, scootering, and rollerblading are hugely popular (see "Tap Your Own Pedal Power," p 164). Hikers and joggers take to parks and the city streets. And getting onto the water is big. In addition to kayaking on the Lachine Canal (see above), a popular option is taking a cruise on the St. Lawrence River. Trips are available from mid-May to mid-October, with companies such as **Le Bateau-Mouche** (www.bateau-mouche.com; ☎ 800/361-9952 or 514/849-9952) and **Croisières AML Cruises** (www.croisieresaml.com; ☎ 866/856-6668) offering 60-minute, 90-minute, and evening trips. Adult fares start at C$25. The boats leave from piers in Vieux-Port.

chemin Remembrance; www.lemontroyal.qc.ca; ☎ 514/843-8240), the small information center on the road that runs between the park and the Notre-Dame-des-Neiges Cemetery to the north. ⏱ 1 hr. There are several entry points to the park, including at av. des Pins and rue Peel. Métro: Peel for the south side, Côte-des-Neiges for the north. Bus: #11 travels along chemin Remembrance.

⑤ Drum with the Tam Tams. If you're free on a Sunday afternoon from early May to late September, join this enormous gathering of musicians. Tam Tams attracts a few hundred drummers who congregate around the statue of Sir George-Etienne Cartier near avenue du Parc at the corner of rue Rachel, on Parc Mont-Royal's most northeastern side. Anyone is free to watch or join in. As the mass of percussionists builds around the steps of the statue, the rest of the park

fills with sunbathers and picnickers who turn the impromptu concert into a festive social event. You'll also find vendors hawking

Every Sunday in summer, Montréalers gather in Parc Mont-Royal for the Tam Tams drum sessions.

Ice skating in Parc La Fontaine.

homemade jewelry and art, and kooky LARPers (Live Action Role Players) putting on whimsical faux battles with foam weapons. Although the City of Montréal doesn't manage the event, it sanctions it and oversees security. *Inside Parc Mont-Royal at av. du Parc and rue Rachel.*

Parc La Fontaine

Many locals come to this green oasis on the Plateau to relax alongside its lake, bike its paths, or play some tennis. A popular open amphitheater, the **Théâtre de Verdure,** is back in business after a renovation. Many people also come simply to find some quiet among the flower beds that bloom bright.

⑥ ★ Enjoy some leisure time in pristine landscaping. Parc La Fontaine is one of the city's oldest parks, and arguably its prettiest. On its northern side, the green space is especially handsome, with canopies of green shading broad, well-used paths. Illustrating the traditional dual identities of the city's populace, some of the park is landscaped in a formal French manner, while other sections have a more casual English style. Bike paths crisscross the park and loop around a slip of a lake. In winter, there's free ice skating (skate rentals are available). ○ *1 hr. The park can be*

entered anywhere on its perimeter. *Métro: Mont-Royal.*

⑦ Relax at a waterside café. The restaurant **Espace La Fontaine**, along the western side of Parc La Fontaine's lake, is a popular spot for weekend brunch and early evening drinks. ○ *1 hr. www. espacelafontaine.com. Inside Parc La Fontaine, near Ave. du Parc La Fontaine.*

⑧ Plan a night at Théâtre de Verdure. Sunset does not send park visitors heading for the exits. Instead, many stay after dark because of this open-air theater— long one of the best places to see a show in the city. Théâtre de Verdure has had stop-and-start renovations since 2014 and is expected to reopen in 2020. In the past it has offered free programming in the summer months, and guests were invited to pack a bottle of wine and a picnic basket to take it all in under the night sky. Look for updates at www.accesculture.com/evenement/theatredeverdure. *Inside Parc La Fontaine, near ave. du Parc La Fontaine.*

Summertime pleasures in Parc La Fontaine.

Kid-Centric Montréal

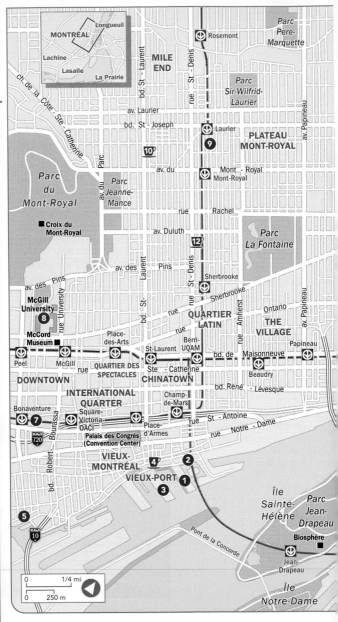

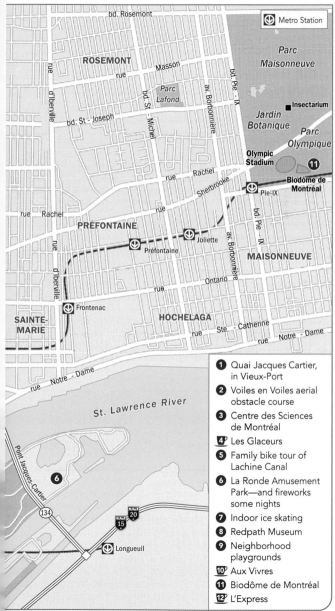

1 Quai Jacques Cartier, in Vieux-Port
2 Voiles en Voiles aerial obstacle course
3 Centre des Sciences de Montréal
4 Les Glaceurs
5 Family bike tour of Lachine Canal
6 La Ronde Amusement Park—and fireworks some nights
7 Indoor ice skating
8 Redpath Museum
9 Neighborhood playgrounds
10 Aux Vivres
11 Biodôme de Montréal
12 L'Express

Montréal is as much a playground for children as it is for adults. A good number of the city's museums and attractions, including those listed below, are tailored to the tiniest sightseers. There are also expanses of grass for running around on in the city's big parks (see p 36), the **Jardin Botanique** (p 53), and on the main campus of McGill University (enter at 845 rue Sherbrooke ouest). START: **Métro: Place d'Armes or Champs-de-Mars.**

1 ★★★ **Quai Jacques Cartier, in Vieux-Port.** This is the happening spot! Head straight to this pier at the eastern end of Vieux-Port, which is now dominated by **La Grande Roue de Montréal Ferris wheel.** In summer months it's supplemented by quadricycle rentals, a miniature electric train, a zipline circuit, a giant labyrinth maze, pedal boats, jetski rides, cruises, and a caravan of food trucks. (See p 13 bullet 11 for details.) There are far fewer offerings here in the cold months, but they include a popular skating rink as well as the Ferris wheel, which runs year-round. ① *1+ hr. Vieux-Port, at Quai Jacques Cartier. www. oldportofmontreal.com.* ☎ *800/971-7678 or 514/496-7678. Métro: Place d'Armes or Champ-de-Mars.*

2 ★★ **Voiles en Voiles aerial obstacle course.** Right in front of

the Ferris wheel and behind a wall of vendor kiosks, you'll see the masts of what looks like a gigantic pirate ship. This is a self-contained mini theme park, with aerial rope walks, bridges, climbing walls, and a playground with inflatable rooms and waterslides. Part of the facility looks like a pirate ship and another like a royal ship. Guests are equipped with harnesses and helmets, and both adults and kids can participate (adults who do not participate can enter for free). The standard ticket is for a 4-hour visit, although there are options for 1 and 2 hours. ① *4 hr. Vieux-Port, Place des Vestiges, on Quai de l'Horloge. www.voilesenvoiles.com.* ☎ *514/473-1458. Admission for 4 hours C$49 for everyone 6 years and older, with discounts for younger children and families. Anyone who is*

Museum Programming for Kids

In addition to the specifically kid-centric museums listed here, several larger Montréal museums have material tailored for children. In Vieux-Montréal, the history museum **Pointe-à-Callière** has kid-friendly material on the earliest city life in the 1600s, including a permanent exhibit on pirates and an archaeo-adventure workshop space; see p 13 and www.pacmusee.qc.ca/en/plan-your-visit/family-activities. Downtown, **Musée des Beaux-Arts** has free family activities, including painting and movies, every Saturday and Sunday; see p 19 and www.mbam.qc.ca/calendrier/en/activities-family. Older children will get a kick out of the city's wax museum, **Musée Grévin Montréal**, also downtown. In addition to sections on historic New France characters, it has rooms with famous figures including Barack Obama, Katy Perry, and Justin Trudeau. See p 73.

The Best Bang for Your Buck

Many of Montréal attractions that appeal to children are expensive, and families on a budget will want to be careful about what they say yes to and what they decline.

The new **Ferris wheel**, for instance, is pricey at C$25 adults, C$20 kids 3–17 and seniors, and C$63 for a family of four. We overheard one girl ask her parent, "Are we basically paying eighty bucks to be sitting down?" Yeah, you are. A better option for many will be the **Voiles en Voiles aerial obstacle course**, right in front of the Ferris wheel. Admission is more reasonable for what you get: 4 hours for C$49 for each person who participates, with discounts for very young children and families. We also always like the **Jardin Botanique** (p 53), which costs C$57 for a family of five and can provide a full day of activity.

There are free options, of course. The **hike to the top of Mont Royal** (p 80) is relaxed enough that it can be done with a stroller, and it passes through beautiful woods and fields. The **McGill University campus** offers green grass downtown for kids to run around in. The **free Redpath Museum** (p 48) is right on the McGill campus—and it has dinosaurs!

not participating can enter for free. Online booking recommended. Late June–Aug daily; Sept–Oct weekends; check website for hours. Métro: Place d'Armes or Champ-de-Mars.

❸ ★★ Centre des Sciences de Montréal. Also in Vieux-Port, the Montréal Science Centre is a family-friendly complex that approaches science and technology in a hands-on way. Some of its programming is geared toward children and young teens, while other exhibits will tap the inner kid

Kids love the hands-on exhibits at the Centre des Sciences de Montréal.

Flying high at La Ronde amusement park.

in all visitors. The permanent exhibition "Clic!" is really just a play-space for kids under 7 (and it's a good one). There's an **IMAX Telus** theater onsite and a small gift shop, and a food court next door offers nine options. ⏱ *2 hr. Vieux-Port, 2 rue de la Commune ouest, on Quai King Edward. www.montrealscience centre.com.* ☎ *877/496-4724 or 514/496-4724. Admission C$22 adults, C$17 ages 13–17; C$11 ages 3–12; free for children 2 and under; C$55 family of 4 package. Daily 10am–5pm. Métro: Place d'Armes.*

The rise in cupcake shops was one of the great trends of the early 21st century, and it's still in full bloom at **7 Les Glaceurs.** This cheery café across the street from the Basilique Notre-Dame sells luscious options such as vanilla-sucre à la crème and praline, which features caramelized hazelnut frosting. You can also pick up ice cream made by Montréal favorite Bilboquet. Open daily from 11am to 6pm. *453 rue St-Sulpice. www.lesglaceurs.ca.* ☎ *514/504-1469. $.*

5 ★★ Family bike tour of Lachine Canal. The Vieux-Port bike rental shop ÇaRoule/**Montréal on Wheels** offers a 10km (6-mile) "Young Family Bike Tour" of the Lachine Canal and Parc Jean-Drapeau, going past the Biosphere and the Formula One racetrack. The cost is C$259 for a 9am–4pm tour for two adults and two kids, with bikes, guide, and ice cream stop included. ⏱ *7 hr. Vieux-Port, 27 rue de la Commune est. www.caroulemontreal.com.* ☎ *877/866-0633 or 514/866-0633. Métro: Place d'Armes.*

6 ★★ La Ronde Amusement Park—and fireworks some nights. Located on Parc Jean-Drapeau, which sits in the St. Lawrence River near Vieux-Port's waterfront, La Ronde Amusement Park is part of the American-owned Six Flags theme-park empire and has rollercoasters galore, 10 kiddie rides, and a small *Tchou Tchou Train*. For eight evenings in the summer—at 10pm most Wednesdays and Saturdays in late June and July—the park hosts a **fireworks**

Other Great Options with Children

Other great activities for children, depending on their ages, include these, listed elsewhere in this book: **taking a food tour** (p 32), visiting the **Atwater or Jean-Talon food market** (p 94), exploring the **Biosphère** (p 56) (not to be confused with the Biôdome, p 49), seeing a sky show at the **Planétarium Rio Tinto Alcan** (p 56), or dancing to outdoor music at the summertime Sunday afternoon **Piknic Électronik** (p 63).

competition called L'International des Feux Loto-Québec. Fireworks can be enjoyed for free from almost anywhere in the city overlooking the river, but visitors can also purchase tickets to watch from an open-air theater at La Ronde. ⏱ 5 hr. 22 chemin Macdonald, Parc Jean-Drapeau on Île Ste-Hélène. www. laronde.com. ☎ 514/397-2000. Admission C$72; free for children 2 and under. Discounts of C$8–C$20 with online purchase. Parking C$28–C$30. Daily 11am–9pm in summer; confirm hours on website. Métro: Parc Jean-Drapeau, then bus no. 767, or Papineau, then bus no. 769.

❼ ★★ Indoor ice skating. Escape the city's stifling heat in summer or freezing cold in winter at **Atrium Le 1000,** a year-round facility in a downtown office building. The cozy rink is surrounded by plenty of eateries and has skate rentals on-site. It attracts a full mix of patrons: groups of giggling teenagers, middle-aged friends chatting and skating side by side, young children teetering in helmets. **Tiny Tots Time,** typically

Skaters flock to the ice rink at Atrium Le 1000.

Saturday and Sunday from 11:15am to 1pm, is reserved for children 12 and younger and their parents. ⏱ *1 hr. 1000 rue de la Gauchetiere ouest. www.le1000.com.* ☎ *514/ 395-0555. Admission C$7.50 adults; C$5 ages 12 and under; C$20 family of 4. Skate rental C$7. Wed–Sun; check website for hours. Métro: Bonaventure.*

❽ ★★ **Redpath Museum.** The main campus of Canada's most prestigious school, **McGill University,** is downtown, on the north side of rue Sherbrooke. The front entrance includes an expanse of lawn that's excellent for kids who want to run around. Just inside the campus is this well-regarded museum, the oldest building in Canada (1882) constructed specifically as a museum. The small venue draws kids with exhibits of dinosaurs and mummies. Admission is by contribution. ⏱ *1 hr. 859 rue Sherbrooke ouest. www.mcgill.ca/ redpath.* ☎ *514-398-4861. Free admission (suggested donation C$10 adults, C$20 families). June–Aug daily 9am–2pm; rest of the year weekdays 9am–5pm; weekends 11am–5pm. Métro: McGill.*

❾ ★★ **Neighborhood playgrounds.** If you're traveling with toddlers who simply want to run around on a playground on a warm day, head to the less-touristy neighborhoods such as Plateau Mont-Royal, Mile End, and Outremont, the neighborhood west of Mile End. Parks are well-maintained and many include playgrounds. One option: Take the Métro to the Laurier stop, where the Plateau meets Mile End. This is an attractive residential neighborhood. Walk south on rue Berri one block to **Parc Albert-Saint-Martin.** This compact urban playground includes a play area for kids 18 months to 5 years old and another for 5- to 12- year-olds. The park is also a 10-minute walk from our favorite doll store, **Raplapla,** p 92, and the kid-friendly vegan restaurant **Aux Vivres** (below). ⏱ *1½ hr. Parc Albert-Saint-Martin is at the corner of rue Berri and rue de Bienville. Métro: Laurier.*

Kids with a sampling of whimsical dolls from Raplapla.

Exploring the Jardin Botanique.

Kids will love the wraps, burgers, and juice concoctions at ⑩ **Aux Vivres**, a cheery vegan restaurant. The main restaurant is bright and busy, and there's a small back terrace. A large selection of foods is also available to go, including lunch boxes, nori rolls, salads, and homemade desserts. *4631 bd. St-Laurent. www. auxvivres.com.* ☎ *514/842-3479.*

⑪ ★★★ **Biodôme de Montréal.** Closed for 2019 for a major renovation, the new Biodome is expected to open in 2020. The venue has long been one of our favorites in the city and is great fun for all ages. It re-creates four ecosystems including a tropical rainforest—with golden lion tamarin monkeys that swing on branches only an arm's length away—and a polar environment. It's next door to the **Stade Olympique (Olympic Stadium)**, p 66. Also nearby and good for kids is the **Insectarium de Montréal**, on the grounds of the **Jardin Botanique** (p 53). Note that the Insectarium is also undergoing renovations and is not expected to reopen until summer 2021. ⏱ *3 hr. 4777 av. Pierre-de-Coubertin (next to Stade Olympique). www.espacepour lavie.ca/en/biodome.* ☎ *514/868-3000. Check website for new hours and prices. Métro: Viau.*

Open for breakfast, lunch, and dinner 7 days a week, ⑫ **L'Express** is the most classic of Parisian-style bistros and a fun treat for every age. From the black-and-white-checkered floor to the grand, high ceilings to the classic cuisine, this is where Old France meets New. Popular dishes include homemade ravioli, steak tartare, and profiteroles in maple syrup. Children are welcome. *3927 rue t-Denis. www.restaurant lexpress.com.* ☎ *514/845-5333.*

Romantic Montréal

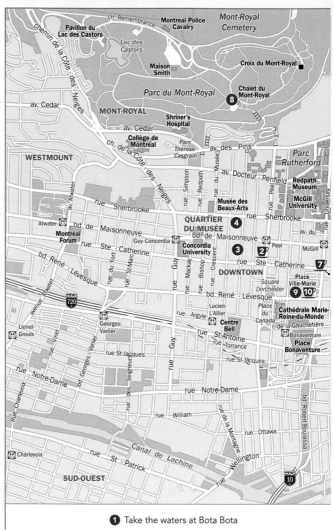

ch. Remembrance
Montreal Police
Cavalry

Pavillon du
Lac des Castors

Mont-Royal
Cemetery

Lac des
Castors

Croix du Mont-Royal ■

Maison
Smith

Chalet du
Mont-Royal
8

Parc du Mont-Royal

av. Cedar

MONT-ROYAL

Shriner's
Hospital

WESTMOUNT

av. Cedar

Collège de
Montréal

Parc
Thérèse-
Casgrain

av. des Pins

Parc
Rutherford

av. Docteur - Penfield

Redpath
Museum

McGill
University

Musée des
Beaux-Arts

rue Sherbrooke

QUARTIER
DU MUSÉE
4

av. du

Atwater
Montréal
Forum

rue Sherbrooke

bd. de Maisonneuve

bd. de Maisonneuve

McGill

rue Ste - Catherine

Guy-Concordia
Concordia
University
3

Peel

2²

rue Ste - Catherine

DOWNTOWN

7²

Square
Dorchester

Place
Ville-Marie
9 **10²**

bd. René - Lévesque

bd. René - Lévesque

Place
du
Canada

Cathédrale Marie-
Reine-du-Monde

Lucien-
L'Allier

rue Argyle

Centre
Bell

rue
St-Antoine

rue Torrance

Place
Bonaventure

Bonaventure

r. de la Gauchetière

Georges-
Vanier

Lionel-
Groulx

rue St-Jacques

rue St-Jacques

rue Notre-Dame

rue Notre-Dame

rue William

rue Ottawa

Canal de Lachine

rue St - Patrick

rue Wellington

Charlevoix

SUD-OUEST

1 Take the waters at Bota Bota

2² Lunch at Ferreira Café

3 Check into Le Mount Stephen Hotel

4 Spring for afternoon tea at Ritz-Carlton Montréal

5 Find some sweets for your sweet

Sir George-Étienne Cartier Monument

Parc Jeanne-Mance

rue Marie--Anne

rue Rachel

rue Duluth

PLATEAU MONT-ROYAL

❺

rue Rachel

Parc La Fontaine

Percival Molson Memorial Stadium

av. des Pins

rue Roy

❻→

rue Cherrier

av. Milton

rue Prince--Arthur

🔽 Sherbrooke

rue Sherbrooke

Parc Persillier-Lachapelle

rue Ontario

rue Sherbrooke

Université du Québec à Montréal (UQAM)

Place-des-Arts
Prés-Kennedy

QUARTIER DES SPECTACLES

Grande Bibliothèque du Québec

LATIN QUARTER

bd. de Maisonneuve

🔽 Place-des-Arts

🔽 St-Laurent

🔽 Berri-UQAM

THE VILLAGE

Square Phillips

Place-des-Arts

Complexe Desjardins

Place de la Paix

Université du Québec à Montréal (UQAM)

rue Ste--Catherine

🔽 Beaudry

bd. René--Lévesque

bd. René--Lévesque

INTERNATIONAL QUARTER

rue de la Gauchetière

🔽 Square-Victoria-OACI

av. Viger

🔽 Place-d'Armes

🔽 Champ-de-Mars

av. Viger

Palais des Congrès (Convention Center)

Champ de Mars

rue St-Antoine

rue Notre-Dame

Montréal World Trade Centre

Banque de Montréal

Vieux Palais de Justice

Hôtel de Ville

Parc Ville-de-la-Flèche

Parc Dalhousie

rue Notre-Dame

Basilique Notre-Dame

ⓘ

Notre-Dame-de-Bon-Secours

VIEUX-MONTRÉAL

Marché Bonsecours

Place d'Youville

Pointe-à-Callière (Montréal Museum of Archaeology & History)

VIEUX-PORT

Quai Jacques Cartier

Quai de l'Horloge

Parc du bassin Bonsecours

St. Lawrence River

Quai King Edward

Quai Alexandra

❶

Parc de la Cité du Havre

0   1/4 mi
0   250 m

ⓘ Information

🔽 Metro Station

❻ Steal away to the Jardin Botanique

7⃣ Henri Brasserie Française

❽ Bask in the expansive views atop Mont Royal

❾ Watch twilight turn to darkness

10⃣ Les Enfants Terribles

Romance is in the eyes of the beholder, making this is a tricky tour to propose. Sitting hand in hand on a quiet park bench might be all you need for a moment to be luminous—while your best friend might dream of an opulent dinner or an evening in a fancy hotel. Options here range from the modest to the luxurious. START: **Métro: Square-Victoria-OACI.**

Taking in the waters at Bota Bota is a great way to unwind.

❶ Take the waters at Bota Bota. Bath complexes are common throughout Scandinavia, less so in North America. This all-season spa is housed in a converted boat docked on the far western end of Vieux-Port. It offers a luxurious water circuit of dry saunas, steam rooms, Jacuzzis, showers, and outdoor terraces, offering stunning views of the Old Port. Access to the boat's "water circuit" is C$40 to C$65 for 3 hours depending on day and time and includes access to all the water facilities and lounges. Massages and facials are available, too. An extension—onto dry land—includes gardens. ⏱ *2+ hr. The boat is docked in the water near the corner of rue de la Commune ouest and rue McGill. www.botabota.ca.* ☎ *855/284-0333 or 514/284-0333. Mon–Thurs 10am–10pm, Fri–Sun 9am–10pm. Métro: Square-Victoria-OACI.*

❷ Lunch at Ferreira Café. In a city where French food and its derivations rule, the fleshy mounds of aromatic Portuguese grilled squid and black cod and the lush blue-and-saffron Mediterranean decor create an experience that is downright sexy. Try their take on the classic *bacalhau à brás*, which mixes cod, string potatoes, olives, and poached eggs. A late-night menu for C$30 is available after 10pm every evening but Sunday. *See p 104.*

❸ Check into Le Mount Stephen Hotel. Sumptuous examples of 19th-century neo-Renaissance architecture welcome you at the entry of this expertly preserved hotel and historic monument.

Modern takes on classic Portuguese seafood awaits at Ferreira Café.

Tea for two—swanky and romantic—at the Ritz-Carlton Montréal.

Meanwhile, the new tower of guest rooms, practically invisible from the street, features luxe accommodations outfitted with the latest technologies. The hospitable hotel staff will go the extra mile. *See p 135.*

❹ Spring for afternoon tea at Ritz-Carlton Montréal. A sumptuous tea service is presented at the Ritz daily at 12:30pm and 3:30pm in its gilded Palm Court. Each guest gets tea, scones, finger sandwiches, and mini pastries (C$36 per person). A glass of champagne is available for an additional C$13 to C$102. ⏱ *1½ hr. 1228 rue Sherbrooke ouest. www. ritzmontreal.com.* ☎ *514/842-4212.*

❺ Find some sweets for your sweet. Local chocolatier **Les Chocolats de Chloé** spices up offerings with saffron, figs and balsamic vinegar, lime zest, and Espelette pepper. The chocolates are sold at the company shop in the Plateau, a short walk from the gorgeous **Parc La Fontaine**. Head there with your bag of treats to take in the scenic ponds on the quaint English (west) half and dreamy garden paths in the distinctly French (east) side—the park is a microcosm of Montréal, from its bilingual nature to its laid-back atmosphere. *See p 93 and p 41.*

❻ Steal away to the Jardin Botanique. You'll be hardpressed to find an area in the botanical gardens that isn't conducive to cuddling. In summer, the Rose Garden is awash in color, and the paths are lush and verdant. In winter, the garden's nine greenhouses stay steamy. In September and October, a gorgeous evening event fills the Chinese, Japanese, and First Nations Gardens with lanterns and multimedia illumination. You might want to avoid the Toxic Plants Garden—unless you're putting your friend on notice or have a wicked sense of humor. ⏱ *2 hr. See p 25, bullet* ❸.

Founded in 1879, the swank Maison Birks jewelry store has been a luxurious mainstay of downtown Montreal. For years the handsome building it is housed in had vast sections that were not open to the public. No longer. A new hotel, Hotel Birks Montréal (https://hotel birksmontreal.com), opened in the building in 2018, and with it a grand and opulent brasserie. With high ceilings, bold interior columns, and white curlicue decor, **7️⃣ Henri Brasserie Française** features an oyster bar and separate menus for breakfast, lunch, brunch, dinner, dessert, and cocktails. Floor-to-ceiling windows look out on a small park, Phillips Square. It's a perfect spot for a cocktail or more. *1240 rue Phillips Square. www.restaurant henri.com.* ☎ *514/544-3674. $$.*

Jardin Botanique's beautiful Chinese Garden is the perfect spot for a romantic stroll.

⑧ Bask in the expansive views atop Mont Royal. The lookouts along rue Camillien-Houde, the road that travels across Parc Mont-Royal, and the **front terrace** of the **Chalet du Mont-Royal** at the very top, offer panoramic views of Montréal and the St-Lawrence River. There are several options for getting up here and back down—see our suggested walk on p 80, or ride by car or bus. *Parc Mont-Royal, see p 39, bullet ④.*

⑨ Watch twilight turn to darkness. Free city views are available from atop Mont Royal ⑧, but perhaps more dramatic are the 360-degree views on display at the **city's new observatory** (in French, *observatoire*). The 46th floor of prominent skyscraper Place Ville Marie (p 29) was turned into a public observatory a few years ago. It features striking views of Mont Royal and the Oratoire St-Joseph, along with Vieux-Montréal, the Olympic Stadium, and locales far beyond. The admission fee includes access to a terrace on the 44th floor. *Observatoire Place Ville Marie,*

1 Place Ville Marie. www.observatoire 360.com. ☎ *514/544-8200. Admission C$19 adult, C$15 children 13–17, C$9 children 6–12, free children 5 and under. Check website for hours, which change seasonally. Métro: Square-Victoria-OACI.*

On the 44th floor of Place Ville-Marie—two floors below the Observatoire Place Ville Marie— **⑩ Les Enfants Terribles** offers spectacular views and is a splashy destination for a nighttime drink or meal. During our brunch visit, we enjoyed the house specialty of shrimp toast made with small crustaceans from the Gaspé Peninsula. This outpost of a fine enough regional chain was packed during daylight hours with family gatherings and gabby tables of two. In the evenings, the restaurant—and, in warm months, its outdoor terrace—are buzzy, festive locales for a date. *1 Place Ville Marie (entrance to elevator at bd. Robert-Bourassa). www.jesuisun enfantterrible.com.* ☎ *514/544-8884. Lunch and dinner daily, Sat–Sun brunch. Métro: Square-Victoria-OACI. $$.*

Environmental Montréal

A conservation mindset has been part of the Montreal identity for a long time. A sustainability plan for 2016–2020 set goals and actions for the city to reduce its greenhouse gas emissions by 80% by 2050, increase vegetation and biodiversity, and ensure access to "human-scale" neighborhoods. Citizens definitely walk the walk: 47% of morning rush-hour travel in 2008 was already by foot, bicycle, or mass transit, and the goal is to boost that number to 55% by 2021. Visitors will find ample opportunity to join in on the efforts. START: **Métro: Parc Jean-Drapeau.**

The Biosphère highlights how to design human-scale neighborhoods and understand climate change.

1 Biosphère. Geodesic domes popped up across the world's landscape during the 20th century for industrial and even residential use. This building, located on Île Ste-Hélène (just a 20-min. walk from Vieux-Montréal), was designed by American architect Buckminster Fuller to serve as the American Pavilion for Expo 67. A fire destroyed the sphere's acrylic skin in 1976, and for almost 20 years it served no purpose other than as a harbor landmark. But in 1995, the city of Montréal joined with Environment Canada (known today as

Environment and Climate Change Canada; www.ec.gc.ca) to convert the space. It's now a museum dedicated to raising awareness and engagement on environmental issues and, specifically, climate change. ⏲ *2 hr. 160 chemin Tour-de-l'Isle (Île Ste-Hélène). www.ec.gc.ca/biosphere.* ☎ *855/773-8200 or 514/283-5000. Admission C$15 adults, C$12 seniors, C$10 students 18 and over, free for children 17 and under. Métro: Parc Jean-Drapeau.*

2 Planétarium Rio Tinto Alcan. Explore the night sky and beyond. This planetarium, which

Montréal is a Composting Leader

Many municipalities make it easy for residents to recycle, but Montréal has taken waste management a step further: It collects compostable waste separately, providing composting bins for residents to use alongside their recycling bins and trash cans. Almost half of all household waste in the Québec province is compostable (it's also known as green waste or organic waste), and the provincial government has set a goal of getting 60% of that trash into compost facilities instead of landfills.

got a full overhaul in 2013, is part of the **Space for Life (Espace pour la vie)** complex that includes the **Jardin Botanique** (p 53) and the **Biosphere**, a four-season ecosystem that got its own major renovations in 2019. About half the shows are in English and half in French. Trailers are posted at the website. ⏱ *1 hr. 4801 ave. Pierre-De Coubertin. www. espacepourlavie.ca.* ☎ *855/518-4506 or 514/868-3000. Admission C$21 adults, C$15 students 18 and older, C$11 children 5–17 years, free for kids 4 and under, C$57 family of 5. Packages available with other Espace pour la vie musuems. Thurs–Sat 9:30am–9pm; Sun–Wed 9:30am–6pm. Metro: Viau.*

❸ **A passion for biking.** Montréal has 400 miles of bike trails within the city itself, used for both commuting and pleasure. Locals and guests use the popular self-service bicycle rental program **BIXI** (an abbreviated combination of the words *bicyclette* and *taxi*). After registering (and putting a deposit down via credit card), users pick up BIXI bikes from designated stands throughout the city and drop them off at any other stand, for a small fee. Some 7,250 bikes are in operation and available at 600 stations in Montréal's central boroughs. In

May, the **Montréal Bike Fest** (p 164) sponsored by Vélo Québec includes a 5-day bike-to-work celebration and nighttime ride (Tour la Nuit). *Stands are located throughout the city, including at Métro: Mont-Royal. See p 165.*

❹ **Volunteer conservation on Parc Mont-Royal.** The group Les amis de la montagne (Friends of

Renting a BIXI bike is a popular Montréal pastime.

Go With the Weather Flow

Winters and summers are long in Montréal—while spring and fall are sweet but short-lived. Winter lasts from November until late March, and summer from June through September. The cold months often include blizzards, freezing rain, and ice storms. In July and August, the summer humidity can often be stifling. On the most extreme days, many locals prefer to get around through the **Underground City:** Located below much of downtown, it has miles of shops, restaurants, and connections to the subway and shopping malls (see p 91). But equal numbers of people are game to go with the flow and embrace every kind of climate. Take your inspiration from them!

the Mountain) puts on activities year-round to share the history and culture of the park and to help maintain its trails and flora. On Saturday mornings from mid-May through October it hosts environmental stewardship activities that anyone can volunteer for. Activities include monitoring shrub plantings in spring and inventorying Monarch butterfly milkweed. *Parc Mont-Royal. www.lemontroyal.qc.ca. See p 39.*

⑤ Vegan options galore.
French-Canadian food has traditionally been meat-centric, but today there are lots of options for vegans and those who want to eat that way occasionally. **5A Aux Vivres,** on the Plateau, was founded in 1997 and is now the benchmark by which other city

vegan restaurants are judged. (Its tagline: "Once a pioneer, now an iconic institution.") In the Latin Quarter, **5B Resto Vego** puts out an expansive by-the-weight buffet each day. **5C Lola Rosa** is a popular four-venue chain with outposts on the Plateau and in Place-des-Arts. And **5D Invitation V**, in the heart of Old Montréal, takes vegan up a notch, with a more formal presentation—nothing about it looks "alternative." *Aux Vivres, see p 102. Resto Vego, see p 107. Lola Rosa: www. lolarosa.ca for addresses and hours of all locations. Invitation V: 201 rue St Jacques. www.invitationv.com. ☎ 514/271-8111. Lunch Tues–Sun, dinner Tues–Sat. Métro: Place d'Armes. $.*

Young Creatives Montréal

0 ——— 1/4 mi
0 ——— 250 m

⊕ Metro Station

MILE END

Rosemont

St.-Laurent
bd.

St.-Denis
rue

ch. de la Côte-Ste-Catherine

Laurier

bd. St.
Joseph

⊕ Laurier

PLATEAU
MONT-ROYAL

Jardin
Botanique

Plateau
Mont-Royal   Map
Area

Down-
town
Parc
Mont-Royal

Parc
Sir-Wilfrid-
Laurier

Papineau

Parc
Jeanne-
Mance

av. du

⊕ Mont - Royal

Mont-Royal

av.

Parc
du
Mont-Royal

■ Croix du
Mont-Royal

rue   Rachel

St.-Denis

av. Duluth

Parc
La Fontaine

du

av.

Laurent

rue des Pins

av. des Pins

⊕ Sherbrooke

rue des Pins

Sherbrooke

Papineau

av. des Pins

4²

St.

McGill
University

McCord
Museum ■

rue University

⊕

⊕ Peel

QUARTIER
DES
SPECTACLES

bd.

QUARTIER
LATIN

Sherbrooke

Amherst

rue

Ontario

THE
VILLAGE

av.

8

⊕
McGill

⊕
Place-
des-Arts

St-Laurent

⊕ Berri-UQAM
rue Ste-
Catherine

bd. de Maisonneuve ⊕
Papineau

DOWNTOWN

9A² 9B² 10 11

CHINATOWN

Beaudry

⊕

INTERNATIONAL
QUARTER   Place-
d'Armes

Champ-
de-Mars

bd. René - Lévesque

(134)

⊕ Bonaventure

Square-
Victoria-
OACI

⊕

⊕

Palais des Congrès
(Convention Center)

rue St - Antoine

rue Notre - Dame

720

12²

VIEUX-MONTRÉAL

1 Dive into vintage
   shopping
2 Kick back with a taste
   of Prague
3 Take a food tour
   of Mile End
4² Juliette et Chocolat
5 Lose yourself in the
   city's residential streets
6 Stop by the sister
   venues Casa del Popolo
   and La Sala Rosa

7 Pick up some vinyl
8 Dip into the gallery
   La Guilde
9A² Taverne F
9B² Brasserie T
10 Indulge in a night
    at the opera
11 Check out contemporary
    art—after midnight
12² Joe Beef
13 Cap off the weekend
    at Piknic Électronik

Parc
Jean-
Drapeau

Île
Sainte-
Hélène   Biosphère ■

⊕
Jean-
Drapeau

Île
Notre-Dame

13

Visitors in their 20s and 30s may want to head to Plateau Mont-Royal and into Mile End, the neighborhood just beyond. This is where many of the city's artists and entrepreneurs live and play. START: **Métro: Mont-Royal.**

❶ Dive into vintage shopping.
The Plateau and Mile End do right by secondhand, thrift, and vintage fashions. At least a dozen shops, some highly curated, some chaotically packed, can be found along boulevard St-Laurent from avenue du Mont-Royal up to rue Bernard, and on nearby side streets. We like **Local 23** (see p 96), **Kay** (157 rue Bernard ouest), and **Citizen Vintage** (5330 boulevard St-Laurent), but the best part of this kind of shopping? The inventory changes all the time. Note that many shops do not open until noon. ⏱ *3 hr. Bd. St-Laurent from av. du Mont-Royal est to rue Bernard ouest. Métro: Mont-Royal, Laurier, or Rosemont.*

❷ Kick back with a taste of Prague.
Exuding a relaxed cool, the Mile End bar Bílý Kun brings in students and professionals who sit elbow to elbow at small tables. The room is lit by candles at night, and in summer ceiling fans twirl and picture windows open to the street. Decor is quirky (hello, mounted ostrich heads), and absinthe drink options are on the menu. If you're visiting in the day, stop by the little shops along the same street. There's lots of used clothing and kitschy stuff. ⏱ *2 hr. See p 87.*

❸ Take a food tour of Mile End.
Here's a fun way to see this artsy neighborhood: Take a walking tour with **Local Montréal Food Tours.** The six-stop tour includes falafels from the vegan **Green Panther** (La Panthère Verte) restaurant, charcuterie, bagels, homemade gnocchi, and ice cream. It's a

Quirky and hip, Bílý Kun is a great place to grab a drink after exploring the surrounding shops.

3-hour tour covering 2.3km (1.4 miles). A slightly shorter evening tour has five stops. ⏱ *3 hr. Starts at La Panthère Verte, at 160 rue St. Viateur est. https://localfoodtours.com/montreal.* ☎ *438/600-0501. C$59 for six-taste tour, C$52 for five-taste tour. Check the website for days and times. Métro: Rosemont.*

❹ Juliette et Chocolat
fills the broad need of coffee house, luncheonette, and purveyor of exceptional chocolate desserts. Chocolate comes in all forms: hot and cold beverages, crêpes, dense brownies (10 kinds!), and fondue. *3600 bd. St-Laurent. www.julietteetchocolat.com.* ☎ *438/380-1090. Sun–Thurs 11am–11pm; Fri–Sat 11am–midnight. Métro: Sherbrooke. $.*

Cycling in the Plateau, one of Montréal's most picturesque and romantic neighborhoods.

with a full calendar of eclectic offerings from around the city and beyond. ① *At least 30 min.*

❼ Pick up some vinyl. Year in and year out, **Beatnick Records**, a little storefront shop, is ranked a top city record store for new and rare LPs. Selections include rock, electro, psychedelic, jazz, and country, with artists from Aretha Franklin to Johnny Cash to Lou Reed and way beyond. ① *30 min. 3770 rue St-Denis. www.beatnick music.com and www.facebook.com/ DisquesBeatnick.* ☎ *514/842-0664. Métro: Sherbrooke.*

❽ Dip into the gallery La Guilde. A 2017 move out of its former brownstone home gave La Guilde Canadienne des Métiers d'Art (the Canadian Guild of Crafts) contemporary street-level digs and a slimmed-down name (it now just

❺ Lose yourself in the city's residential streets. Just walk with no agenda? *Naturellement!* The tree-lined streets of the Plateau and Mile End are ablaze with gold and scarlet leaves in the fall, thick with fresh snow in the winter, and lushly green in spring and summer—the perfect backdrop in any season for a leisurely stroll. ① *2 hr. Métro: Laurier.*

❻ Stop by the sister venues Casa del Popolo and La Sala Rosa. Spanish for "The House of the People," the cozy Casa del Popolo is set in a scruffy storefront. It serves coffee and vegetarian food, operates a laid-back bar, and has a small first-floor stage. For many it's a refuge from the trendier, expensive venues farther south on boulevard St-Laurent. Across the street, sister performance space La Sala Rosa is a terrific music venue

A pleasant park setting where Plateau Mont-Royal meets Mile End.

goes by "La Guilde"). The gallery emphasizes First Nations art and exhibits artists both emerging and well-known. It's across the street from the grand **Musée des Beaux-Arts** (p 91), which has its own dazzling special exhibitions. ⏱ *15 min. 1356 rue Sherbrooke ouest. www. laguilde.com.* ☎ *514/849-6091. Admission free. Métro: Peel.*

Directly on the sidewalk of Place des Arts are two restaurants housed in unique glass boxes: **9A Taverne F**, a Portuguese restaurant specializing in *petiscos* (small plates to be shared among friends), and **9B Brasserie T**, where you can make a creative meal out of just the appetizers, charcuteries, and tartares. At night in warm months, a pool of water alongside the restaurants and the length of a city block has a "dancing waters" lightshow. *Taverne F, 1485 Rue Jeanne-Mance. www.tavernef.com.* ☎ *514/289-4558. $$. Brasserie T, see p 103.*

⑩ Indulge in a night at the opera. In Place des Arts, L'Opera de Montréal offers an ongoing "34 and under" promotion of up to 50% off all tickets. Productions can be edgy and avant-garde, making them the perfect introduction for opera newbies. The same discount is offered at other Place des Arts companies, including Orchestre Symphonique de Montréal and Orchestre Métropolitain du Grand Montréal. *See p 124.*

⑪ Check out contemporary art—after midnight. For its "Les Nocturnes du MAC," the Musée d'Art Contemporain de Montréal stays open until 2am, with live music, drinks, and tours of the exhibition galleries. The events happen a few times a year. ⏱ *2 hrs. See*

www.macm.org/en/cactivite/ nocturne-event/.

If you're sporting sleeve tattoos, cute little vintage clothes, or a C$200 haircut designed to look like you just fell out of bed, head south and west to **12 Joe Beef.** Foodies will have heard of the glutton-inducing restaurant—think boisterous diner with adventurous food—given that it has been profiled everywhere. The evening's options are written on a chalkboard, but if you're game, this a good place to leave yourself in the kitchen's capable hands, with parameters such as "seafood to start" or "meat for a main course." The management runs two other equally stellar operations on the same block: Liverpool House restaurant, at #2501, and Le Vin Papillon wine bar, at #2519. Reservations are essential. *2491 rue Notre-Dame ouest. www.joebeef.ca.* ☎ *514/935-6504. Main courses C$25–C$55. Tues–Sat 5:30–11pm. Métro: Lionel-Groulx. $$.*

Venison carpaccio at Joe Beef.

⓭ Cap off the weekend at Piknic Électronik. Every Sunday afternoon into evening from mid-May through September, Piknic Électronik presents an outdoor electronic music dance party at Parc Jean-Drapeau, an easy 10-minute subway ride from the city. Tickets are C$19 at the door, and the shows run from 2pm to 9:30pm. ◷ *At least 2 hr. Plaine des Jeux on Parc Jean-Drapeau. www. piknicelectronik.com.* ☎ *514/904-1247. Métro: Jean-Drapeau.*

Sport Montréal

Longueuil

MONTRÉAL

Lachine

Lasalle

La Prairie

ch. de la Côte-Ste-Catherine

6

Rosemont

MILE END

bd. St - Laurent

rue St - Denis

Parc Père-Marquette

av. Laurier

bd. St - Joseph

Laurier

Parc Sir-Wilfrid-Laurier

PLATEAU MONT-ROYAL

av. du Parc

av. du

Mont - Royal

Mont-Royal

av. Papineau

Parc du Mont-Royal

Parc Jeanne-Mance

■ Croix du Mont-Royal

rue Rachel

Parc La Fontaine

av. Duluth

av. des Pins

5

av. des Pins

rue St - Denis

bd. St - Laurent

Sherbrooke

Sherbrooke

QUARTIER LATIN

rue Amherst

Ontario

THE VILLAGE

av. Papineau

McGill University

rue University

McCord Museum ■

Place-des-Arts

St-Laurent

Berri-UQAM

Papineau

Peel

McGill

rue

QUARTIER DES SPECTACLES

CHINATOWN

bd. de Maisonneuve

DOWNTOWN

Ste - Catherine

Beaudry

3 **4**

INTERNATIONAL QUARTER

Champ-de-Mars

bd. René - Lévesque

Bonaventure

Bourassa

2

Square-Victoria-OACI

720

Place-d'Armes

rue St - Antoine

rue Notre - Dame

bd. Robert-

Palais des Congrès (Convention Center)

VIEUX-MONTRÉAL

VIEUX-PORT

10

Île Sainte-Hélène

Parc Jean-Drapeau

Biosphère ■

Pont de la Concorde

Jean-Drapeau

| 0 | | 1/4 mi |
| 0 | 250 m | |

Île Notre-Dame

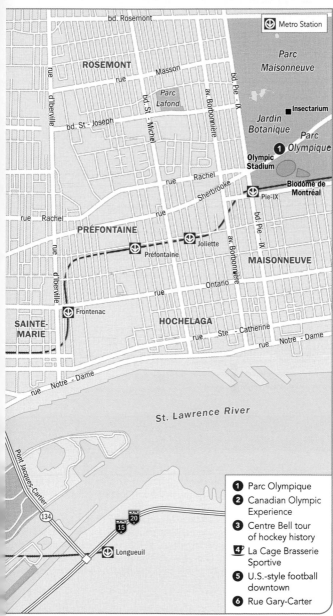

1 Parc Olympique
2 Canadian Olympic Experience
3 Centre Bell tour of hockey history
4 La Cage Brasserie Sportive
5 U.S.-style football downtown
6 Rue Gary-Carter

This city loves its sports. While its first love is the Canadiens hockey team, Montréal also takes pride in having hosted the 1976 Olympic Games. Major league baseball had a team here from 1969 to 2004 (at that point the Expos packed up and moved to Washington, D.C.), and U.S.–style football is played by the Alouettes. Jump in and start cheering. START: **Métro: Viau.**

❶ ★ **Parc Olympique.** Olympics fans make it a point to pilgrimage to Montréal's space-age stadium, the centerpiece of the 1976 Olympic Games. A guided tour describes the Olympics that took place here and use of the center today (for many years it hosted the Montréal Expos baseball team). Its 165m (541-ft.) inclined tower, which leans at a 45-degree angle, has done duty as an observation deck in the past, although it was closed in 2019 for an indefinite period (the building was recently refurbished—adding wiring and windows—and turned into offices). The complex includes swimming pools used by both Olympians-in-training and the general public and a 56,000-seat stadium for sporting events and music concerts. A snazzy outdoor esplanade is now host to circus shows, dance parties, and skateboard festivals. ◷ 1 hr. 4141 Pierre-De-Coubertin ave. www.parcolympique.qc.ca.

Guided tour C$15 adults, C$12 students, C$8 children 5–17, C$37 family of 5. ☎ 877/997-0919 or 514/252-4141. Métro: Viau.

❷ ★ **Canadian Olympic Experience.** Open since 2018, this museum celebrates all things Olympic. The most universally appealing section is the zone where visitors can try out sports virtually, including fencing, bobsledding, and mogul skiing. The rest of the museum is Canadian-centric, with displays about the 200+ individuals who have represented the country at the Olympic Games. It's housed in the headquarters of the Canadian Olympic Committee, and when we visited, the exterior of the skyscraper was lit with multi-color Olympic rings. ◷ 1 hr. 500 bd. René-Lévesque ouest. https://experience.olympic.ca. Admission C$13 adults, C$9 children 7–17, C$39 family of 4. ☎ 866/908-9090 or 514/790-1111. Métro: Square-Victoria-OACI.

Channel Your Own Sporty Spice

Montréal offers lots of options for folks who like their downtime active: Kayaking, paddle boating, skating, and cross-country skiing are all options. Biking, though, is the biggest personal sport. Visitors can grab BIXI bikes for short trips (see p 4), but guided tours are also a fun option. **ÇaRoule/Montréal on Wheels** (27 rue de la Commune est; www.caroulemontreal.com; ☎ 877/866-0633 or 514/866-0633) offers a variety of tours including a 4-hour jaunt that goes from Vieux-Port through the Quartier Latin up to Parc La Fontaine, the Plateau, and Mile End. The cost is C$75, and reservations are required.

Percival-Molson Memorial Stadium, downtown on the McGill University campus, is the home of the CFL Montréal Alouettes.

children 12–17, C$12 children 5–11. Canadiens tickets available at www. nhl.com/canadiens and online resale sales. Métro: Bonaventure.

Given that **4 La Cage Brasserie Sportive** is located on av. des Canadiens du Montréal just down the street from Centre Bell, you know it's the place to be in hockey season. It's packed both before and during games. When it's quieter, bartenders will call up other sports on the TVs for guests who ask. *See p 114.*

5 ★ Football, U.S.–style. The Montréal Alouettes are part of the Canadian Football League, and they play right downtown on the McGill University campus, at Percival-Molson Memorial Stadium. If you don't have tickets, it's easy to get close and take in the atmosphere. ○ *3 hr.*

6 ★ Rue Gary-Carter. Jarry Park, in Little Italy a few blocks from Marché Jean-Talon, was home to the Expos baseball team for 7 years (it now hosts the Rogers Cup tennis tournament). Rue Faillon ouest on the park's southern side was renamed rue Gary-Carter in 2013 to honor the late Hall of Fame catcher, whose career started here. Carter played with the Expos for 11 years, then took his star power to the New York Mets, helping to fuel them to a 1986 World Series victory. *Métro: De Castelnau.*

3 ★ Centre Bell tour of hockey history. Fans who wear the *bleu-blanc-rouge* of their favorite hockey team can tour the Hometown House of the Habs. Tours of the hockey venue are available daily and include stops in the Canadiens' dressing room, the press gallery, and the podium where postgame interviews rehash the agony or the ecstasy of what went down on the ice. ○ *1 hr. 1909 ave. des Canadiens-de-Montréal. www.centrebell.ca/en/page/guided_ tours.* ☎ *855/310-2525. Guided tour C$20 adults, C$15 seniors and*

Historic Montréal

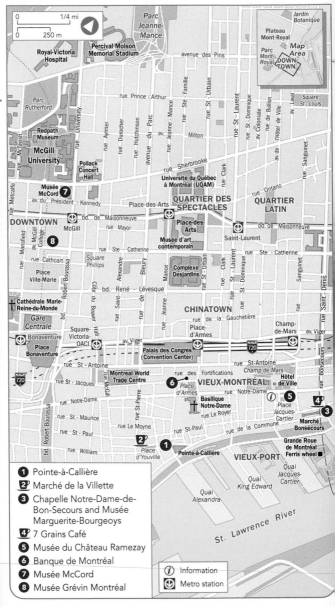

1. Pointe-à-Callière
2. Marché de la Villette
3. Chapelle Notre-Dame-de-Bon-Secours and Musée Marguerite-Bourgeoys
4. 7 Grains Café
5. Musée du Château Ramezay
6. Banque de Montréal
7. Musée McCord
8. Musée Grévin Montréal

ⓘ Information
Ⓜ Metro station

First Nations vs. Europeans. French vs. British. Peace vs. war. Montréal history is thick with both tranquillity and strife. The city wears its history proudly on its sleeve: In no other place in North America does the richness of 400 years of nation building continue to be as discussed, celebrated, and dissected as it is in Montréal and its sister city, Québec City, to the north. START: **Métro: McGill.**

The Pointe-à-Callière history museum sits on the exact location of the city's founding.

❶ ★★★ Pointe-à-Callière. Built on the very site where the original colony of Montréal was established in 1642, this contemporary Museum of Archaeology and History provides details on the region's inhabitants, from Amerindians to French trappers to Scottish merchants to the locals of today. 🕐 1½ hr. See p 44.

Just around the corner from Pointe-à-Callière, **❷ Marché de la Villette** offers a traditional French snack or meal. It started life as an atmospheric boucherie and charcuterie market specializing in cheeses, meats, and breads, and started adding tables. The staff is flirty and welcoming to the waves of locals and tourists who settle in. We return regularly for the hearty cassoulet maison royal with duck confit along with pork belly, homemade sausage, and silky-smooth beans, all topped with crunchy bread crumbs. *324 rue St-Paul ouest.* www.marche-villette.com ☎ 514/807-8084. $$.

❸ ★ Chapelle Notre-Dame-de-Bon-Secours and Musée Marguerite-Bourgeoys. Called the Sailors' Church because so many seamen made pilgrimages here to give thanks for being saved at sea, this chapel was founded by Marguerite Bourgeoys, a nun and teacher. The present chapel was built in 1771 but excavations in 1996 unearthed foundations of her

Ship hanging inside the "Sailors' Church" of Chapelle Notre-Dame-de–Bon-Secours.

Today's First Nations

Native sovereignty and "the land question," notes prominent filmmaker Alanis Obomsawin, "have been issues since the French and English first settled the area. A lot of promises were made and never kept." Obomsawin is a member of the Abenaki Nation who was raised on the Odanak Reserve near Montréal, and over a long career she has provided unflinching looks at that essential tension and the lives of contemporary Native Americans, who are referred to collectively in the Québec province as members of the First Nations. She began making movies for the National Film Board of Canada in 1967 and has produced more than 30 documentaries about the hard edges of the lives of aboriginal people. Termed "the first lady of First Nations film" by the commissioner of the film board in 2008, Obomsawin received the Governor General's Performing Arts Award for Lifetime Artistic Achievement that year.

One of her major works is *Kanehsatake: 270 Years of Resistance* (1993). It details a wrenching incident in 1990 that pitted native peoples against the government over lands about an hour west of Montréal that were slated to be turned into a golf course. The clash degenerated into a months-long armed standoff between Mohawks and the authorities. "What the confrontation of 1990 showed is that this is a generation that is not going to put up with what happened in the past," said Obomsawin. Many of her movies can be viewed at the **National Film Board** website (www.nfb.ca).

original 1675 church, which can be visited. The museum tells the story of Bourgeoys's life and incorporates the archaeological site. Visitors can climb the tower for a view of the port and Old Montréal. Outside the church, take a look at the exterior of **La Maison Pierre du Calvet,** a few steps away at 405 rue Bonsecours. Built in 1725, this house was inhabited by a well-to-do family in its first years. Pierre du Calvet, believed to be the original owner, was a French Huguenot who supported the American Revolution and met here with Benjamin Franklin in 1775. With a characteristic sloped roof and raised end walls that serve as firebreaks, the building is constructed of Montréal gray stone. It has been a hotel and restaurant in recent years and was under renovation in

2019. ⏱ *30 min. 400 rue St-Paul est (at the foot of rue Bonsecours). www.margueritebourgeoys.org/en.* ☎ *514/282-8670. Free admission to chapel. Museum (includes archaeological site) C$12 adults, C$9 seniors and students, C$7 kids ages 6–12, free for children 5 and under. C$30 families. May–Oct daily 10am–6pm; Nov to mid-Jan and Mar–Apr Tues–Sun 11am–4pm. Closed mid-Jan to Feb. Métro: Champ-de-Mars.*

Offering baked goods, breakfast, and lunch, **4** **7 Grains Café** is small and likeable. Tucked into a corner location, it offers sandwiches, crêpes, and casseroles, and has games and a small area where kids can play. *393 rue St-Paul est. www.7 grains.ca.* ☎ *514/861-8181. $.*

Explore 300 years of Montréal history at the Musée du Château Ramezay.

⑤ ★★ Musée du Château Ramezay. Claude de Ramezay, the colony's 11th governor, built this château as his residence in 1705. It was home to the city's royal French governors for almost 4 decades, until Ramezay's heirs sold it to a trading company in 1745. Fifteen years later, British conquerors took it over, and then in 1775 an army of American revolutionaries invaded Montréal and used the château as their headquarters. For 6 weeks in 1776, Benjamin Franklin spent his days here, trying to persuade the Québécois to rise with the American colonists against British rule (he failed). Exhibits about natives and the New World, the fur trade, and New France share space with old portraits, Amerindian artifacts, and other memorabilia related to the economic and social activities of the 18th and 19th centuries.

🕐 1 hr. 280 rue Notre-Dame est. www.chateauramezay.qc.ca. ☎ 514/861-3708. *Admission C$11 adults, with discounts for students, children, and seniors; free for children 4 and under. June–Oct daily 9:30am–6pm; Nov–May Tues–Sun 10am–4:30pm. Métro: Champ-de-Mars.*

⑥ ★ Banque de Montréal. The grand bank and teeny bank exhibit in this building are worth stopping into when you're passing through Place d'Armes in Vieux-Montréal. This is Montréal's oldest bank building, dating from 1847. From 1901 to 1905, American architect Stanford White extended the original building, and in this enlarged space, he created a lavish, vast chamber with green-marble columns topped with golden capitals. The public is welcome to stop in for a look. The bank also houses a

Stanford White's commanding Banque de Montréal.

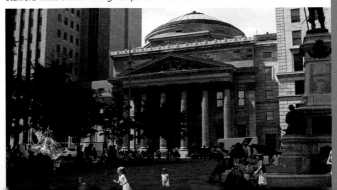

Catch a glimpse of Canadian history at Musée McCord.

quirky exhibit that illustrates early bank operations. It has on display mechanical cast-iron penny banks and sample counterfeit bills. It's just off the main lobby to the left, and admission is free. ① *15 min. 129 rue St-Jacques.* ☎ *514/877-6810. Museum open Mon–Fri 10am–4pm.*

❼ ★★ **Musée McCord.** The McCord is fresh at each visit. It boasts an fascinating permanent exhibition, "Wearing Our Identity: The First People's Collection." It presents a respectful look at the relationship of the region's First Nations to their clothing, which often is made of animal pelts. Temporary exhibitions are edgier and have included the first major retrospective of fashion photographer Horst (a frequent contributor to

Marguerite Bourgeoys, Canada's First Female Saint

One of the "first women" of Montréal is Marguerite Bourgeoys (1620–1700), a teacher who traveled from France in the mid–17th century to join the nascent New France colony of 50 people. She was 33 when she arrived. She built schools for both the settlers and native children, and cofounded the Congregation of Notre-Dame, Canada's first nuns' order. The settlement prospered, contained until the 1800s in the area known today as Vieux-Montréal. Bourgeoys was canonized by Pope John Paul II in 1982, becoming the Canadian church's first female saint.

The **Musée Marguerite-Bourgeoys** ★ is devoted to relating Bourgeoys' life and work. It's housed in a restored 18th-century crypt in the Chapelle Notre-Dame-de-Bon-Secours, in Vieux-Montréal. For the chapel's 350th birthday, Marguerite's remains were brought to the church and interred in the altar.

1759: Britain Takes Québec City from France

It can't be overstated how much the British and French struggle for dominance in the 1700s and 1800s for North America—the New World—continues to shape the character of the Québec province today. A bit of history is in order. In 1607, a group of British entrepreneurs under a charter from King James I sailed west and founded the British colony of Jamestown, in what would later become Virginia. French explorer Samuel de Champlain arrived in Québec City a year later, determined to establish a French colony on the North American continent as well.

By the 1750s, the constant struggle between Britain and France for dominance in the Canadian region had escalated. The French appointed General Louis Joseph, marquis de Montcalm, to command their forces in Québec City. The British sent an expedition of 4,500 men in a fleet under the command of General James Wolfe. The British troops surprised the French by coming up and over the cliffs of Québec City's Cap Diamant, and the ensuing skirmish, fought on September 13, 1759, lasted 18 to 25 minutes, depending on whose account you read. It resulted in 600 casualties, including both generals.

The battle had a significant impact on the future of North America. Britain was victorious, and as a result, the continent remained under English influence for more than a century. That authority carries on today: Queen Elizabeth II's face graces all Canadian currency.

"Burning of Hayes House, Dalhousie Square, Montreal," by James Duncan, at Musée McCord.

Vogue in the 20th century) and a collection of "queer baroque" ceramics works. Also available to the world at large are online collections that provide a taste of the depth of its offerings. A strong museum shop features locally made bags and jewelry, Aboriginal artwork, and children's toys. Most exhibitions are small and won't take visitors more than 15 minutes each, but there usually are a couple of temporary shows in addition to the permanent display. ⏱ *1 hr. See p 19, bullet* ❻.

❽ ★★ **Musée Grévin Montréal.** This is a different way to take in your history: An offshoot of the popular Musée Grévin wax museum

Wax figure of Julie Payette, a Canadian astronaut, at the Musée Grévin wax museum.

in Paris, this Canada-centric version is filled with lifelike replicas of figures, grouped by theme. Early on there's a heavy focus on Canadian personalities and historic New France characters dating back to Québec's beginnings in the 16th century. Later, entertainers including Lady Gaga, Jimi Hendrix, and Brad Pitt fill a star-studded room. (Children under six might get spooked by the unmoving but lifelike statues.) ⏱ *at least 30 min. 705 rue Ste-Catherine oust (inside the Centre Eaton mall, 5th floor). www.grevin-montreal.com.* ☎ *514/788-5211. Admission C$20 adults, with discounts for students and seniors; C$14 for children ages 6–12; free for children 5 and under. Mon–Sat 10am–6pm; Sun 11am–5pm. Métro: McGill.* ●

The Language of Separatism

Two defining tensions of Canadian life are language and culture, and they continue to be thorny issues. Many Québécois have long believed that the only way to maintain their rich French culture in the face of the Anglophone (English-speaking) ocean that surrounds them is to make their province a separate, independent state. Indeed, Québec's role within the Canadian federation has been the most debated and volatile topic of conversation in Canadian politics for the past 50 years. The tension is long-simmering: After France lost power in Québec to the British in the 18th century, a kind of linguistic exclusionism developed, with wealthy Scottish and English bankers and merchants denying French-Canadians access to upper levels of business and government. A real bias continued well into the 20th century.

The separatist movement began in earnest when René Lévesque founded the Parti Québécois (PQ) in 1968. The PQ became the governing party in 1976, and a year later passed Bill 101, which all but banned the use of English on public signage. Today English is widely spoken in Montréal and both English and French are used in the written materials for almost all hotels, restaurants, and other venues that cater to tourists. But French is still the state language across the Québec province, and all signs are required to be in French.

Little Italy & Mile End

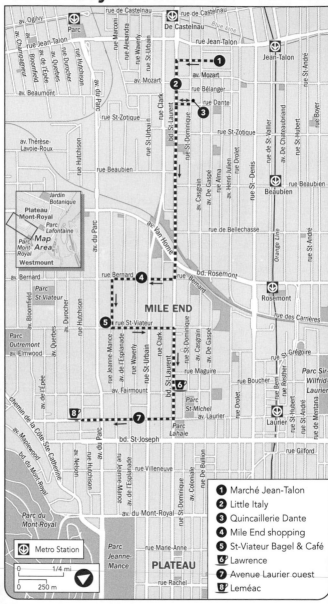

1 Marché Jean-Talon
2 Little Italy
3 Quincaillerie Dante
4 Mile End shopping
5 St-Viateur Bagel & Café
6 Lawrence
7 Avenue Laurier ouest
8 Leméac

Previous page: Shopping for fruit at Marché Jean-Talon.

Most cities are best explored on foot, and Montréal is one of North America's most pedestrian-friendly. There's much to see in the concentrated districts. This tour is essentially a browsing and grazing trek, designed to sample two flourishing neighborhoods where many of the city's younger families and creatives work and play and live. Little Italy is bounded by rue Jean-Talon on the north, rue de Bellechasse on the south, boulevard St-Laurent on the west, and rue St-Denis on the east. Mile End is bounded more or less by avenue Van Horne to the north, avenue du Mont-Royal to the south, rue Hutchison to the west, and rue St-Denis to the east. START: **Métro: Jean-Talon.**

❶ **Marché Jean-Talon.** Start with nibbles and grazes at one of North America's largest open-air markets. Jean-Talon covers the gamut of locally grown produce, stunning flowers, and ready-to-devour delicacies. Walls go up as a barrier to winter's chill, making it a perfect place to mill around no matter the season. *7070 av. Henri-Julien. www.marchespublics-mtl.com.* ☎ *514/937-7754.*

❷ **Little Italy.** If you haven't had your coffee yet, head south from Jean-Talon into Little Italy and try a stand-up espresso at one of the many cafés along the main (boulevard St-Laurent) or side streets (like rue Dante). The Italian population has thrived here since the early 1900s, and remnants of Art Deco architecture as well as shops with cured meats, fresh pasta, or cannoli remain. *www.petiteitalie.com.* ☎ *514/439-4591.*

❸ **Quincaillerie Dante.** As you head southeast through Little Italy toward the Mile End neighborhood, pop in to this family-run institution for Italian kitchen gear sought out by professional and home chefs alike. Items like hand-cranked pasta machines remain stalwartly low-tech. *6851 rue St. Dominique. www.quincailleriedante. com.* ☎ *514/271-2057.*

❹ **Mile End shopping.** Mile End is peppered with trendy food

Street café in Mile End.

destinations, vintage shops, bookstores, and microbrasseries. Head to rue Bernard, which runs east-west, and walk west away from the Main. Be sure to stop into **Drawn & Quarterly** bookstore, at 211 rue Bernard ouest; see p 92. If you stay on St-Laurent, keep an eye out for shops selling artisan leather bags, clothing, and home goods. *www. mtl.org/en/explore/neighbourhoods/ plateau-and-mile-end.*

❺ **St-Viateur Bagel & Café.** No Montréal visit is complete without tasting one of the city's signature bagels. At St-Viateur, bagels are shaped by hand, dressed with seeds or spices, and baked in a wood-fired oven. In addition to this original flagship shop, which is open 24 hours, there's a sit-down

The famed St-Viateur Bagel & Café.

cafe with sandwiches, salads, soups, wine, and beer at 1127 avenue du Mont-Royal est. *263 rue St.-Viateur ouest. www.stviateurbagel. com.* ☎ 514/276-8444.

6 Lawrence. A satisfying pick for brunch, lunch, or dinner, Lawrence serves up innovative yet reliable "modern British" dishes and friendly service. It was cool at launch and, one major renovation later, remains so today, with a little more luxe. *5201 bd. St-Laurent. www.lawrencemtl.com.* ☎ 514/503-1070. **$$.**

7 Avenue Laurier ouest. Fancy footwear for kids. Imported treats from high-end grocery stores. Designer clothing for women and men. Plus, a few charming spots to stop off for refreshments—from hot chocolate to microbrews to French chardonnay. That's what you'll find along one of the city's poshest stretches of shops along avenue Laurier ouest from boulevard St-Laurent to Côte Ste-Catherine. Even if it's too pricey to actually shop, this is a fun street to browse, away from the hustle of downtown's department stores and underground mega-malls. *Av. Laurier between bd. St-Laurent and rue Durocher. www.laurierouest.com.*

8 Leméac. Fitting for a crisp glass of wine at the bar or a classic dish of steak frites, Leméac captures the French flair that expressly draws so many visitors to Montréal. It's a classic bistro that is competent, elegant, yet refreshingly at ease. Seek out patio seating in

Walking Vieux-Montréal & Downtown

Vieux-Montréal and the city's commercial downtown are major Montréal neighborhoods—they're arguably the top must-sees for visitors. Our Best Full-Day Tours chapter (p 7) offers highlights of these areas: Day one covers Vieux-Montreal and day two covers downtown and the Quartier des Spectacles arts district. Each tour can be walked in 1 to 2 hours if you don't stop at any of the sights, but each can also fill the better part of a day if you visit shops, museums, and restaurants along the way.

Jewish Montréal

At the turn of the 20th century, Montréal was home to more Jews than any other Canadian city, attracting an especially large Yiddish-speaking population from Eastern Europe. Today Toronto has nearly twice as many Jewish residents, but vestiges of the community's history and ongoing practices remain here.

Cultural and educational destinations include the **Jewish Public Library** (www.jewishpubliclibrary.org; ☎ 514/345-2627), with the largest circulating collection of Judaica in North America, and the **Montréal Holocaust Museum** (www.museeholocauste.ca; ☎ 514/345-2605). Both are located at 5151 Côte-Ste-Catherine. Just across the street is the **Segal Centre for Performing Arts** (p 126), which presents plays in Yiddish. The **Museum of Jewish Montréal** (www.museemontrealjuif.ca; ☎ 514/840-9300) has a free gallery at 4040 St-Laurent and leads historical walking and food tours.

Edibles abound, of course. One could start the day with a bagel from either **St-Viateur Bagel & Café** (1127 av. Mont-Royal est) or **Fairmont Bagel** (74 av. Fairmont ouest), a few blocks farther north, or opt for a fountain soda from **Wilensky Light Lunch** (34 rue Fairmount ouest). For any meal, there's always **Schwartz's** (3895 bd. St-Laurent). See chapter 5, p 97, for restaurant details.

warm weather and plan to splurge on dessert: The kitchen prepares as many as 15 options, including chocolate and banana cake with house-made popcorn ice cream. It's open 11:45am to midnight Monday through Friday and from 10am on weekends for brunch, and includes an extensive post-10pm menu. After a meal here, you won't have to dream of France because you'll fall in love with Québec. *1045 av Laurier ouest. www.restaurantlemeac.com.* ☎ *514/270-0999. $$$.*

The bar at Leméac restaurant.

Parc du Mont-Royal

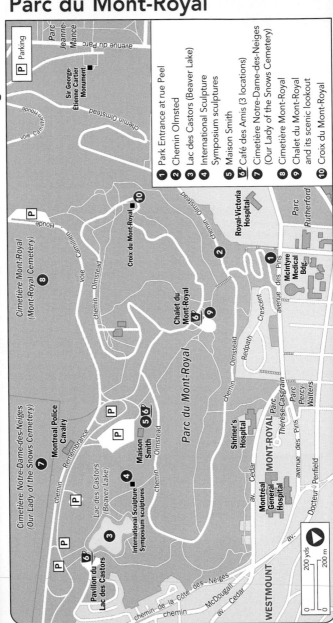

1. Park Entrance at rue Peel
2. Chemin Olmsted
3. Lac des Castors (Beaver Lake)
4. International Sculpture Symposium sculptures
5. Maison Smith
6. Café des Amis (3 locations)
7. Cimetière Notre-Dame-des-Neiges (Our Lady of the Snows Cemetery)
8. Cimetière Mont-Royal
9. Chalet du Mont-Royal and its scenic lookout
10. Croix du Mont-Royal

P Parking

Mont-Royal, the small mountain for which Montréal is named, is a popular park for walkers, runners, and anyone seeking panoramic views of the city. Visitors can drive into the 200-hectare (494-acre) park (there is limited parking) or take bus no. 11, which travels across chemin de la Remembrance. But those in reasonably good shape can enter the park from its base and walk to the top in about 45 minutes, which includes time for some stops along the way. The walk we describe here is on a broad, lightly graded bridle path, with options to take shortcuts of steeper stair-cases. If you're carrying a phone with Internet access, there are additional maps at www.lemontroyal.qc.ca/carte/en/index.sn. Rest-rooms and food are available at three spots—see ⑥⑥ for details.

START: Corner of rue Peel and avenue des Pins (also listed as Pine Ave on English maps).

❶ Park entrance at rue Peel.
A spacious entrance of steps and beautiful plantings greets visitors at the start of this walk into the woods. If you're heading up with a bike or stroller—as we have done—there's another entrance about 30m (100 ft.) to the left without steps. Hearty souls can choose the quickest and most strenuous approach, taking the steepest sets of stairs at every opportunity, and going directly to the Chalet du Mont-Royal and its lookout at the top (see #9). Those who prefer to take their time and gain altitude slowly should use the initial switchback path, called "Le Serpentin." Don't be worried about getting lost; the park is small enough that you'll regain your sense of direction no matter which combination of routes you take.
Corner of rue Peel and av. des Pins.

❷ ★ Chemin Olmsted. After a few minutes on the switchbacks, you'll find yourself on a road-sized path that loops through the park. Chemin Olmstead was named for the park's initial designer, American landscape architect Frederick Law Olmsted (1802–1903), who also designed Central Park in New York City. It's actually the only part of Olmsted's design that became a reality; the rest of the park wasn't

completed to his scheme. Walkers, joggers, mountain bikers, and police officers on horseback all use this thoroughfare. It's closed to cars, making it a joy for those looking for a haven of peace and quiet in the city.

❸ ★ Lac des Castors (Beaver Lake). Beaver Lake's name refers to the once-profitable fur industry, not to the actual presence of the long-gone animals. In summer, the lake is surrounded by sunbathers and pic-nickers, and you can rent a wooden rowboat. In the winter, a large out-door skating rink next to Beaver Lake Pavilion (the lake itself cannot support

The bronze and granite Monument à George-Étienne-Cartier is topped by the winged Greek deity La Renommée.

Notre-Dame-des-Neiges, Montréal's largest cemetery.

skaters) has rentals for skates, cross-country skis, and snowshoes. See 6 for restaurant information.

4 International Sculpture Symposium sculptures. On the grassy rise to the east of Beaver Lake sit stone and metal sculptures erected in 1964 as part of the International Sculpture Symposium in Montréal. A collection of artists was given marble, granite, or metal to shape their abstract visions, and a limited amount of time to complete their work. The representation of four priestesses, made in Italian marble by Yerassimos Sklavos (1927–67), is one of the most striking pieces. Not far from the sculptures, see if you can find two granite plaques (out of a total of five such plaques spread around the park) that have poetic phrases or humorous quips by Montréaler Gilbert Boyer chiseled into the rock. *Near Beaver Lake.*

5 ★ Maison Smith. The park's year-round information center has restrooms, a cafe, a gift shop, and a educational displays about the history, flora, and fauna of Mont-Royal. The center has a parking lot for those who choose to drive to the park instead of walk. On Saturdays from May through October, 10am to noon, there are volunteer conservation activities that anyone can join in on. *1260 chemin Remembrance. www.lemontroyal.qc.ca.* ☎ *514/843-8240.*

6 Café des Amis. This cafe has three locations in the park: Beaver Lake Pavilion (**3**, above), Maison Smith (**5**), and Chalet du Mont-Royal (**9**, below). The Beaver Lake location is a large restaurant with floor-to-ceiling glass walls to take in the views and is open daily until 6pm in spring and fall, until 9pm in summer, and closed mid-December to mid-March. The Maison Smith location is a small cafe with a lovely terrace for dining alfresco in warm months. It's open daily until 5pm year-round. The Chalet location is a food counter and is open daily until 5pm year-round. ☎ *514/843-8240.*

7 Cimetière Notre-Dame-des-Neiges (Our Lady of the Snows Cemetery). Many famous Montréalers have been laid to rest in the city's largest, and mostly Catholic, cemetery. Included are the Molson crypts, where members of the influential Canadian brewing family are buried. Other prominent residents include statesman Sir

A skyline view from Mont-Royal.

George-Etienne Cartier, poet Emile Nelligan, architect Ernest Cormier, and Canadian hockey star Maurice "The Rocket" Richard. The cemetery's website offers a search function to locate specific graves. *4601 chemin Côte-des-Neiges. www.cimetiere nddn.org.* ☎ *514/735-1361.*

❽ Cimetière Mont-Royal. Smaller than its Catholic neighbor to the west, Mont-Royal Cemetery was founded in 1852 by a group of Christian (but non-Catholic) denominations. The beautifully terraced cemetery was designed to resemble a garden and makes for peaceful strolling. Among those interred here is Anna Leonowens, the British governess who was the real-life inspiration for the musical *The King and I.* *1297 chemin de la Fôret. www.mount royalcem.com.* ☎ *514/279-7358.*

❾ ★★ Chalet du Mont-Royal and scenic lookout. At the top of the mountain is this rustically atmospheric chalet, with a front terrace that offers a popular panoramic view of the city and the St. Lawrence river. The chalet was constructed from 1931 to 1932 and has been used for receptions and concerts. Inside, take a look at the 17 paintings hanging just below the ceiling: They relate the region's history and the story of the French explorations of North America.

❿ Croix du Mont-Royal. Legend has it that Montréal founder

At play in Parc Mont-Royal.

Paul de Chomedey, Sieur de Maisonneuve, erected a wooden cross here in 1643 after the young colony survived a flood threat. The present incarnation, installed in 1924, is made of steel and is 33m (108 ft.) tall. It is visible to much of the city and illuminated by LED lights at night. Beside the cross is a plaque marking where a time capsule was interred in August 1992, during Montréal's 350th anniversary celebration. Some 12,000 children ages 6 to 12 filled the capsule with messages and drawings depicting their visions for the city in the year 2142, when Montréal will be 500 years old and the capsule will be opened. *To return to downtown Montréal, go back along the path toward the chalet terrace. On the left, just before the terrace, is a path to a staircase that descends to where the tour began. The walk down by this route takes about 15 minutes. Or, pick up the no. 11 bus, which travels along chemin de la Remembrance.*

An autumn scene in Parc Mont-Royal.

Little Burgundy & Marché Atwater

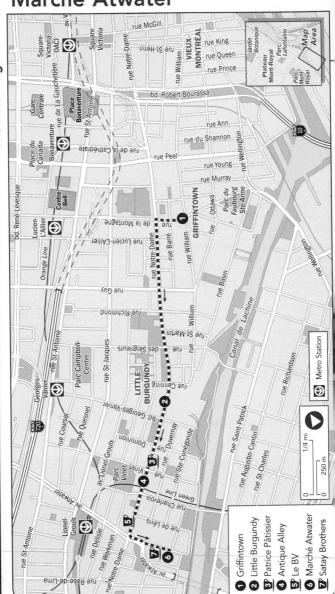

1 Griffintown
2 Little Burgundy
3 Patrice Pâtissier
4 Antique Alley
5 Le BV
6 Marché Atwater
7 Satay Brothers

Metro Station

The blossoming neighborhoods west of Vieux-Montréal can be explored with a 45-minute stroll. This walk past Griffintown and through Little Burgundy is a straight shot west on rue Notre-Dame and passes good antique shops and loads of bistros (making it a fine option for brunch, lunch, or dinner). It concludes at Marché Atwater, a major food and vegetable market that's open year-round. START: **Métro: Square Victoria.**

1 Griffintown. As you walk west from Vieux-Montréal on rue Notre-Dame, you'll pass new high-rises and, at boulevard Robert-Bourassa, a small greenway with unique stairway sculptures (you can climb them) for a bird's-eye view of the city. You'll pass under a highway, and then into the Griffintown neighborhood. To the south (your left), it's peppered with newer condominium complexes. *Rue Notre-Dame from rue McGill to rue Guy.*

2 Little Burgundy. About 20 minutes into your walk, after crossing rue Guy, you'll find new cafes, chic bars, and exceptional restaurants. They have sprouted like mushrooms after a spring rain in this neighborhood of Little Burgundy (in French, Petite-Bourgogne). Especially at weekend brunch time, this section of rue Notre-Dame is thick with the city's creative crowd and a buzzing energy. *Rue Notre-Dame from rue Guy to av. Atwater.*

3 Patrice Pâtissier. Sumptuous pastries and stylish lunch and brunch fare keep this small cafe in the heart of Little Burgundy busy. Stop in for a perfectly elegant Kouign-amann, cannelé, or fruit tartelette. *2360 rue Notre-Dame ouest. www.patricepatissier.ca.* ☎ 514/439-5434. $.

4 Antique Alley. Rue Notre-Dame in Little Burgundy used to be thick enough with antique shops to warrant the nickname Antique Alley. There are fewer antique shops here today, but those that remain are chock-a-block with high- and low-end collectibles. They include Deuxiemement (#1880), Grand Central (#2448), and Old Times (#2617). Alongside are high-end lighting-fixture shops and lots of expensive facial care boutiques. *Rue Notre-Dame, from rue Seigneurs to ave Atwater. Find a map of the antique shops at lesquartiersducanal. com/en/explore.*

Dessert at Patrice Pâtissier.

Food vendors at Marché Atwater.

5 Le BV. The "BV" in the name stands for bon vivant—which means both the good life and a social person with cultivated taste. Both are good descriptions for the scene at this restaurant, which is packed on weekends serving up chic, healthy options. It's open 10am to 11pm Saturday and Sunday, and for dinner Monday through Friday. *2705 rue Notre-Dame ouest. www.lebv.ca.* ☎ *514/316-4585. $$.*

6 Marché Atwater. Send your senses into overdrive at this indoor-outdoor market: Stroll the stalls offering flowers for planting and fiddleheads in spring, maple sugar candies, spices from around the world, samosas to go, green tea chocolate from **Chocolats Privilège**, plus exquisite selections from the *poissonnerie* and *fromageries.* See p 93 for more. *138 av. Atwater. www.marche-atwater.com.* ☎ *514/937-7754. Métro: Lionel-Groulx.*

From mid-May to mid-October, Atwater opens up an outside space with picnic tables under canopies and a handful of takeout vendors. **7 Satay Brothers** specializes in Singaporean street food, including sumptuous meat skewers with cucumber and peanut sauce, perfect steamed buns with pork, and papaya salad. It's open daily 10:30am to 5pm in warm months; cash only. Sit at the bar to watch the food prep in action. *138 Atwater Avenue. www.sataybrothers.com.* ☎ *514/933-3507. $.* ●

The Best Shopping

Shopping Best Bets

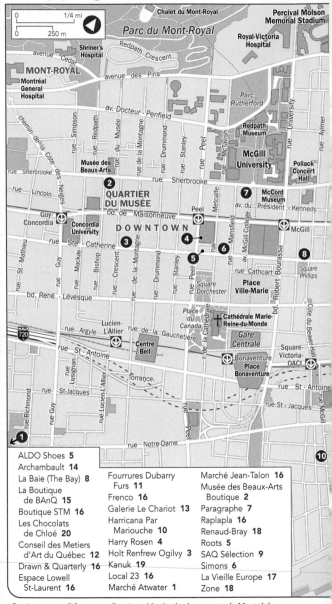

0 ——— 1/4 mi
0 ——— 250 m

Chalet du Mont-Royal

Percival Molson Memorial Stadium

Parc du Mont-Royal

Royal-Victoria Hospital

Shriner's Hospital

Redpath Crescent

avenue Cedar

MONT-ROYAL

Montréal General Hospital

avenue des Pins

Parc Rutherford

chemin de la Côte des Neiges

av. Docteur - Penfield

Redpath Museum

McGill University

rue Simpson
rue Redpath
rue du Musée
rue de la Montagne
rue Drummond
rue Stanley
rue Peel
rue McTavish
rue University
rue Aylmer

Musée des Beaux-Arts

rue Sherbrooke

Pollack Concert Hall

rue Sherbrooke

rue Lincoln

②

QUARTIER DU MUSÉE

McCord Museum

av. du Président - Kennedy

⑦

Guy-Concordia **Ⓜ**

Concordia University

bd. de - Maisonneuve

Peel **Ⓜ**

DOWNTOWN

McGill **Ⓜ**

④

⑥

⑧

rue Ste - Catherine

③

rue St-Mathieu
rue Guy
rue Mackay
rue Bishop
rue Crescent
rue de-la-Montagne
rue Drummond
rue Stanley
rue Peel
av. McGill College
rue Mansfield
rue Metcalfe
rue Robert-Bourassa

⑤

rue Cathcart

Square Phillips

bd. René - Lévesque

Square Dorchester

Place Ville-Marie

Côte du Beaver-Hall

Place du Canada

Cathédrale Marie-Reine-du-Monde

Lucien-L'Allier **Ⓜ**

rue Argyle
rue de-la-Gauchetière

Gare Centrale

Square-Victoria-OACI **Ⓜ**

rue St-Antoine

Centre Bell

Bonaventure **Ⓜ**
Place Bonaventure

rue Lusignan
rue Lucien-L'Allier

Torrance

rue St - Antoine

rue St-Jacques

rue-St-Jacques

rue Richmond
rue Guy
rue St-Jacques

rue Peel

①

rue - Notre-Dame

⑩

Previous page: Gift store at Boutique Musée des beaux-arts de Montréal.

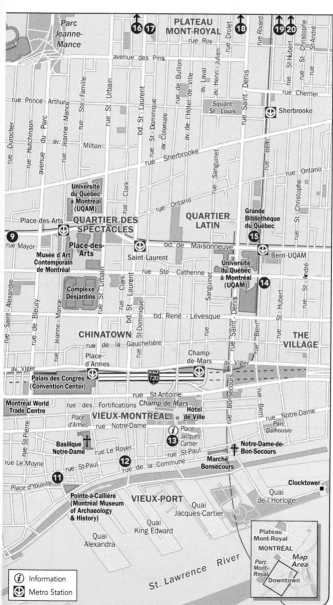

Parc Jeanne-Mance

PLATEAU MONT-ROYAL

16 17
18
19 20

rue Roy

avenue des Pins

rue Prince-Arthur

rue Durocher
rue Hutchinson
avenue du Parc
rue Jeanne-Mance
rue Ste-Famille
rue St-Urbain
bd. St-Laurent
rue St-Dominique
av. Coloniale
rue de-Bullion
av. de l'Hôtel-de-Ville
av. Henri-Julien
av. Laval
rue Saint-Denis
rue Drolet
rue Rivard
rue St-Hubert
rue St-Christophe
St-André

Square St-Louis

rue Cherrier

Sherbrooke

Milton

rue Sherbrooke

rue Berri

rue Ontario

rue St-Christophe

Université du Québec à Montréal (UQAM)

Place-des-Arts

rue Mayor

9

rue Ontario

QUARTIER LATIN

Grande Bibliothèque du Québec

15

QUARTIER DES SPECTACLES

Place-des-Arts

Musée d'Art Contemporain de Montréal

Saint-Laurent

bd. de Maisonneuve

Berri-UQAM

rue Ste-Catherine

Université du Québec à Montréal (UQAM)

14

rue St-André

rue St-Hubert

rue Berri

rue Sanguinet

Complexe Desjardins

rue Clark
bd. St-Laurent
rue St-Dominique

bd. René-Lévesque

rue Saint-Denis

CHINATOWN

rue de la Gauchetière

St-Dominique

THE VILLAGE

Place-d'Armes

Champ-de-Mars

av. Viger

av. Viger

rue Bonsecours

rue Berri

Palais des Congrès (Convention Center)

720

Montréal World Trade Centre

rue St-Antoine

rue des Fortifications Champ de Mars

rue Notre-Dame

Parc Dalhousie

Place d'Armes

VIEUX-MONTRÉAL

Hôtel de Ville

Basilique Notre-Dame

rue Le Royer

rue Notre-Dame

Place Jacques-Cartier

13

Notre-Dame-de-Bon-Secours

rue Le Moyne

rue St-Paul

rue St-Paul

12

Marché Bonsecours

rue St-Pierre

rue Le Royer

rue de la Commune

11

Place d'Youville

Pointe-à-Callière (Montréal Museum of Archaeology & History)

VIEUX-PORT

Clocktower

Quai de l'Horloge

Quai Jacques-Cartier

Quai King Edward

Quai Alexandra

St. Lawrence River

i Information

Metro Station

Plateau Mont-Royal

MONTRÉAL

Parc Mont-Royal

Map Area

Downtown

Shopping Best Bets

Best **Crafts from the Québec Region**
★★ Conseil des Metiers d'Art du Québec, 20 rue St-Paul ouest (p 91)

Best **Affordable Québec Memorabilia**
★★ Items with images from the library's collection, at BAnQ Boutique, 475 bd. De Maisonneuve est, in the Grande Bibliothèque's hall (p 96)

Best **Montréal-Made Leather Goods**
★★★ Espace Lowell St-Laurent, 5298 bd. St-Laurent (p 95)

Best **Department Store for Montréal Designer Fashion**
★★ Simons, 977 rue Ste-Catherine ouest (p 93)

Best **Luxury Mega Store**
★★ Holt Renfrew Ogilvy, 1307 rue Ste-Catherine ouest (p 93)

Best **Functional Historic Item**
★★ Hudson's Bay "point blanket" from La Baie (The Bay), 585 rue Ste-Catherine ouest (p 92)

Best **Handcrafted Dolls**
★★★ Raplapla, 69 rue Villeneuve ouest (p 92)

Best **Source for Inuit Sculpture**
★★ Galerie Le Chariot, 446 Place Jacques-Cartier (p 91)

Best **Source for Transit System Souvenirs**
★★ Boutique STM, Online only, at www.boutiquestm.com.

Best **Vintage Clothing Shopping**
★ Local 23, 23 rue Bernard ouest (p 96)

Best **Destination for High-End Shopping**
★★ Avenue Laurier has boutiques for browsing and restaurants for recharging, Avenue Laurier, between bd. St-Laurent and av. de l'Epée

Best **Store for Warding off Winter**
★ Kanuk, 485 rue Rachel est (p 96)

Best **Destination Food Markets**
★★★ Marché Atwater, 138 rue Atwater (p 93) and ★★★ Marché Jean-Talon, 7070 av. Henri-Julien (p 94)

Best **Chocolate Shop**
★★ Les Chocolats de Chloé, 546 rue Duluth est (p 93)

Best **Old-World Food Shop**
★ La Vieille Europe, 3855 bd. St-Laurent (p 94)

Best **Museum Shop**
★★★ Musée des Beaux-Arts Boutique, 1390 rue Sherbrooke ouest (p 91)

Fresh, colorful fruit at Marché Atwater.

Shopping A to Z

Arts & Crafts

★★ Conseil des Metiers d'Art du Québec VIEUX-MONTREAL

This small, bright boutique right on the most touristed footpath of Old Montréal is a primary distributor for members of the CMAQ, an organization of nearly 1,000 professional artists and craftspeople across Québec. Offerings include jewelry (we love the brushed-aluminum earrings and necklaces of J.R. Franco), wooden housewares, pottery, and stone carvings. *20 rue St-Paul ouest.* www.metiersdart.ca. ☎ 438/385-7787. *Métro: Place-d'Armes.*

★★ kids Galerie Le Chariot

VIEUX-MONTREAL Sculptures by Inuit artists are on display and for sale here, with small pieces—carved bears, seals, owls, tableaus of mothers and children—running C$125 to C$600. *446 Place Jacques-Cartier (in the center of the plaza).* galerielechariot.wix site.com/lechariotmetierdart. ☎ 514/875-6134. *Métro: Place-d'Armes.*

★★★ kids Musée des Beaux-Arts Boutique DOWNTOWN

An unusually impressive museum shop, the boutique of the city's major fine-arts museum sells everything from folk art to furniture. It's a perfect destination for gifts made by Québec artists, such as leather passport covers handcrafted in Montréal by Holdur, wooden cooking paddles by Littledeer, and felt laptop and tablet sleeves by designer Cindy Cantin. *1390 rue Sherbrooke ouest.* www.mbam. qc.ca. ☎ 514/285-1600. *Métro: Peel.*

Books & Toys

★★ Drawn & Quarterly PLATEAU

This Mile End bookstore is a cultural hub, with book-launch parties and book clubs for young readers, teens,

Montréal's Underground City

Montréal's harsh winters and sticky summers were the motivating force behind the construction of underground tunnels that created a network of subterranean shops, cafes, and entrances to hotels and Métro stations. This monumental achievement in urban planning stretches for nearly 33km (21 miles). It can be intimidating to newcomers: No singular entity manages the Underground City network, so signage and even the numbering of levels can differ from one section to the next. People using wheelchairs or strollers may face navigational challenges.

Place Ville Marie, the original anchor, debuted in 1962, and for many years there was no prettier way to enter the underground city than through one of its outdoor glass pyramids. Major renovations in 2018 and 2019 raised the bar again, creating a swanky, new mixed-use space including a giant food hall. (This same building houses a way-way-*above*-ground observatory deck on the 46th floor, with fantastic views—see p 29.)

To head *souterrain* from street level, look for blue signs with a white arrow pointing down or signs marked "RESO." You can also enter from malls that operate both at street level and below ground.

Mile End's Drawn & Quarterly is a vibrant community bookstore.

sci-fi fans, and more. It specializes in graphic novels, including those from its own publishing company, but also carries novels, essays, and fine-arts books. A sister shop, **La Petite Librairie Drawn & Quarterly,** is a children's bookstore that opened in 2017 just down the block at #176. *211 rue Bernard ouest. mtl.drawnand quarterly.com.* ☎ *514/279-2224. Métro: Rosemont or Outremont.*

★ **Paragraphe** DOWNTOWN Though it caters to university students, Paragraphe is also stocked with a good selection of English-language novels and classics. It hosts a busy schedule of in-store author appearances, especially during the school year. *2220 av. McGill College. www. facebook.com/paragraphebookstore.* ☎ *514/845-5811. Métro: McGill.*

★★★ kids **Raplapla** MILE END Sweet dolls for infants and young children made from organic cotton are the specialty of this Frommer's favorite. The adorable rectangular-shaped Monsieur Tsé-Tsé doll is our pick for ambassador for the Montréal handcraft movement. These are sold from the company's small studio-boutique and online at Etsy. *69 rue Villeneuve ouest. www.raplapla.com and www.etsy.com/ca-fr/shop/raplapla.* ☎ *514/563-1209. Métro: Mont-Royal.*

★ kids **Renaud-Bray** PLATEAU For those who know French or want to brush up, the large Renaud-Bray bookstore has primarily French-language stock and also sells newspapers and magazines from all over the world. *4380 rue St-Denis. www. renaud-bray.com.* ☎ *514/844-2587. Métro: Mont-Royal.*

Department Stores

★★ **La Baie (The Bay)** DOWNTOWN No retailer has an older or more celebrated pedigree than the Hudson's Bay Company, whose name was shortened to "The Bay" and then transformed into "La Baie" by Québec language laws. The company was incorporated in Canada in 1670 but is now under a corporate umbrella with Saks Fifth Avenue, and other brands. Plans have stalled (for now) for a big renovation of the store along with the introduction of a new Saks in the same building. Still, it's worth a trip if you're in the market for the famous Hudson's Bay "point blanket," which runs C$325 to C$550. *585 rue Ste-Catherine ouest. www.hbc. com.* ☎ *514/281-4422. Métro: McGill.*

★★ **Holt Renfrew Ogilvy** DOWNTOWN In the heart of Montréal's "Golden Square Mile," this new luxury department store merges two longtime anchors of the neighborhood. Holt's, a high-end chain of Canadian department stores founded in 1837, will be closing its

A baby on a "bed" of Monsieur Tsé-Tsé dolls at Raplapla doll store.

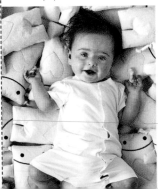

Historic department store "La Baie."

store on rue Sherbrooke and joining forces with Ogilvy in the building that Ogilvy has occupied since 1912. Ogilvy has long been a vibrant example of a classy breed of department store that appeared to be fading from the scene (sparkly chandeliers, a bagpiper announcing the noon hour), so it will be fascinating to see the merged operation. *Retail Insider* says the space will be the largest luxury retail superstore in Canada, "by far." *1307 rue Ste-Catherine ouest. www.holtrenfrew. com.* ☎ *514/842-7711. Métro: Peel.*

★★ **Simons** DOWNTOWN This Québec City–based department store offers one-stop-shopping for clothes from Montréal designers, including Marie-Ève Lecavalier (her line is Lecavalier + Édito), the Asian-influenced UNTTLD (whose atelier is on 2020 rue William in Little Burgundy), and Denis Gagnon (whose showroom is at 170 rue Saint-Paul ouest). In business since 1840, the family-owned Simons chain also has an in-house label, Twik, that is a must for teens. *977 rue Ste-Catherine ouest. www. simons.ca.* ☎ *514/289-1840. Métro: Peel.*

Edibles
★★ **Les Chocolats de Chloé** PLATEAU If you approach chocolate the way certain aficionados approach wine—that is, on the lookout for the best of the best—then

this teeny shop will bring great delight. Perhaps Caramel Crac (crunchy caramel coated with dark chocolate)? Or little fish-shaped chocolates ("Sardines Pralinées") filled with hazelnut paste? *546 rue Duluth est. www.leschocolatsdechloe.com.* ☎ *514/849-5550. Métro: Mont-Royal.*

★ **Frenco** PLATEAU Your body will rejoice at this small health-food grocery. In addition to grains and other bulk food items, it now has an onsite cafe with coffee and ultra-healthy smoothies and an assortment of vegan fast food. *3985 bd. St-Laurent. www.frenco.ca.* ☎ *514/ 285-1319. Métro: St-Laurent.*

★★★ **Marché Atwater** DOWNTOWN Atwater market is an indoor-outdoor farmer's market that's open daily. A long interior shed is bordered by stalls stocked with gleaming produce and flowers. The two-story center section is devoted to vintners, butchers, and bakeries. **La Fromagerie Atwater** (☎ 514/932-4653) lays out more than 850 local and international cheeses—with hundreds from Québec alone—as well as pâtés and charcuterie. See our tour to walk there on p 84. *138 av. Atwater. www. marche-atwater.com.* ☎ *514/937-7754. Métro: Lionel-Groulx.*

★★★ **Marché Jean-Talon** MILE END As with the Marché Atwater, above, Marché Jean-Talon is a must-visit for food fans. Stalls, some permanent and some seasonal, sell smoked seafood, cured meat, fresh flowers, local wine and cheese, and delicacies such as sprays of fresh lavender and trays of pastel-hued macarons. **La Boite aux Huitres** (www. laboiteauxhuitres.ca; ☎ 514/277-7575) shucks oysters while you wait, and **Aqua Mare** (☎ 514/277-7575), just adjacent, sells fish 'n' chips, fried calamari, shrimp, and éperlans (smelt). *7070 av. Henri-Julien, north of Mile End. www.marchespublics-mtl.com.* ☎ *514/937-7754. Métro:Jean-Talon.*

★ **SAQ Sélection** DOWNTOWN Wine and spirits (although not beer) are heavily regulated by the provincial government and sold in SAQ outlets. The Express outlets offer the most popular libations and are open until 10pm, while the Sélection shops have more choices, including new wines and expensive bottles. Consider Québec's unique ice cider (cidre de glace), made from apples harvested after the first frost. The winery Domaine Pinnacle, an hour and a half from Montréal, makes a favorite version of this regional treat. *440 bd. De Maisonneuve ouest. www.saq.com.* ☎ *514/873-2274. Métro: Place-des-Arts.*

★ **La Vieille Europe** PLATEAU Create the mother of all picnic lunches with the delectable cheeses and cold cuts found here—or pick up some fancy food gifts. La Vieille Europe has been holding court here since 1959, with much of the gourmet fare imported from France, England, and Germany. *3855 bd. St-Laurent. www.facebook.com/LaVieilleEurope.* ☎ *514/842-5773. Métro: St-Laurent.*

Fashion

Also see "Department Stores" earlier in this chapter. Shopping in the bohemian Plateau and Mile End neighborhoods should send you home with a dash of local style. We especially like avenue Laurier, between boulevard St-Laurent and avenue de l'Epée: It's home to products from the ateliers of young Québécois designers as well as Parisian boutiques.

★ **ALDO Shoes** DOWNTOWN Montréal-based and internationally known, ALDO shoes have been around since 1972 and are practical and moderately priced. There are ALDO outlets in city malls and stand-alone shops including this large one downtown. *1007–1009 rue Ste-Catherine ouest. www.aldoshoes. com.* ☎ *514/499-1809. Métro: Peel.*

★★★ **Espace Lowell St-Laurent** MILE END An OMG cool shop with Lowell MTL artisan leather goods, Montréal-made fashion by atelier b and others, and handcrafted housewares. *5298 bd. St-Laurent. www.lowellmtl.ca.* ☎ *514/544-6518. Métro: Laurier.*

★★ **Fourrures Dubarry Furs** VIEUX-MONTRÉAL Montréal has a long history in the fur trade, and the husband-and-wife team here carry on that tradition with a reputation for stellar, no-pressure customer service. The collection has items small and large: wool hats with fur trim, fur headbands and earmuffs, and capes and coats in fur, shearling, and leather. *206 rue St-Paul ouest. www.dubarryfurs.com.* ☎ *514/844-7483. Métro: Place d'Armes.*

★★ **Harricana Par Mariouche** VIEUX-MONTRÉAL Designer Mariouche Gagné takes her unique cue from the city's long history with the fur trade: She recycles fur coats, cashmere scarves, and even wedding gowns into funky garments, hats, and keychain fobs. A leader in the eco-luxe movement, Gagné's

Fourrures Dubarry Furs is a reminder of Montréal's fur-trading past.

Harry Rosen has been a Canadian retailer since 1954.

boutique now includes hats made in collaboration with Montréal milliner Canadian Hat. *416 rue McGill. www.harricana.qc.ca.* ☎ *514/282-1616. Métro: Place d'Armes.*

★★ **Harry Rosen** DOWNTOWN Since 1954, this Canadian retailer has been a leader at making men look good in its own bespoke suits as well as brands like Armani and Zegna. Renovations at this flagship store have given it a brighter, flasher facade. *1455 rue Peel, in the shopping mall Les Cours Mont Royal. www.harryrosen. com.* ☎ *514/284-3315. Métro: Peel.*

★ **Kanuk** PLATEAU One of the top Canadian manufacturers of high-end winter jackets makes its clothes right in the heart of Plateau Mont-Royal. Heavy-duty coats go for over C$1,000. More modestly priced winter caps make nice (and cozy) souvenirs. Customers can give clothes a trial run in an onsite cold room chilled to -25°F. *485 rue Rachel est. www.kanuk.com.* ☎ *877/284-4494 or 514/284-4494. Métro: Mont-Royal.*

★ **Local 23** MILE END This is one of a half-dozen really great vintage or secondhand options clustered together in Mile End. Here, you get jaunty, colorful garments that span the decades, especially the '90s. *23 rue Bernard ouest. www.local23.ca.* ☎ *514/270-9333. Métro: Rosemont.*

★ **kids Roots** DOWNTOWN Back in 1973, Toronto-based Roots began making footwear with so-called "negative heels"—the heel slightly lower than the toe. Although negative heels are long gone, much of the footwear offered by the company today does have low-to-flat heels. This shop also sells clothing for women, men, and kids. *1025 rue Ste-Catherine ouest. www.roots.com.* ☎ *514/845-7995. Métro: Peel.*

Housewares

For photos of the work of some of the city's most innovative artisans, check out Design Montréal's catalogue "Code Souvenir Montréal" at designmontreal.com.

★ **Atelier-D** ONLINE STORE Designer Jonathan Dorthe works in wood to make contemporary hand-crafted furniture and housewares: boxes, checkerboards, trays,

Jonathan Dorthe's wooden Penta Tray at Atelier-D.

The Boutique at Grande Bibliothèque.

Boutique STM sells Montréal transit–branded souvenirs.

laser-cut plywood hanging lamps. *Online only. www.atelier-d.ca.*

★★ **La Boutique de BAnQ** LATIN QUARTER The city's central library, the Grande Bibliothèque, is located in the college neighborhood of UQAM (Université du Québec à Montréal). Inside the library is a boutique showcasing housewares, bags, and T-shirts, some emblazoned with breezy images from the institution's archives: a 1730 map of "New France" Canada, cookbook illustrations from 1943, a 1900 illustration by Henri Julien of the beloved Canadian folk tale *canot d'écorce qui vole* (The Canoe that Could Fly). *475 bd. De Maisonneuve est, in the Grande Bibliothèque's hall. www.banq.qc.ca/services/boutique_ de_banq/.* ☎ *514/873-1100. Métro: Berri-UQAM.*

★★ **Boutique STM** ONLINE STORE Maps, bags, and mugs of a subway system (or a favorite subway stop) are unique and inexpensive tokens of a trip. Boutique STM sells route posters, keychains, and more

depicting Montréal's buses and metro and is also opening a brick-and-mortar **store** (9494 bd. St-Laurent, Suite 900; ☎ **514/375-1956**); call for hours. *www.boutiquestm.com.*

★ **Zone** PLATEAU A Québec company with seven locations, this housewares store features colorful bowls and plates, furnishings, and more. Think Crate & Barrel with Québécois style and flair. *4246 rue St-Denis. www.zonemaison.com.* ☎ *514/845-3530. Métro: Mont-Royal.*

Music

★ **Archambault** QUARTIER DES SPECTACLES The Archambault chain calls itself Québec's largest retailer of musical instruments. This outlet sells sheet music, books, and English- and French-language CDs along with instruments. It has a good variety of Québécois music you'd be hard-pressed to find outside the province. *510 rue Ste-Catherine est. www.archambault.ca.* ☎ *514/849-6201. Métro: Berri-UQAM.* ●

Archambault is Québec's largest retailer of musical instruments.

Dining Best Bets

Best **Restaurant in Montréal**
★★★ Bouillion Bilk $$ *1595 bd. St-Laurent (p 103)*

Best **Buzzworthy Hot Resto**
★★★ Pastel $$$ *124 rue McGill (p 106)*

Best **Parisian-Style Bistro**
★★ L'Express $$ *3927 rue St-Denis (p 104)*

Best **Classic White-Tablecloth Experience**
★★★ Europea $$$ *1227 rue de la Montagne (p 104)*

Best **Contemporary Québécois**
★★★ Le Club Chasse et Pêche $$$ *423 rue St-Claude (p 103)*

Best **Modern Italian**
★★★ Graziella $$$ *116 rue McGill (p 105)*

Best **Hearty Sandwich**
★★★ Olive + Gourmando $ *351 rue St-Paul est (p 106)*

Best **Bakery**
★★★ Première Moisson $ *860 av. du Mont-Royal est (p 107)*

Best **Vegan**
★★★ Aux Vivres $ *4631 bd. St-Laurent (p 102)*

Best **Breakfast**
★★ Eggspectation $ *1313 de Maisonneuve ouest (p 104)*

Best **Old-Time Diner**
★★ Beauty's Luncheonette $ *93 av. du Mont-Royal ouest (p 102)*

Best **Bagel**
★★ Fairmount Bagel $ *74 av. Fairmont ouest (p 104)*

Best **Modern British**
★★★ Lawrence $$ *5201 bd. St. Laurent (p 105)*

Best **Portuguese/Seafood**
★★★ Ferreira Café $$ *1446 rue Peel (p 104)*

Best **Polish**
★★ Stash Café $$ *200 rue St-Paul ouest (p 108)*

Best **Homage to Pork**
★★ Au Pied de Cochon $$$ *536 rue Duluth (p 102)*

Best **Pizza**
★★ Magpie Pizzeria $ *16 rue Maguire (p 105)*

Best **24-Hour Poutine**
★ La Banquise $ *994 rue Rachel est (p 102)*

Best **Room with a View**
★ Les Enfants Terribles $$ *1 Place Ville Marie (entrance to elevator at bd. Robert-Bourassa) (p 54)*

Best **Montréal Landmark (for its Smoked Meat)**
★★★ Schwartz's $ *3895 bd. St-Laurent (p 108)*

Previous page: MaGuire Pasta special from Magpie Pizzeria.

Dining in the Plateau & Mile End

Au Pied de Cochon 9
Aux Vivres 5
La Banquise 10
Beauty's Luncheonette 4
L'Express 8
Fairmount Bagel 3
Lawrence 2
Magpie Pizzeria 1
Premiere Moisson 6
Schwartz's 7

Dining in Downtown & Vieux-Montréal

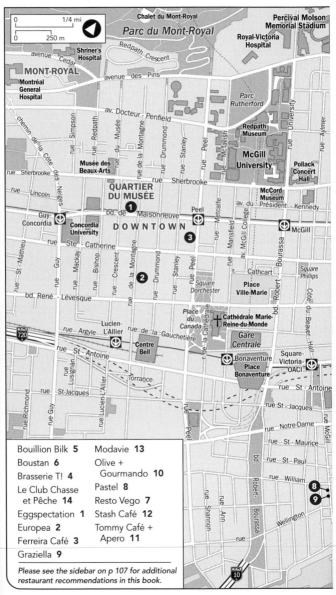

Bouillion Bilk **5**	Modavie **13**
Boustan **6**	Olive + Gourmando **10**
Brasserie T! **4**	Pastel **8**
Le Club Chasse et Pêche **14**	Resto Vego **7**
Eggspectation **1**	Stash Café **12**
Europea **2**	Tommy Café + Apero **11**
Ferreira Café **3**	
Graziella **9**	

Please see the sidebar on p 107 for additional restaurant recommendations in this book.

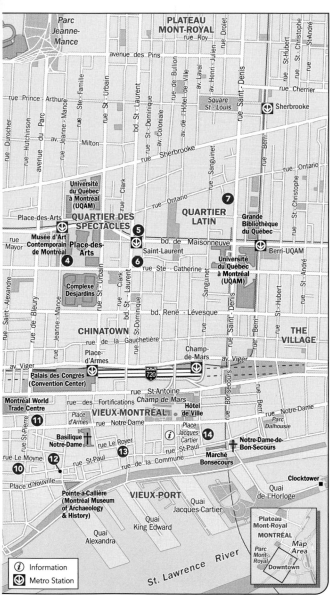

Restaurants **A to Z**

Two notes: First, in addition to the restaurants detailed in this chapter, **we recommend lots of other venues in this book**. See the sidebar "More Restaurant Recommendations" p 107. And second, restaurants whose names begin with *Le, La,* or *Les*—French variations on the English word "The"—are listed alphabetically by the next word.

★★ **Au Pied de Cochon**

PLATEAU *CONTEMPORARY QUEBECOIS* Some of the best meals at "the Pig's Foot," a casual-looking, upscale, always packed restaurant, unsurprisingly feature cuts of pork—though massive amounts of beef, chicken, lamb, duck, and especially foie gras are also used to create inventive dishes. Celebrity chef Martin Picard runs a seasonal **cabane à sucre (sugar shack)** an hour outside the city as well. Reservations at both restaurants are recommended. *536 rue Duluth. www.restaurantaupied decochon.ca.* ☎ *514/281-1114. Main courses C$23–C$44. Dinner Wed–Sun. Métro: Sherbrooke. Map p 99.*

★★★ kids **Aux Vivres** MILE

END *VEGAN* Cheery and casual, the consistently excellent Aux Vivres offers flavors from every continent, all imagined through vegan fare: Greek-style gyro with souvlaki-style tempeh, baked-to-order Indian chapati with veggie butter, a BLT

with bacon made from coconut. There are also salads, rice bowls, and juice and smoothie options, and a patio out back when it's warm. Next door, the restaurant operates a market with to-go vegan foods. *4631 bd. St-Laurent. www. auxvivres.com.* ☎ *514/842-3479. Most items under C$12. Lunch and dinner daily. Map p 99.*

★ kids **La Banquise** PLATEAU

LIGHT FARE Open 24 hours a day, this hippie-meets-hipster diner is a city landmark for its *poutine,* with 31 variations on the standard French fries with gravy and cheese curds. Add-ons range from smoked meat to chicken and peas, and there are vegetarian and vegan options, too. The regular size is plenty big for most appetites. It also serves burgers and, during breakfast hours, eggs, crêpes, and French toast. *Poutine* is known as a post-*drinking-after-*2am binge food, but La Banquise is also kid-friendly. It's located on the north end of the Plateau's pretty **Parc La Fontaine** (p 99), where people of all ages can head to walk off a meal. *994 rue Rachel est. www.labanquise.com.* ☎ *514/525-2415. Poutine plates C$8–C$19; most other items less than C$10. Cash only. Daily 24 hr. Map p 99.*

★★ kids **Beauty's Luncheonette**

PLATEAU *LIGHT FARE* An iconic

Poutine—French fries with gravy and cheese curds—is the specialty at La Banquise, open 24 hours a day.

A dish of Brussels sprouts, potatoes, Les Métayères (Canadian cheese), paprika, and pomegranate at Bouillion Bilk.

diner with banquette seating, Beauty's has been in business here since 1942. Its signature dish is quintessentially Montréal: the Mish-Mash omelet with hot dog, salami, fried onions, and green pepper. It's packed at weekend brunch. *93 av. du Mont-Royal ouest. www.beautys. ca.* ☎ *514/849-8883. Most items under C$15. Breakfast and lunch daily. Métro: Mont Royal. Map p 99.*

★★★ **Bouillion Bilk** QUARTIER DES SPECTACLES *CONTEMPORARY QUEBECOIS* Hidden behind a run-down storefront on a shabby stretch of St-Laurent, this exceptional restaurant is worth finding immediately. Even on weekdays, lively crowds fill the simply adorned space where astute yet easygoing waitstaff deliver balanced cocktails or local beer. Then, mind-blowing handmade pasta and crispy, salted scallops. The menu changes, but that's what we had and we're still referring to it as our best meal of the year. *1595 bd. St-Laurent. www.bouillon bilk.com.* ☎ *514/845-1595. Reservations recommended. Small plates*

C$18–C$24, main courses C$28–C$39. Lunch Mon–Fri, dinner daily. Métro: Saint-Laurent. Map p 101.*

★ **Boustan** QUARTIER DES SPECTACLES *MIDDLE EASTERN* Since 1986, Bouston has held court on rue Crescent as a popular pitstop for fast, filling Lebanese shawarma, kebabs, and vegetarian falafel. In 2014 new owners began opening additional shops in and around Montréal, including this location just off the Place des Arts. It's a dependable, welcome option for a quick bite, and it's open until 4am daily. *19 rue Ste-Catherine est. www.boustan.ca.* ☎ *514/844-2999. Main courses C$6–C$14. Lunch Mon–Sat, dinner daily. Métro: Saint-Laurent. Map p 101.*

★★ **Brasserie T!** QUARTIER DES SPECTACLES *BRASSERIE* Housed in a unique all-glass box perched on a sidewalk on Place des Arts, Brasserie T! overlooks a "dancing waters" fountain in warm months. You can make a creative meal out of just the charcuteries, tartares, and appetizers (go for the garlic sea snails and pan-seared foie gras). *1425 rue Jeanne-Mance. www.brasserie-t.com.* ☎ *514/282-0808. Main courses C$16–C$29. Lunch and dinner daily. Métro: Place-des-Arts. Map p 101.*

★★★ **Le Club Chasse et Pêche** VIEUX-MONTREAL *CONTEMPORARY QUEBECOIS* Chef Claude Pelletier is one of the city's stars, and he serves up highlight-of-the-trip meals. His menu changes frequently, but always includes a *chasse et pêche*

Classic beef tartare and fries at Brasserie T!.

dish (hunting and fishing, or what we'd call "surf and turf" in the U.S.). The stone and brick dining room is dark and masculine, while the platings are carefully constructed and almost delicate. The wine list is 18 pages long. The nondescript entrance is easily missed, marked only by a small sign with a crest on it. *423 rue St-Claude. www.leclubchasseetpeche. com.* ☎ *514/861-1112. Main courses C$34–C$42. Dinner Tues–Sat. Métro: Champ-de-Mars. Map p 101.*

★★ **kids Eggspectation** DOWN-TOWN *BREAKFAST/LIGHT FARE* The atmosphere is funky and prices are okay for the large portions. Regional offerings include the "Sugar Shack" plate with eggs, ham, baked beans, potatoes, a *crepe bretonne*, and Québec maple syrup, and the "Montréal Benny," eggs Benedict with smoked meat. Other locations of this endearing chain include 190 Ste-Catherine ouest at the Quartier des Spectacles and 12 rue Notre Dame est in Vieux-Montréal. *1313 de Maison-neuve ouest. www.eggspectation. com.* ☎ *514/842-3447. Most items less than C$15. Breakfast and lunch daily. Métro: Peel. Map p 100.*

★★★ **Europea** DOWNTOWN *CONTEMPORARY FRENCH* Montréal has a handful of celebrity chefs, and Europea's Jérôme Ferrer is justifiably one of them. While many upscale restaurants have fallen by the wayside, this venue—a member of the prestigious Relais & Châteaux association—remains one of the special celebration spots in the city. For the full treatment, order the extravagant 11-course *grande experience*: In the past it has included a lobster cream "cappuccino," maple bark–stewed foie gras, and a squid, octopus, and scallop dish called "sea bed myths and legends." At lunch, a three-course option costs C$35. *1227 rue de la Montagne.*

www.europea.ca. ☎ *514/398-9229. Reservations recommended. All meals fixed-price: C$60 early evening, C$150 dinner, several options at lunch. Lunch Mon–Fri, dinner daily. Métro: Peel. Map p 100.*

★★ **kids L'Express** PLATEAU *BIS-TRO* No obvious sign announces L'Express, perhaps because all Montréal knows exactly where this most classic of Parisian-style bistros is located. It's eternally busy and open until at least 2am every day of the week, with an atmosphere that hits all the right notes: checkered floor, high ceiling, mirrored walls, just the right kind of noisy, *soupe de poissons, croque-monsieur*. Walk-ins can often find a seat at the zinc-topped bar. *3927 rue St-Denis. www. restaurantlexpress.com.* ☎ *514/845-5333. Main courses C$14–C$30. Breakfast, lunch, and dinner daily. Métro: Sherbrooke. Map p 99.*

★★ **kids Fairmount Bagel** MILE END *BAKERY* Montréal's bagels are justifiably renowned for their dense, sweet dough. Bakers hand-roll each bagel, which is then dropped in boiling water sweetened with a touch of honey and baked in big wood-fired ovens. Fairmount's poppyseed is its original flavor, though sesame is also popular. Founded in 1919, this shop is small and to-go only, but worth visiting to see the bakers in action. It's open 24 hours a day, 7 days a week—even on Jewish holidays. *74 av. Fairmount ouest. www.fairmount bagel.com.* ☎ *514/272-0667. Most bagels under C$1. Cash only. Daily 24 hr. Métro: Laurier. Map p 99.*

★★★ **Ferreira Café** DOWN-TOWN *SEAFOOD/PORTUGUESE* Ferreira exudes a warm, festive, Mediterranean grace, and excels with its take on Portuguese classics, including oysters (*huîtres à la portugaise*), roasted black cod (*morue noire rôtie*), and fish and seafood

Portuguese classics, like this roasted black cod, are highlights of the cozy, romantic Ferreira Café.

bouillabaisse. A smaller, late-night menu is also available. For lighter fare, Ferreira's sister venue, **Café Vasco de Gama,** on the same block (at 1472 rue Peel), offers big breakfasts, a variety of salads, and delectable desserts indoors—as well as sidewalk tables in warm months (open daily into the early evening). *1446 rue Peel. www.ferreiracafe.com.* ☎ *514/848-0988. Main courses C$26–C$55. Lunch Mon–Fri, dinner daily. Métro: Peel. Map p 100.*

★★★ **Graziella** VIEUX-MONTREAL *ITALIAN* Chef-owner Graziella Battista and her staff prepare modern Italian dishes served in understated yet beautiful presentations, like little works of art. Our top recommendations are the fall-off-the-bone *osso buco* and the homemade pasta dishes, such as *gnocchi al limone e basilico* (lemon-basil ricotta gnocchi) or rabbit and mushroom tortelli. The room is pretty and the service sophisticated. Reservations recommended. *116 rue McGill. www.restaurant graziella.ca.* ☎ *514/876-0116. Main courses C$37–C$42. Lunch Tues–Fri, dinner Tues–Sat. Métro: Square-Victoria-OACI. Map p 100.*

★★★ **Lawrence** MILE END *BISTRO* Emblematic of everything that's exciting about the Mile End dining scene, Lawrence takes modern British cuisine to a new level. Its hugely popular English breakfast and brunch are what most people rave about (although the lunch and dinner menus are equally outstanding). Brunch offers masterful turns on pub standards like bubble and squeak (boiled potatoes, cabbage,

vegetables) and kedgeree (haddock, curried rice, hard-boiled egg), while lunch and dinner get a touch of classic French technique. *5201 bd. St. Laurent. www.lawrence mtl.com.* ☎ *514/503-1070. Main courses C$17–C$26. Lunch Tues–Fri, dinner Tues–Sat, brunch Sat–Sun. Métro: Laurier. Map p 99.*

★★ kids **Magpie Pizzeria** MILE END *PIZZA* We love the wood-fired pizza here as much as the rustically hip atmosphere. Its Margherita is classic, its prosciutto and arugula pizza is fresh, and its "spanakopizza" is a unique blend of spinach, dill, onions, feta, and lemon. And unlike most pizza joints, this one is serious about dessert, with offerings such as a *tarte à la lime,* a key lime pie with basil whipped cream. In addition to the original Mile End location, there's a second Magpie at 1237 rue Amherst in the Village. *16 rue Maguire. www.pizzeriamagpie. com.* ☎ *514/507-2900. Pizzas C$14–C$21. Lunch Tues–Fri, dinner Tues–Sun. Métro: Laurier. Map p 99.*

★★ **Modavie** VIEUX-MONTREAL *MEDITERRANEAN* In the middle of the most touristed street in the most touristed part of the city, this restaurant caters heavily to acationers.

The sunny lemon hues in Graziella's restaurant.

Wood-fired pizzas at Magpie.

It does it with cheer. Modavie's menu features both French bistro classics and Italian-influenced pasta dishes, with excellent steak frites and a section of the menu dedicated to lamb. (We were also impressed seeing saffron risotto on the children's menu.) There is live jazz every evening and a weekend jazz brunch. *1 rue St-Paul ouest. www.modavie. com.* ☎ *514/287-9582. Main courses C$15–C$42. Lunch and dinner daily. Métro: Place d'Armes. Map p 101.*

★★★ kids **Olive + Gourmando** VIEUX-MONTREAL *BAKERY/LIGHT FARE* Eminently appealing, Olive + Gourmando is a local favorite. Croissants, scones, and biscuits sit side by side with creative sandwiches and plates, from a grilled cheese with Gouda and caramelized onions to homemade vegan burgers. The owners have opened two notable ventures in recent years: **Un Po' Di Più**, an Italian-style aperitivo bar with drinks and refined small plates as well as coffee and pastries, right on the main drag of the Old Port (www. caffeunpodipiu.com; 3 rue de la Commune est), and the restaurant

Foxy, in the Griffintown neighborhood just west of Vieux-Montréal (www.foxy.restaurant; 1638 rue Notre-Dame ouest). *351 rue St-Paul ouest. www.oliveetgourmando.com.* ☎ *514/350-1083. Most items under C$16. Breakfast and lunch until 5pm weekdays and 6pm weekends. Métro: Square-Victoria. Map p 101.*

★★★ **Pastel** VIEUX-MONTREAL *CONTEMPORARY QUEBECOIS* Pastel has been awash in accolades since it opened in summer 2018. *Eater Montreal* named it the 2018 Restaurant of the Year. The city's most esteemed food critic, Lesley Chesterman, declared that Pastel's sushi rice capped with lobster in chive emulsion was the dish of the year: Owners Kabir Kapoor and chef Jason Morris were already well-known in the city, and this venture is equal parts industrial-experimental and classical-sophisticate. It's ideal for special occasions. *124 rue McGill. www.restopastel.com.* ☎ *514/395-9015. Fixed-price menus only: C$140 10-course, C$90 7-course, C$50 5-course. Dinner Wed–Sun. Métro: Square Victoria. Map p 100.*

Bargain Hunters: Look for the *Table d'Hôte*

Always consider the table d'hôte fixed-price meals at restaurants. Ubiquitous in Montréal, they comprise a meal of two or four courses, usually priced at just a little more than the cost of a single a la carte main course. Restaurants at all price ranges offer them, and they represent the best value around. They're cheaper still at lunch—an economical way to sample top establishments.

More Restaurant Recommendations

In addition to the restaurants detailed in this chapter, we recommend these venues in other chapters of the book: **3 Brasseurs** (p 21), **7 Grains Café** (p 70), **Bonaparte Restaurant** (p 12), **Le BV** (p 86), **Café des Amis** (p 82), **Café Vasco Da Gama** (p 21), **Deville Dinerbar** (p 31), **Les Enfants Terrible** (p 54) **Les Glaceurs** (p 46), **Henri Brasserie Française** (p 53), **Invitation V** (p 58), **Jardin Nelson** (p 115), **Java U** (p 19), **Joe Beef** (p 62), **Juliette et Chocolate** (p 60), **Leméac** (p 78), **Marché de la Villette** (p 69), **Patrice Pâtissier** (p 85), **Ritz-Carlton Montréal** (p 53), **St-Viateur Bagels** (p 33), **Satay Brothers** (p 35), and **Taverne F** (p 62).

★★★ **kids** **Première Moisson**
PLATEAU *BAKERY* Another of Montréal's great bakeries and certainly its best chain: Première Moisson crafts 36 varieties of breads and baguettes alone (including green olive and chive baguettine; *flammenkueche* focaccia; maple cream and pecan turnover; and spelt and chia-seed bread) along with mind-bogglingly beautiful pastries. It has about a dozen branches throughout the city. *860 av. du Mont-Royal est. www.premieremoisson.com.* ☎ *514/523-2751. Most breads under C$5. Breakfast, lunch, and early dinner daily. Métro: Mont-Royal. Map p 99.*

★★ **kids** **Resto Vego** QUARTIER LATIN *VEGETARIAN* Just a few blocks from Université du Québec à Montréal, rue St-Denis is thick with inexpensive restaurant options. Vego is a favorite: vegetarian food served buffet-style, and you pay by the

weight. Dishes include vegetarian lasagna, quesadillas, and puff pastry with asparagus and mushrooms, with dozens of hot options (and luscious desserts). *1720 rue St-Denis. www.restovego.ca.* ☎ *514/845-2627. Pay by the weight: C$2.80 per 100g, or about C$13 for a dinner portion, with a maximum price of C$20. Lunch and dinner daily. Métro: Sherbrooke. Map p 100.*

★★★ **kids** **Schwartz's** PLATEAU *DELI* Many are convinced that this legendary Montréal eatery is the only place to indulge in the guilty treat of *viande fumée*—a brisket that's called, simply, smoked meat. Most guests also order sides of fries and mammoth garlicky pickles. It's one of many city landmarks created by Jewish immigrants, in this case Reuben Schwartz in 1928, making it Canada's oldest deli. Tables are communal and packed tight, so come prepared to rub elbows with strangers.

Olive + Gourmando.

The Best Dining

Cheese, Please

The cheeses of Québec are renowned for their rich flavors and textures, and many can only be sampled in Canada because they are often unpasteurized—made of *lait cru* (raw milk)—and therefore subject to strict export law. When dining in Montréal, do try some as a final course, such as the buttery **Le Cendré de Lune** from Alexis de Portneuf, 2½ hours north in the Laurentiens (p 150); or the creamy **Ermite** blue, made by monks at the Abbaye de Saint-Benoît-du-Lac, 1½ hours west of Montréal (p 159). Find out more from **Plaisirs Gourmets** (www.fromagesduquebec.qc.ca), a group that distributes and promotes Québec's artisan cheeses.

Schwartz's is open until 12:30am during the week, later on weekends. *3895 bd. St-Laurent. www.schwartzs deli.com.* ☎ *514/842-4813. Sandwiches and meat plates C$8–C$26. Cash only. Breakfast, lunch, and dinner daily. Métro: Sherbrooke. Map p 99.*

★★ **kids Stash Café** VIEUX-MONTRÉAL *POLISH* Alongside Vieux-Montréal's many French restaurants and houses of *nouvelle cuisine* sits this old-fashioned gem serving traditional Polish cuisine. Prices are affordable—main courses are almost all in the C$15-to-C$18 range, a rarity in this part of town. We recommend the *golabki* (cabbage leaves stuffed with pork and rice in a savory tomato sauce) and the *pierogis* (dumplings filled with beef, cheese and potato, or mushrooms and cabbage). Weekend brunch features eggs and Polish sausage, French toast, and a charcuterie plate. A pianist plays nightly, starting at 6pm. *200 rue St-Paul ouest. www.restaurantstashcafe. ca.* ☎ *514/845-6611. Main courses C$15–C$25. Lunch and dinner daily. Métro: Place d'Armes. Map p 101.*

★★ **kids Tommy Café + Apéro** VIEUX-MONTRÉAL *BAKERY/LIGHT FARE* With an all-white rococo ceiling, assorted other architectural curlicues, and a giant hanging plant that looks like a chandelier with dripping green vines, Tommy "cafe and apéro" (coffee shop and bar) offers a bright and dramatic setting. There's croissants and other pastries, avocado toast, quiche, and the like. *200 rue Notre-Dame ouest. www. tommymontreal.com.* ☎ *514/ 903-8669. All items C$4–C$12. Breakfast, lunch, and dinner daily. Métro: Place d'Armes. Map p 101.* ●

Schwartz's Deli has been serving its signature smoked meat sandwiches since 1928.

Nightlife Best Bets

Above: Dieu de Ciel. Previous page: Crowds at Montréal's famed Festival International de Jazz de Montréal.

Best **Cozy Plateau Terraces**
★★ Buvette Chez Simone, *4869 av. du Parc (p 114)* and ★★ Vices & Versa, *6631 bd. St-Laurent (p 116)*

Best **Hotel Cocktail Bar**
★★ Bar George in Le Mount Stephen Hotel, *1440 rue Drummond*

Best **Bar in Old Fur Warehouse**
★★ Bar Furco, *425 rue Mayor (p 114)*

Best **Terrace Along the Lachine Canal**
★★ McAuslan Brewing, *5080 rue St-Ambroise (p 116)*

Best **Downtown Wine Bar**
★★ Pullman, *3424 av. du Parc (p 116)*

Best **Low-Key Jazz Venue**
★★ Upstairs Jazz Bar & Grill, *1254 rue Mackay (p 118)*

Best **Speakeasy-Style Jazz Venue**
★★ Maison du Jazz, *2060 rue Aylmer (p 118)*

Best **Daytime Jazz Garden**
★★ Le Jardin Nelson, *407 Place Jacques-Cartier (p 115)*

Best **LGBTQ Dance Club**
★ Complexe Sky, *1478 rue Ste-Catherine est (p 117)*

Best **Fans During Habs Games**
La Cage Brasserie Sportive, *1212 av. des Canadiens du Montréal (p 114)*

Best **Craft Beers**
★★ Dieu du Ciel, *29 av. Laurier ouest (p 115)*

Best **Late-Night Menu in a Sexy Setting**
★★★ Ferreira Café, *1446 rue Peel (p 52)*

Best **Crescent Street Terrace for People-Watching**
★★ Sir Winston Churchill Pub, *1459 rue Crescent (p 116)*

Best **Live Celtic Music**
★ Hurley's Irish Pub, *1225 rue Crescent (p 118)*

Best **Montréal Indie Rock Scene**
★★ La Sala Rossa, *4848 bd. St-Laurent (p 118)*

Best **Drag Club**
★★ Cabaret Mado, *1115 rue Ste-Catherine est (p 117)*

Best **Paris-Style Bistro Open Until at Least 2am**
★★ L'Express, *3927 rue St-Denis (p 104)*

Best **Upscale Cocktails**
★★ Bar Henrietta, *115 av. Laurier ouest (p 114)*

Best **Swimming-Pool-Themed Bar**
★★ Club Pelicano, *1076 rue de Bleury (p 115)*

Nightlife in Plateau & Mile End

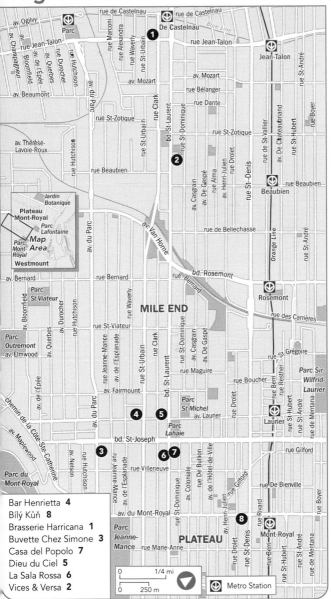

Bar Henrietta **4**
Bílý Kůň **8**
Brasserie Harricana **1**
Buvette Chez Simone **3**
Casa del Popolo **7**
Dieu du Ciel **5**
La Sala Rossa **6**
Vices & Versa **2**

Nightlife in Downtown & Vieux-Montréal

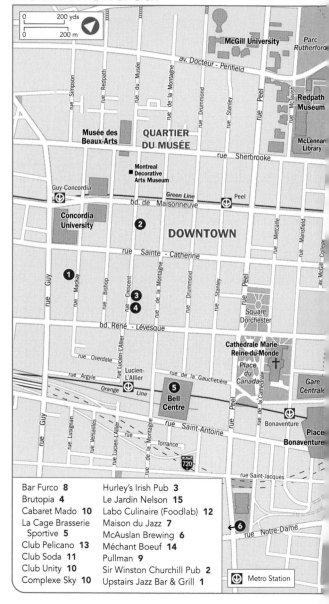

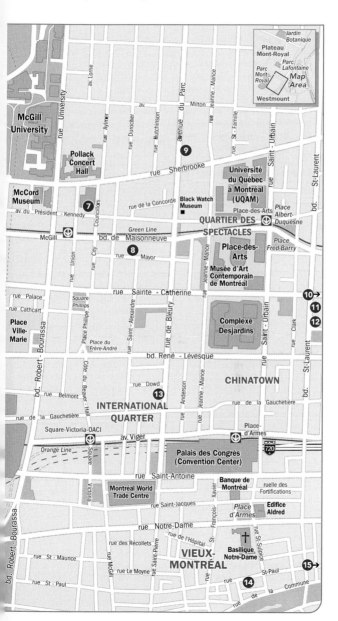

Jardin Botanique
Plateau Mont-Royal
Parc Lafontaine
Parc Mont-Royal
Map Area
Westmount

McGill University

Pollack Concert Hall

rue University
av. Lorne
rue Aylmer
rue Durocher
rue Hutchinson
avenue du Parc
Milton
Jeanne - Mance
St - Famille
Saint - Urbain
St-Laurent bd.

av. du Président - Kennedy

rue Sherbrooke

McCord Museum

7

rue de la Concorde

9

Black Watch Museum ■

Université du Québec à Montréal (UQAM)

Place Albert-Duquesne

Place-des-Arts

Councillors

Green Line

McGill

bd. de Maisonneuve

QUARTIER DES SPECTACLES

Place Fred-Barry

rue Union
rue City

rue **8** Mayor

Place-des-Arts

Musée d'Art Contemporain de Montréal

Jeanne - Mance

rue Palace
rue Cathcart

Square Phillips

rue Sainte - Catherine

10→

Place Ville-Marie

bd. Robert - Bourassa

Place Phillips

rue Saint-Alexandre

rue de Bleury

Complexe Desjardins

Saint - Urbain

rue Clark

St-Laurent

11
12

Côte du Beaver - Hall

Place du Frère-André

bd. René - Lévesque

rue Dowd

Anderson

CHINATOWN

rue Belmont

13

INTERNATIONAL QUARTER

Jeanne - Mance

rue de la Gauchetière

bd.

rue de la Gauchetière

Square-Victoria-OACI

Orange Line

Square

av. Viger

Place-d'Armes

Victoria

Palais des Congrès (Convention Center)

720

bd. Robert - Bourassa

rue Saint-Antoine

Montréal World Trade Centre

Banque de Montréal

ruelle des Fortifications

rue Saint-Jacques

Xavier

Place d'Armes

Edifice Aldred

rue Notre-Dame

rue des Récollets

rue de l'Hôpital

François-

St-

VIEUX-MONTRÉAL

Basilique Notre-Dame

St-Sulpice

rue des Récollets

rue St - Maurice

rue McGill

rue Le Moyne

15→

rue St - Paul

14

rue St - Paul

rue de la Commune

Nightlife A to Z

Bars

★★ **Bar Furco** QUARTIER DES SPECTACLES Industrial-chic Berlin meets an old Montréal fur warehouse. That's the inspiration for this downtown hotspot near Quartier des Spectacles for cocktails and wine (the food menu kicks in after 5pm). Attractive 20- and 30-somethings even wait in line to soak up Furco's vintage-mod vibe. *425 rue Mayor. www.barfurco. com.* ☎ *514/764-3588. Métro: Place-des-Arts or McGill. Map p 113.*

★★ **Bar Henrietta** MILE END Classy and friendly with soft light on a chic shopping street, the tapas-y Henrietta—offering oysters, toasts, and similar small plates—attracts a professional crowd. This is definitely the place to try a fancy cocktail from its mixologists, such as the "Belle Jaune" ("Beautiful Yellow"), with gin, lemon, thyme syrup, and cucumber. *115 av. Laurier ouest. www.barhenrietta.com.* ☎ *514/276-4282. Métro: Laurier. Map p 111.*

★★ **Bílý Kun** PLATEAU Pronounced "Billy Coon" and named after a bar in the Czech Republic, this is a bit of Prague in Montréal. Decor leans avant-garde (mounted ostrich heads hold court over the room), and drink options include Czech beers and a cocktail with absinthe and apples. Students and older professionals jam in for the relaxed candlelit atmosphere. There's live jazz or classical music from 6 to 8pm most nights and DJs on Thursdays, Fridays, and Saturdays until 3am. *354 av. Mont-Royal est. www.bilykun.com.* ☎ *514/845-5392. Métro: Mont-Royal. Map p 111.*

★★ **Brasserie Harricana** MILE END Way north near Little Italy, this large, bright craft brewery boasts two dozen beers and ciders on tap. Small (5-oz.) pours are available, making it fun to build your own flight of beers. The well-executed food menu features gussied-up pub food like meat pie, monkfish burger, and beer-can-roasted chicken. Serving lunch and dinner. *95 rue Jean-Talon ouest. www. brasserieharricana.com.* ☎ *514/303-3039. Métro: Jean-Talon. Map p 111.*

★ **Brutopia** DOWNTOWN Featured among Brutopia's home-brewed beers are its own version of an Irish stout, an IPA, and flavored concoctions such as Maple Vanilla Porter. Brutopia is right on the crowded party street of rue Crescent but maintains the atmosphere of a basic neighborhood bar. There are three floors and some terrace seating. Bands cram in and perform every night, with open mic on Sundays. *1219 rue Crescent. www. brutopia.net.* ☎ *514/393-9277. Métro: Lucien-L'Allier. Map p 112.*

★★ **Buvette Chez Simone** PLATEAU Industrial chic defines the interior bar, while a terrace framed by greenery is a coveted spot in sunny summer weather. The menu has a satisfying selection of small eats, including charcuterie and cheeses, as well as a strong selection of wines by the glass. *4869 av. du Parc. www.facebook.com/ BuvetteChezSimone.* ☎ *514/750-6577. Métro: Laurier. Map p 111.*

★ **La Cage Brasserie Sportive** DOWNTOWN Part of a national chain, this outpost is located in the Bell Centre and attracts the Canadiens faithful: During the hockey season, you'll find yourself surrounded by a sea of red, white, and blue jerseys—if you can find a seat. *1212 av. des Canadiens du Montréal. www.cage.ca.* ☎ *514/925-2255. Métro: Lucien-L'Allier. Map p 112.*

Outdoor patio of Jardin Nelson.

★★ Club Pelicano QUARTIER DES SPECTACLES

Located in the basement below restaurant Tiradito, Club Pelicano has a fun Art Deco swimming pool theme and cool vibe. Québec microbrews are featured as well as kitschy "poolside" cocktails with names such as "Missionary's Downfall." *Eater Montréal* named it the 2018 bar of the year. *1076 rue de Bleury. www. clubpelicano.com.* ☎ *514/861-1515. Métro: Place d'Armes. Map p 113.*

★★ Dieu du Ciel MILE END

There are dozens of *brasseries artisanale* in Montréal, but Dieu du Ciel is a favorite. This little neighborhood hangout offers an alternating selection of about 20 beers, and 4-ounce glasses make it easy to sample a few. Dieu du Ciel's brewery and bottling plant are now located about an hour north in Saint-Jérôme and its beers are sold throughout the province. *29 av. Laurier ouest. www. dieuduciel.com.* ☎ *514/490-9555. Métro: Laurier. Map p 111.*

★★ Le Jardin Nelson VIEUX-MONTREAL

Touristy, sure, in this most touristy part of the city, but in the summer, this outdoor dining option on Old Montréal's central Place Jacques Cartier is mighty appealing. Le Jardin Nelson is fronted by a people-watching porch adjacent to the plaza, but you want a table in its tree-shaded garden court, which sits behind a stone building dating from 1812. A pleasant hour or two can be spent listening to live jazz, played every afternoon and evening. Food includes pizzas, onion soup, and crêpes. When the weather's nice, it's open as late as 1am. Closed mid-October through mid-April. *407 Place Jacques-Cartier. www. jardinnelson.com.* ☎ *514/861-5731. Métro: Champ-de-Mars. Map p 113.*

★★ Labo Culinaire (Foodlab) QUARTIER DES SPECTACLES

Hidden away on the top floor of the Société Des Arts Technologiques, this venue hosts parties and business events, but it's also open Tuesday through Saturday from 5pm for drinks and food. In warm weather, come for the rooftop terrace and accompanying art-world creatives. *1201 bd. St-Laurent.*

Celebrate warm weather on the rooftop terrace at Labo Culinaire (Foodlab).

A late-night menu at Méchant Boeuf bar-brasserie kicks in at 11pm.

www.sat.qc.ca/foodlab. ☎ 514/884-2033. Métro: Saint-Laurent. Map p 113.

★★ **McAuslan Brewing** SAINT HENRI Much farther west than anything else listed in this book—in the artsy Saint Henri neighborhood just beyond **Marché Atwater** (p 35)—this brewery gets our nod because of its wonderful onsite **St-Ambroise Terrasse** pub. It's directly on the Lachine Canal, making it a terrific destination for a warm-day bike ride. Although the outdoor terrace is closed in the winter, the brewery also has an indoor pub, **L'Annexe,** open year-round. McAuslan makes the St-Ambroise and Griffon brand beers and offers tours at this facility. *5080 rue St-Ambroise. www.mcauslan.com.* ☎ 514/939-3060. Métro: Place Saint-Henri (25-min. walk). Map p 112.

★ **Méchant Boeuf** VIEUX-MONTREAL A young, stylish crowd piles into the bar of this brasserie during happy hour (featuring C$1 oysters) and doesn't seem to leave (a DJ keeps everyone moving with nonstop techno-pop). The menu has shareable appetizers, but the real focus is on beef: burgers, mini sliders, short ribs, and steaks. There's a substantial late-night menu starting at 11pm, and a brunch menu, too. *124 rue St-Paul ouest. www.mechant-boeuf.com.* ☎ 514/788-4020. Métro: Champs-de-Mars. Map p 113.

★★ **Pullman** DOWNTOWN Take advantage of 2- and 4-ounce pours at the sleek Pullman wine bar to try out some new options—there are more than 50 wines by the glass. A spiffy

tapas menu offers grilled cheese bedazzled with port and charcuterie prepared with the precision of a sushi chef. The multilevel space creates pockets of ambience, from cozy corners to tables drenched in natural light. *3424 av. du Parc. www.pullman-mtl.com.* ☎ 514/288-7779. Métro: Place des Arts. Map p 113.

★★ **Sir Winston Churchill Pub** DOWNTOWN In business for over 50 years, this gigantic rue Crescent landmark, with its New Orleans–style terraces (open in warm months), is usually packed with people taking in the street scene and the passing parade of humanity. Its three floors have DJs and occasional live music, TVs for sports fans, and a top-floor lounge, but try to snag one of those second-floor terrace spots if it's your first visit. *1459 rue Crescent. www.swcpc.com.* ☎ 514/288-3814. Métro: Guy-Concordia. Map p 112.

★★ **Vices & Versa** LITTLE ITALY An appealing backyard terrace and a menu of upwards of 40 microbrews makes this unpretentious joint a popular, low-key

The bar at Pullman.

Montréal's Monster Jazz Fest

The central Quartier des Spectacle arts district is the main big stage for the ★★★ **Festival International de Jazz de Montréal**, one of the monster events on the city's arts calendar. It costs serious money to hear big stars such as Buddy Guy, Norah Jones, or Chick Corea, but hundreds of free outdoor performances also take place during the 11-day June/July party, many right on downtown streets and plazas. Visit www.montrealjazzfest.com or call ☎ 855/299-3378 or 514/871-1881 for information.

favorite. Food options are several steps up from standard pub grub. *6631 bd. St-Laurent. www.viceset versa.com.* ☎ *514/272-2498. Métro: Beaubien. Map p 111.*

Dance Clubs

★ **Club Unity** THE VILLAGE Like the nearby **Complexe Sky** (below), the popular Club Unity has huge dance floors and a rooftop terrace. It attracts both LGBTQ and straight partiers. *1171 rue Ste-Catherine est.* ☎ *514/523-2777. www.clubunity. com. Métro: Beaudry. Map p 113.*

★ **Complexe Sky** THE VILLAGE Montréal is one of the LGBTQ capitals of the world, and Sky is a central meeting place. Sky has two floors of dancing and a first-floor bistro bar, **Le Branché.** The *cinq à sept* (5–7pm)

crowd takes to the rooftop terrace for after-work drinks, while late-night patrons come up for a breather from the downstairs dance clubs in the early morning. *1478 rue Ste-Catherine est.* ☎ *514/529-6969. www.complexe sky.com. Métro: Beaudry. Map p 113.*

Music Venues

In addition to the small venues listed here, check chapter 7, "The Best Arts & Entertainment," for the city's larger performance spaces for classical music and arena rock

★★ **Cabaret Mado** THE VILLAGE Year in and year out, Montréal's premiere drag club keeps on keeping on, popular with gay men, bachelorette parties, and fans of the fabulous. The club is named after Québec's reigning Queen, Mado Lamotte. Most performers do their

Dancing at Club Unity.

The Montréal Jazz Festival unifies the city's residents and visitors.

shows in French. *1115 rue Ste-Catherine est. www.mado.qc.ca.* ☎ *514/525-7566. Cover usually C$5–C$10. Métro: Beaudry. Map p 113.*

★ **Casa del Popolo** PLATEAU Self-described as "part fair-trade café, part music venue, part resto-bar and part art gallery," the storefront Casa del Popolo is a laid-back space that holds 55 and has a cozy first-floor stage for its intimate shows. *4873 bd. St-Laurent. www.casadel popolo.com.* ☎ *514/284-3804. Cover C$5–C$15. Métro: Laurier. Map p 111.*

★ **Club Soda** QUARTIER LATIN A long-established rock club in the old red-light district of the Latin Quarter on the edge of the Quartier des Spectacles, Club Soda hosts national acts, cover bands, and parts of the city's music and comedy festivals. *1225 bd. St-Laurent. www.clubsoda. ca.* ☎ *514/286-1010. Tickets from C$12. Métro: St-Laurent. Map p 113.*

★ **Hurley's Irish Pub** DOWNTOWN On the southern end of Rue Crescent, Hurley's has a street-level terrace and several semi-subterranean rooms where Celtic musicians perform nightly. It pours gallons of Guinness and takes pride in its "drunken debauchery." *1225 rue Crescent. www.facebook.com/ HurleysIrishPub.* ☎ *514/861-4111. Métro: Lucien L'Allier. Map p 112.*

★★ **Maison du Jazz** DOWNTOWN Since 1980, this New Orleans–style venue has presented jazz of the swinging mainstream variety, and the gilded speakeasy decor

is fun. It puts on shows every night, at 6pm and 9pm every Friday and Saturday and 7pm other evenings. Lunch and dinner are served, with options for ribs, burgers, and *poutine* fancied-up with crispy fried chicken or *saucisses Toulouse.* Reservations recommended. *2060 rue Aylmer. www.houseofjazz.ca.* ☎ *514/842-8656. Cover C$10. Métro: McGill. Map p 113.*

★★ **La Sala Rossa** PLATEAU A bigger venue than its sister space **Casa del Popolo** (see above), La Sala Rossa offers a calendar of interesting rock, experimental, and jazz music. The same family business operates **La Vitrola,** at 4602 St-Laurent, and **La Sotterenea,** at 4848 St. Laurent, with schedules for all four venues bundled onto one calendar. Together they make up the heart of the Montréal indie music scene. *4848 bd. St-Laurent. www.casadel popolo.com.* ☎ *514/844-4227. Cover C$5–C$30. Métro: Laurier. Map p 111.*

★★ **Upstairs Jazz Bar & Grill** DOWNTOWN Little jazz clubs that offer music every night are part of the lifeblood of big cities, and the Upstairs Jazz bar more than fills that role for Montréal. It started as a piano bar but now has broader programming that includes flamenco and Latin jazz. Sets begin as early as 7pm. You actually have to walk downstairs to enter. *1254 rue Mackay. www.upstairsjazz.com.* ☎ *514/931-6808. Cover C$8–C$16. Métro: Guy-Concordia. Map p 112.* ●

Houston Person on sax at Upstairs Jazz.

Arts & Entertainment Best Bets

Best **Circus Companies**
★★★ Cirque du Soleil *(p 121)* and ★★★ Les 7 Doigts *(p 124)*

Best **Circus Festival**
★★ Montréal Complètement Cirque *(p 161)*

Best **Opportunity to Hear French Chanson**
★★ Les FrancoFolies de Montréal festival, held in June *(p 160)*

Best **Ballet Company**
★★ Les Grands Ballets Canadiens, *Place des Arts, with performances at Salle Wilfrid-Pelletier and Théâtre Maisonneuve (p 125)*

Best **Opera Company**
★★★ L'Opera de Montréal, *Place des Arts, Salle Wilfrid-Pelletier, 175 rue Ste-Catherine ouest (p 124)*

Best **Orchestra Companies**
★★ Orchestre Symphonique de Montréal (OSM) and ★ Orchestre Métropolitain du Grand Montréal, *Place des Arts, Maison symphonique de Montréal, 1600 rue St-Urbain (p 124)*

Best **English-Speaking Theater**
★★ Centaur Theatre, *453 rue St-Francois-Xavier (p 126)*

Best **Music Festival**
★★★ Festival International de Jazz de Montréal, held in June and July *(p 160)*

Best **Jewish Cultural Events**
★ Segal Centre for Performing Arts, *5170 Côte-Ste-Catherine (p 127)*

Best **Comedy Entertainment**
★★ Festival Juste pour Rire (Just for Laughs Festival) festival, held in July *(p 160)*, and ★★ The Comedy Nest, *2313 Ste-Catherine ouest (p 125)*

Best **Venue for Sports & Big-Name Concerts**
★★ Centre Bell, *1909 av. des Canadiens-de-Montréal (p 126)*

Best **Destination for Games of Chance**
★ Casino de Montréal, *Parc Jean-Drapeau (p 121)*

Best **Humungous Movie Screen**
★ IMAX Telus Theatre, *in the Centre des Sciences de Montréal, Quai King Edward (p 126)*

Best **Free (or Almost Free) Classical Music**
★★ Pollack Hall, *555 rue Sherbrooke ouest (p 125)*

Below: The Casino de Montréal. Previous page: Orchestre Symphonique de McGill at Salle Pollack.

Casino
★ **Casino de Montréal** PARC JEAN-DRAPEAU   The province's original casino is housed in a splashy complex recycled from the French and Québec pavilions from the 1967 World's Fair. The buildings provide a dramatic setting for poker, blackjack, roulette, and 3,000 slot machines. There's Latin music every Friday and Saturday evening. Visitors must be at least 18. *Parc Jean-Drapeau, 1 ave. du Casino. www. casinosduquebec.com.* ☎ *800/665-2274 or 514/392-2746. Free admission. Métro: Parc Jean-Drapeau. Map p 122.*

Circus
★★★ **Cirque du Soleil**   The circus company Cirque du Soleil, now a global powerhouse, is based in Montréal. Each show is a celebration of pure skill with acrobats, trapeze artists, and performers costumed

Montréal has cultivated some of the world's best circus performers.

to look like creatures not of this world—iguanas crossed with goblins, peacocks born of trolls. Although there isn't a permanent show in Montréal, the troupe usually comes through the city at least once a year, setting up circus tents on Quai Jacques-Cartier in Vieux Port. *www.cirquedusoleil.com.* ☎ *877/924-7783. Tickets from C$67.*

Montréal's Quartier Des Spectacles

The cultural district known as Quartier des Spectacles lies just north of Vieux-Montréal and on the eastern edge of downtown. It has blossomed since the 2017 completion of a 10-year development project and is a central location for Montréal's major festivals and other events. Its center is the **Place des Arts complex**—an indoor-outdoor space of concert halls, museums, open-air plazas, restaurants, and shops—but its artistic reach spills out into the broader neighborhood with video projections onto building facades, dramatic red lighting on sidewalks (a nod to the neighborhood's former life as a red-light district), dancing waters on one central plaza, an annual springtime installation of *21 Balançoires/21 Swings* (a swing set that plays musical notes), and the transformation of a section of rue Ste-Catherine into a pedestrian-only thoroughfare in spring and summer. The website www.quartierdesspectacles.com has loads of details and the latest on what's new.

In addition to the venues and production companies listed here, additional listings for performing arts can be found in chapter 6, "The Best Nightlife," and "Festivals & Special Events" on p 160.

Arts & Entertainment in Montréal

Les 7 Doigts **6**
Casino de Montréal **7**
Centaur Theatre **8**
Centre Bell **3**
Cirque du Soleil **10**
The Comedy Nest **2**
Les Grands Ballets
  Canadiens **6**
IMAX Telus Theatre **9**
L'Opera de Montréal **6**

Orchestre Métropolitain
  du Grand Montréal **6**
Orchestre Symphonique de
  Montréal (OSM) **6**
Percival-Molson Memorial
  Stadium **4**
Pollack Concert Hall **5**
Segal Centre for Performing
  Arts **1**

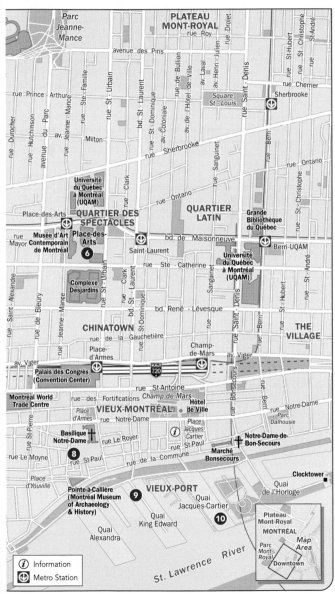

Parc Jeanne-Mance

PLATEAU MONT-ROYAL
rue Roy

avenue des Pins

rue Prince - Arthur

Milton

rue Sherbrooke

Square St - Louis

Sherbrooke

rue Cherrier

rue Ontario

Université du Québec à Montréal (UQAM)

Place-des-Arts

QUARTIER DES SPECTACLES

Musée d'Art Contemporain de Montréal

Place-des-Arts
6

rue Mayor

Saint-Laurent

bd. de Maisonneuve

rue Ontario

QUARTIER LATIN

Grande Bibliothèque du Québec

Berri-UQAM

rue Ste - Catherine

Université du Québec à Montréal (UQAM)

Complexe Desjardins

bd. René - Lévesque

CHINATOWN

rue de la Gauchetière

THE VILLAGE

Place-d'Armes

Champ-de-Mars

av. Viger

av. Viger

Palais des Congrès (Convention Center)

720

Montréal World Trade Centre

rue des Fortifications

rue St-Antoine

Champ de Mars

Hôtel de Ville

Place d'Armes

VIEUX-MONTRÉAL

rue Notre-Dame

rue Notre-Dame

Parc Dalhousie

Basilique Notre-Dame
8

rue Le Royer

rue St-Paul

Place Jacques-Cartier

Notre-Dame-de-Bon-Secours

rue St-Paul

Marché Bonsecours

rue Le Moyne

rue St-Paul

rue de la Commune

Place d'Youville

Pointe-à-Callière (Montréal Museum of Archaeology & History)
9

VIEUX-PORT

Quai Jacques-Cartier
10

Clocktower

Quai de l'Horloge

Quai King Edward

Quai Alexandra

St. Lawrence River

Plateau Mont-Royal

MONTRÉAL

Map Area

Parc Mont-Royal

Downtown

(i) Information

Ⓟ Metro Station

The Best **Arts & Entertainment**

★★★ **Les 7 Doigts** Like Cirque du Soleil, "The 7 Fingers" is a circus troupe based in Montréal that sends shows out around the world. Compared to its better-known competitor, the 7 Fingers is petite in scale, with fewer performers on stage and smaller venues. That means less bombast and a more intimate and up-close theater experience. www.7fingers.com. ☎ 514/521-4477. Tickets from C$36.

Classical Music
★★★ L'Opera de Montréal
QUARTIER DES SPECTACLES Founded in 1980, this outstanding opera company mounts four productions per year in Montréal along with a few shorter engagements, with artists from Québec and abroad. Offerings in 2020 include Mozart's "The Magic Flute" and the edgy modern composition "Written On Skin" by George Benjamin. Lyrics are projected above the stage in both French and English. Performances are held from September through May. There are special prices for people 34 and under. Place des Arts, Salle Wilfrid-Pelletier, 175 rue Ste-Catherine ouest. www.operade montreal.com. ☎ 877/385-2222 or 514/985-2222. Tickets from C$30. Métro: Place-des-Arts. Map p 123.

★ Orchestre Métropolitain du Grand Montréal
QUARTIER DES SPECTACLES This is a world-caliber orchestra of musicians who mostly trained in the province. It performs dozens of concerts a year—primarily at Place des Arts.

The Orchestre Métropolitain du Grand Montréal performs at Place des Arts.

Programs range from Slavik masters to Bach and beyond. *Place des Arts, Maison symphonique de Montréal, 1600 rue St-Urbain. www.orchestre-metropolitain.com. ☎ 866/842-2112 or 514/842-2112. Tickets from C$46. Métro: Place-des-Arts. Map p 123.*

★★ Orchestre Symphonique de Montréal (OSM)
QUARTIER DES SPECTACLES The orchestra's home has an unusual "shoebox" style, with seats on multiple balcony levels surrounding the performers. The symphony's repertoire typically features works by Bach, Brahms, and Verdi. *Place des Arts, Maison symphonique de Montréal, 1600 rue St-Urbain. www.osm.ca. ☎ 888/842-9951 or 514/842-9951.Tickets from C$32. Métro: Place-des-Arts. Map p 123.*

★★ Pollack Hall
DOWNTOWN A stone statue of Queen Victoria perched on her throne guards the entrance to this 1908 landmark building on the McGill University campus. Because many of the classical concerts and recitals performed here are by McGill students or alumni, ticket prices are modest. *555 rue*

The Just for Laughs comedy festival is the largest of its kind in the world.

Jordan Carlos at the Comedy Nest.

Sherbrooke ouest. www.mcgill.ca/music/events. ☎ 514/398-4547. Tickets free to C$40. Métro: McGill. Map p 122.

Comedy

Montréal's Festival Juste pour Rire (Just for Laughs Festival) is the largest comedy fest in the world and has been going strong for over 35 years. It draws headliners such as Trevor Noah, Wanda Sykes, and Hasan Minhaj, and dozens of other stand-up comics. It's held in venues across the city throughout the month of July. Visit www.hahaha.com or call ☎ 888/244-3155 or 514/845-2322.

★★ The Comedy Nest DOWNTOWN   This long-running club entertains patrons with both new-bie comics and world-class headliners. The building it's in, the famed Montréal Forum, was home to Canadiens Hockey for decades. The entrance is on avenue Atwater. 2313 Ste-Catherine ouest, in Forum de Montréal, 3rd floor. www.comedynest.com. ☎ 514/932-6378. Cover from C$5. Métro: Atwater. Map p 122.

Dance

★★ Les Grands Ballets Canadiens QUARTIER DES SPECTACLES Founded in 1957, this prestigious company performs both a classical and a modern repertoire and has brought prominence to many gifted Canadian choreographers and composers. The troupe's annual production of "The Nutcracker" is a big event each winter. Its season runs October through June. Place des Arts, with performances at Salle Wilfrid-Pelletier and Théâtre Maisonneuve. www.grandsballets.com. ☎ 514/849-0269 for information and tickets. Tickets from C$79. Métro: Place-des-Arts. Map p 123.

Film

In Montréal, English-language films are usually presented with French subtitles. However, when the letters VF (for version française) follow the title of a non-Francophone movie, it means that the movie has been dubbed into French. Policies vary regarding English subtitles on non-English-language films, so ask at the box office.

★ IMAX Telus Theatre VIEUX-PORT   Images and special effects are visually dazzling (and dizzying) on this gigantic 3-D screen in the **Centre des Sciences de Montréal** (p 13). Recent films, all rated G, have highlighted volcanos, pandas, and "super hero" dogs. Running time is usually less than an hour. One screening per day is in English and the rest are in French. Quai King Edward, Vieux-Port. www.montrealsciencecentre.com. ☎ 877/496-4724 or 514/496-4724. Movie tickets C$12 adults, C$11 seniors and teens, C$9 child, C$37 family. About 10 shows daily. Métro: Place d'Armes or Champ-de-Mars. Map p 123.

Sports & Rock Venues

★★ Centre Bell DOWNTOWN Seating 21,273 for most events,

IMAX at the Montréal Science Centre.

Centre Bell is the home of the Montréal Canadiens hockey team (nicknamed the Habs) and host to the biggest international rock and pop stars traveling through the city, including Québec native Céline Dion. There are guided tours of the venue for uber-fans. *1909 ave. des Canadiens-de-Montréal. www.centre bell.ca.* ☎ *855/310-2525. Métro: Bonaventure. Map p 122.*

★ **Percival-Molson Memorial Stadium** DOWNTOWN   U.S.–style football is played right downtown at this McGill University stadium, on the eastern slope of Parc Mont-Royal. During the Canadian Football League season, the stadium gets incredibly loud thanks to die-hard, chest-painting fans of the Montréal Alouettes (that's French for "larks"). Tickets to games sell out quickly. *Top of rue University at McGill University campus. www.montrealalouettes. com.* ☎ *844/575-2525 or 514/787-2525 for ticket info. Tickets from C$26. Métro: McGill. Map p 122.*

Theater
★★ **Centaur Theatre** VIEUX-MONTRÉAL   The city's principal English-language theater is housed in a former stock-exchange building from 1903, and celebrated its 50th anniversary in 2018. It presents an exciting slate of works by Canadian playwrights along with fun programs such as a series of single performances on Saturday mornings for children ages 4 to 12. Tickets to major plays are often hard to come by, but check the website to see what's on and what might be available. The season runs October through April. *453 rue St-Francois-Xavier. www.centaurtheatre.com.* ☎ *514/288-3161. Tickets from C$44. Métro: Place d'Armes. Map p 123.*

★ **Segal Centre for Performing Arts** PLATEAU   From about 1900 to 1930, Yiddish was Montréal's third-most-common language. That status has since been usurped by any number of languages, but its dominance lives on here: The centre is home to the **Dora Wasserman Yiddish Theatre,** Canada's only Yiddish-language theater. It also presents concerts, dance, cinema, and other Jewish cultural events. *5170 Côte-Ste-Catherine. www.segal-centre.org.* ☎ *514/739-7944. Tickets from C$30. Métro: Côte-Ste-Catherine or Snowdon. Map p 122.* ●

Entrance to the Centaur Theatre.

Hotel Best Bets

Best **Full-Service Hotel**
★★★ Hôtel Place d'Armes $$ 55 rue St-Jacques ouest (p 135)

Best **Sleek New Hotel**
★★ Hôtel Monville $$ 1041 rue de Bleury (p 134)

Best **Luxury Hotel**
★★★ Le Mount Stephen Hotel $$$ 1440 rue Drummond (p 135)

Best **Romantic Hotel**
★★ Auberge du Vieux-Port $$$ 97 rue de la Commune est (p 131)

Best **Hotels For Families**
★★★ Le Saint-Sulpice Hôtel Montréal $$ 414 rue St-Sulpice (p 135); ★★★ Hôtel Bonaventure Montréal $$ 900 rue de la Gauchetiere ouest (p 132); and ★★ Le Square Phillips Hôtel & Suites $$ 1193 Square Phillips (p 136)

Best **Elegant B&B**
★★ Casa Bianca $$ 4351 av. de L'Esplanade (p 132)

Best **High-Design Hotels**
★★ Hôtel Gault $$ 449 rue Ste-Hélène (p 133) and
★★ Hôtel St-Paul $$ 355 rue McGill (p 135)

Best **Casual Cozy Hotel**
★★ Auberge de La Fontaine $$ 1301 rue Rachel est (p 131)

Best **Inexpensive Option**
★★ HI Montréal Hostel $ 1030 rue Mackay (p 132)

Best **Rooftop Pool & Jacuzzi**
★★ Hôtel Le Crystal $$ 1100 rue de la Montagne (p 133)

Best **Rooftop Terrace**
★★ Hôtel Nelligan $$ 106 rue St-Paul ouest (p 134)

Best **In-House Dining**
★★★ Hôtel de l'ITHQ $$ 3535 rue Saint-Denis (p 134)

Above: Start the day in style with a light breakfast at the restaurant Bonaparte, complimentary for Hôtel Bonaparte guests. Previous page: The Grand Staircase at Le Mount Stephen Hotel.

Accommodations in Vieux-Montréal

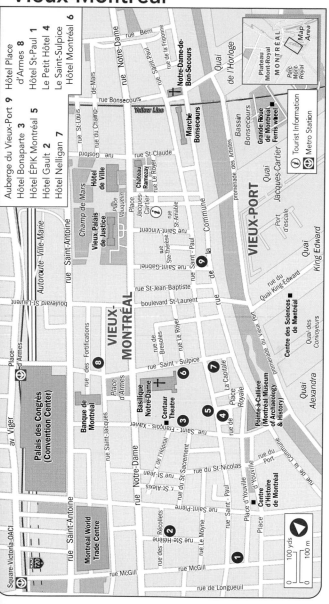

Auberge du Vieux-Port **9**
Hôtel Bonaparte **3**
Hôtel ÉPIK Montréal **5**
Hôtel Gault **2**
Hôtel Nelligan **7**

Hôtel Place d'Armes **8**
Hôtel St-Paul **1**
Le Petit Hôtel **4**
Le Saint-Sulpice **6**
Hôtel Montréal **6**

ⓘ Tourist Information
Ⓔ Metro Station

Accommodations in Downtown & the Plateau

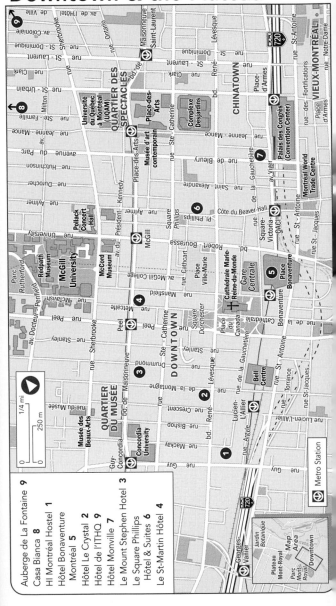

Map Area

Downtown

Plateau Mont-Royal

Parc Mont-Royal

Jardin Botanique

◉ Metro Station

QUARTIER DU MUSÉE

Musée des Beaux-Arts

Concordia University

McGill University

Parc Rutherford

Redpath Museum

Pollack Concert Hall

McCord Museum

DOWNTOWN

Square Dorchester

Place du Canada

Cathédrale Marie-Reine-du-Monde

Gare Centrale

Place Bonaventure

Bell Centre

Square Phillips

Place Ville-Marie

Square Victoria-OACI

Montreal World Trade Centre

Palais des Congrès (Convention Center)

CHINATOWN

Place-d'Armes

VIEUX-MONTRÉAL

Complexe Desjardins

Place-des-Arts

Musée d'art contemporain

QUARTIER DES SPECTACLES

Université du Québec à Montréal (UQAM)

Hôtel de Ville

0   1/4 mi
0   250 m

Hotels **A to Z**

Your glass awaits on the terrace at Auberge du Vieux-Port hotel.

Montréal has many fine chain hotels in its downtown, including **Fairmont, Lowes, Marriott, Ritz, Sheraton, W,** and **Westin** properties. The hotels and smaller *auberges* listed here are unique to the city. Note that names that begin with *Le, La, or Les*—French variations on the English word "The"—are listed alphabetically by the next word.

★★ **Auberge de La Fontaine**

PLATEAU   For visitors who plan to spend time at the restaurants and bars of Plateau Mont-Royal and want a casual option, La Fontaine can't be beat. Set in a greystone mansion, it feels like a cheerful hostel, although all the rooms are private and done up in a soothing palette of sky blue and slate grey. It's located directly on the lovely Parc La Fontaine and one of the city's central bike paths. The breakfast buffet (pastries, cereals, fresh fruit, local cheeses) is one reason guests return to this *auberge* time and time again. Families are warmly accommodated. *1301 rue Rachel est. www.aubergedelafontaine.com.* ☎ *800/597-0597 or 514/597-0166. 21 units. Doubles C$155–C$247. Métro: Mont-Royal. Map p 130.*

★★ **Auberge du Vieux-Port**

VIEUX-MONTREAL   Terrifically romantic. This luxury inn in an 1882 building faces the waterfront, and many rooms (as well as a rooftop terrace) offer unobstructed views of Vieux-Port, a particular treat on summer nights when fireworks light up the river. In addition to elegantly modern comforts, you'll find stone walls and wooden beams. The auberge also offers a selection of studio, one-, and two-bedroom loft-style apartments not far from the hotel, ideal for families and long-term stays. *97 rue de la Commune est.* ☎ *www.aubergeduvieux port.com.* ☎ *514/876-0081. 45 units. Doubles C$162–C$489. Métro: Place d'Armes. Map p 129.*

Airbnb, Vrbo, and B&Bs

Renting an apartment or room from a local is often (but not always) less expensive than staying in a comparable hotel. Both **Airbnb** (www.airbnb.com/s/Montreal) and **Vrbo** (www.vrbo.com) list hundreds of single rooms and whole apartments in Montréal. Bed-and-breakfasts in the city are usually set up as small hotels. The tourism office, **Tourisme Montréal** (www.mtl.org), has a select list of B&Bs that it recommends. (Also check its "Sweet Deal" offers with many of the city's top hotels, at www.mtl.org/en/deals/sweet-deal.)

★★ **Casa Bianca** PLATEAU An architectural landmark, this elegant B&B is full of character. It's on the corner of a tree-lined residential street in Montréal's hip Plateau neighborhood, adjacent to Parc Jeanne-Mance and a stone's throw from Parc du Mont-Royal. If the weather is cooperating, the organic breakfast is served on a breezy patio. Yoga instruction can be planned in advance with an in-house yoga instructor. Rooms are spacious with antique touches, and many have claw-foot bathtubs that add to the homey feel. If you're looking to do some shopping, it's close to the shops and boutiques along boulevard St-Laurent and avenue Mont-Royal. *4351 av. de L'Esplanade.* www.casabianca.ca. ☎ *514/312-3837. 5 units. Doubles C$129–C$279. Métro: Mont Royal. Map p 130.*

★★ **HI Montréal Hostel** DOWNTOWN A member of Hosteling International, HI Montréal offers both shared accommodations and private rooms. Like most hostels, it features a communal kitchen, but this being Montréal, it also has a bar, organized pub crawls, and group bike rides and ice-skating trips for guests. The raucous bar scene of rue Crescent is two blocks away. *1030 rue Mackay.* www.hostel lingmontreal.com. ☎ *866/843-3317 or 514/843-3317. 206 beds. Single bed in a private room C$90–C$130; shared room C$25–C$45. Métro: Lucien-L'Allier. Map p 130.*

Guests at HI Montréal.

★★ **Hôtel Bonaparte** VIEUX-MONTREAL Rooms at the lowest price point are small but bright, and square footage increases as you move up in price. Some units feature gorgeous exposed brick walls, while those on the courtyard side have an appealing view of the Basilique Notre-Dame. (The special Empire Room has a private terrace overlooking the basilica courtyard.) Complimentary breakfast is served in the graceful **Bonaparte** restaurant (p 12). At night, the restaurant dishes out classic French cuisine, with the Dover sole meunière especially recommended. *447 rue St-François-Xavier.* ☎ *514/844-1448.* www.bonaparte. com. *31 units. Doubles C$179–C$399. Métro: Place d'Armes. Map p 129.*

★★★ **kids Hôtel Bonaventure Montréal** DOWNTOWN The Bonaventure is in a concrete monster of an office building, but don't be put off by its Brutalist exterior. The hotel inside is lovely: It takes up the top two floors, and the 397 rooms and suites all have either

The independently owned Hôtel Bonaventure Montréal is a great choice for families in any season.

Vieux-Montréal's rustic charm softens the crisp lines in a loft at Hôtel Épik.

expansive views of the city or a peek at the hotel's delightful rooftop gardens featuring a resident family of ducks (and ducklings in spring), small walking paths, and a corker of a pool—outdoor, heated, and open year-round. Now independently owned, the hotel was part of the Hilton chain until 2015 and has retained some signature Hilton touches, including long hallways with attached conference rooms and a competent in-house restaurant and bar. *900 rue de la Gauchetiere ouest. www.hotelbonaventure.com.* ☎ *800/267-2575 or 514/878-2332. 397 units. Doubles C$189–C$359. Métro: Bonaventure. Map p 130.*

★★ **Hôtel Le Crystal** DOWN-TOWN   A top-floor pool (indoor, ringed by glass windows) and outdoor all-season Jacuzzi on the roof terrace are a big part of the Crystal's appeal. All the rooms are suites, and the smallest, at 495 square feet, is certainly ample for most guests, with a king bed, sofa, and kitchenette. Enveloping sheets and luxurious mattresses are part of the mix, of course. Its location close to the Centre Bell arena (home to the Canadiens hockey team and big

touring musical events) means that many visitors are taking in (or performing at) these shows, and prices tend to soar accordingly. The raucousness of rue Crescent is just around the corner. *1100 rue de la Montagne. www.hotellecrystal.com.* ☎ *877/861-5550 or 514/861-5550. 131 units. From C$195 suite and way up. Métro: Lucien L'Allier. Map p 130.*

★★ **Hôtel ÉPIK Montréal** VIEUX-MONTREAL   For many years this converted 1723 building was the Auberge Les Passants du Sans Soucy, a longtime Frommer's favorite. New owners and renovations have given the property a sleek, modern look. The onsite **Restaurant** Épik serves Italian fare at lunch and dinner and has an outdoor terrace in season. *171 rue St-Paul ouest. www. epikmontreal.com.* ☎ *877/841-2634. 10 units. Doubles C$140–C$329. Métro: Place d'Armes. Map p 129.*

★★ **Hôtel Gault** VIEUX-MONTREAL   Gault has softened the hardest edges of minimalism that it first embraced while retaining its modern, edgy look. Design aficionados will likely love it. Monumental concrete walls and structural austerity are tempered by contemporary

Hôtel Gault mixes sleek, minimalist style and colorful whimsy.

furniture and photography by local artists. Large bedrooms are loft-style, with polished-steel architect lamps. Some of the units have private balconies—a special treat in this evocative, formerly industrial area. *449 rue Ste-Hélène. www.hotel gault.com.* ☎ *866/904-1616 or 514/904-1616. 30 units. Doubles C$178 and way up. Métro: Square-Victoria-OACI. Map p 129.*

★★★ **Hôtel de l'ITHQ** PLATEAU For visitors who've "done" Old Montréal and want access to the Plateau's buzz of everyday Montréal life, there is no better option. Primely located and well-priced, this elegant hotel is expertly run by hospitality students who are learning the Province's signature style at the Institut de tourisme et d'hôtellerie du Québec (ITHQ). Rooms are modern, tidy, and spacious. There's a work desk if needed, but better to throw open the curtains and catch a sunset from the 8th floor, ideally on a Mont Royal–facing terrace. Each stay includes breakfast in the student-run **Restaurant de l'Institut,** a fine choice for any meal, even amid the plethora of neighborhood spots. *3535 rue Saint-Denis. www.ithq.qc.ca/en/ hotel.* ☎ *855/229-8189 or 514/282-5120. 42 units. Doubles from C$179. Métro: Sherbrooke. Map p 130.*

★★ **Hôtel Monville** QUARTIER DES SPECTACLES The eastern pocket of downtown just north of the Palais des Congrès convention center used to be a no-man's land of two-and three-story buildings. Now it's a mini city of hotels. Fresh among them is the Monville, all gleaming 20 stories. An appealing open-plan lobby has dramatic two-story floor-to-ceiling windows and houses a bar and a cafe with takeout items. A small, colorful robot (think R2D2) skitters around the lobby and in and out of the elevator, delivering cold items to guest rooms. Rooms are industrial-chic, in slate grey with cozy touches. Corner suites (such as #1114) offer a little more room and spectacular 180-degree views—at least until another hotel sprouts up. *1041 rue de Bleury. www.hotelmonville.com.* ☎ *844/545-2001 or 514/379-2000. 269 units. Doubles C$169–C$357. Métro: Place d'Armes. Map p 130.*

★★ **Hôtel Nelligan** VIEUX-MONTREAL Many of the Nelligan's bedrooms are dark-wooded, masculine retreats, and all have heaps of pillows and quality mattresses. The common spaces create a communal feel that will make you want to hang out all day—certainly doable considering the many private corners for tucking into. The Nelligan has one of the great hotel rooftop terraces of the city (www.terrassenelligan.com), popular with hotel guests and the general public alike; make reservations if you want to come for brunch. In the evening, tables are first-come, first-served for cocktails or a meal. *106 rue St-Paul ouest. www.hotelnelligan.com.* ☎ *877/788-2040 or 514/788-2040. 105 units. Doubles C$169-C$468. Métro: Place d'Armes. Map p 129.*

A guest room in Hôtel Nelligan.

Guest room at Hôtel Place d'Armes.

★★★ Hôtel Place d'Armes

VIEUX-MONTREAL   Four adjoining buildings make up this romantic hotel, with their elaborate architectural details of the late-19th and early-20th centuries in abundant evidence. Many bedrooms have richly carved capitals and moldings, high ceilings, or original brick walls, and all are decorated in contemporary fashion—deluxe bedding is standard, of course. Amenities could keep you in the hotel the whole trip: The hushed on-site **Rainspa** has a *hammam*—a traditional Middle Eastern steam bath—and offers massages and facials. And there are three appealing in-house dining options: the Japanese sushi restaurant **Kyo Bar**; the airy, elegant, tall-ceilinged **Brasserie 701**, where guests take breakfast; and the 8th-floor **Terrassse Place d'Armes**, which overlooks Old Montréal and is a go-to setting for a cocktail or meal. *55 rue St-Jacques ouest. www.hotelplacedarmes. ouest.* ☎ *844/806-1917 or 514/842-1887. 169 units. Doubles C$171–C$422. Métro: Place d'Armes. Map p 129.*

★★ Hôtel St-Paul

VIEUX-MONTREAL   The chic St-Paul has been a star to design and architecture aficionados since its opening. Minimalism pervades, with simple lines, muted colors, and then a pop of orange or purple. Many rooms face Vieux-Montréal's western edge, with its visually appealing stone and brick buildings. The St-Paul is on a sophisticated stretch of rue McGill, near some of the city's top restaurants, including **Graziella** (at #116; see p 105) and **Pastel** (#124; p 106). *355 rue McGill. www.hotelstpaul. com.* ☎ *866/380-2202 or 514/380-2222. 119 units. Doubles from C$179 and way up. Métro: Square-Victoria-OACI. Map p 129.*

★★★ Le Mount Stephen Hotel

DOWNTOWN   Italianate charm meets high-tech luxury in this recently restored architectural gem, located in the heart of downtown. It was first a residence for Lord George Stephen and then an exclusive social club. Now anyone can sip cocktails in the hand-carved wood-paneled **Bar George** (outfitted with 22k-gold fixtures) or stay overnight in one of the mod, newly constructed guest rooms. In-shower light therapy, heated toilet seats, and pillow menus are de rigueur. *1440 rue Drummond.* ☎ *844/838-8655 or 514/313-1000. www.lemount stephen.com. 85 units. Doubles from C$225. Métro: Peel. Map p 130.*

★★ Le Petit Hôtel

VIEUX-MONTREAL   Le Petit Hôtel aims to be the quirky entry to Vieux-Montréal's hospitality landscape. Many elements—from the comic-book artwork in the cafe to the rooms being categorized as "S, M, L, and XL" to the room-and-bike-tour special offer—skew toward a younger demographic. Other elements provide architectural ballast, including the dramatic stone walls found throughout the property and the handsome custom-designed Québec-made furniture. Breakfast is served in the small lobby cafe. *168 rue St-Paul ouest. www.petit hotelmontreal.com.* ☎ *877/530-0360 or 514/940-0360. 28 units. Doubles C$162–C$516. Métro: Place d'Armes. Map p 129.*

★★★ 🅺🅸🅳🆂 Le Saint-Sulpice Hôtel Montréal

VIEUX-MONTREAL   Each of the 108 units at this

Deluxe balcony room at Le Saint-Sulpice.

top-notch, uniquely Montréalais boutique hotel is a suite with fully equipped kitchen. Even the smallest feel like decked-out efficiency apartments, ideal for families. They include French windows that can be opened, a rarity in this city. The lobby has a well-stocked bar, and the hotel's **Sinclair Restaurant,** which focuses on contemporary French cuisine, serves both indoors and on an especially lovely private outdoor terrace in warm months. Customer service is of the highest order here, as the concierge staff are all members of the prestigious Clefs d'Or organization. *414 rue St-Sulpice. www.lesaintsulpice.com.* ☎ *877/785-7423 or 514/288-1000. 108 units. Suites from C$175 and way up. Métro: Place d'Armes. Map p 129.*

★★ kids **Le Square Phillips Hôtel & Suites** DOWNTOWN The Square Phillips is one of the great downtown hotel options for families, especially on weekends when business travelers have cleared out. Even the smallest of rooms are decent-sized studios, with a full kitchen including a large fridge and stove. The heavy-duty walls of this former warehouse are handy for muffling the noise: Rooms here are close to a lot of action (both the busy shopping street rue Ste-Catherine and the Quartier des Spectacles arts district are around the corner) but seem insulated from the outside world. There's an indoor rooftop pool and a self-service laundry room available. *1193 Square Phillips. www.squarephillips.com.* ☎ *866/393-1193 or 514/393-1193. 164 units. Studios C$159–C$484. Métro: McGill. Map p 130.*

★★ **Le St-Martin Hôtel** DOWNTOWN High-rises on this downtown block are tall, so rooms don't have much of a view, but that won't matter for most guests, particularly given the modern interiors and touches like standalone bathtubs and electric fireplaces. A narrow, outdoor "dipping pool" is heated and open year-round. The in-house restaurant **Gustave** spills out onto a lovely sidewalk terrace in the warm months for alfresco dining. *980 boul. de Maisonneuve ouest. www.lestmartin montreal.com.* ☎ *877/843-3003 or 514/843-3000. 123 units. Doubles from C$229. Métro: Peel. Map p 130.* ●

The indoor pool at Square Phillips.

Québec City

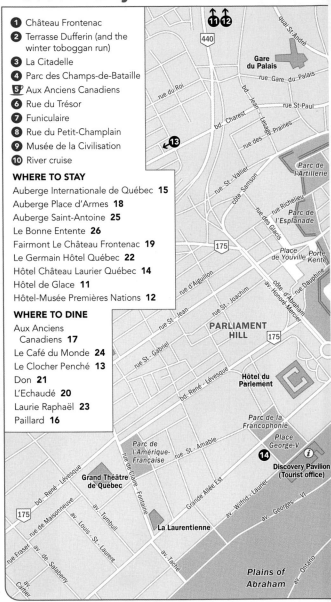

1. Château Frontenac
2. Terrasse Dufferin (and the winter toboggan run)
3. La Citadelle
4. Parc des Champs-de-Bataille
5. Aux Anciens Canadiens
6. Rue du Trésor
7. Funiculaire
8. Rue du Petit-Champlain
9. Musée de la Civilisation
10. River cruise

WHERE TO STAY

Auberge Internationale de Québec **15**
Auberge Place d'Armes **18**
Auberge Saint-Antoine **25**
Le Bonne Entente **26**
Fairmont Le Château Frontenac **19**
Le Germain Hôtel Québec **22**
Hôtel Château Laurier Québec **14**
Hôtel de Glace **11**
Hôtel-Musée Premières Nations **12**

WHERE TO DINE

Aux Anciens Canadiens **17**
Le Café du Monde **24**
Le Clocher Penché **13**
Don **21**
L'Echaudé **20**
Laurie Raphaël **23**
Paillard **16**

Previous page: Ice skating at Manoir Hovey.

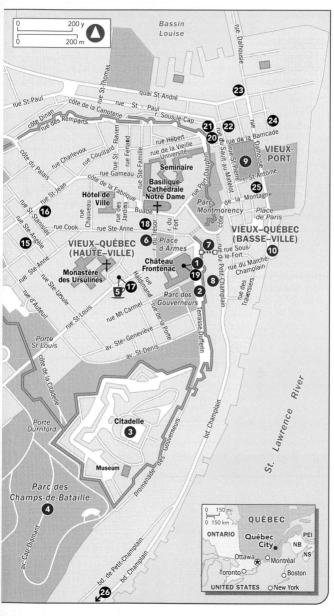

0 200 y
0 200 m

Bassin Louise

rue St-Thomas
rue St-Paul
côte de la Canoterie
côte Dinan
rue des Remparts
rue Charlevoix
côte du Palais
rue Couillard
rue St-Jean
côte de la Fabrique
rue Chauveau
rue St-Stanislas
rue Ste-Angèle
rue St-Jean
rue Cook
rue Ste-Anne
rue Ste-Anne
rue Ste-Ursule
rue d'Auteuil
rue St-Louis
rue Mt-Carmel
rue de la Porte
av. Ste-Geneviève
av. St-Denis

quai St-André
rue St-Paul
r. Sous-le-Cap
rue Hébert
rue de la Vieille Université
rue Ste-Famille
rue Ferland
rue Ste-Flavien
rue Gameau
côte de la Fabrique
rue des Jardins
Buade
r. du Trésor
r. du Fort
rue Ste-Anne

Seminaire
Basilique-Cathédrale Notre Dame
Hôtel de Ville
Parc Montmorency

VIEUX-PORT

rue du Sault-au-Matelot
r. St-Pierre
r.-St-Antoine
rue de la Barricade
rue Dalhousie

VIEUX-QUÉBEC (BASSE-VILLE)
Place de Paris
de la Montagne
Place Royale
rue Sous-le-Fort
rue du Marché Champlain
rue des Traversiers

VIEUX-QUÉBEC (HAUTE-VILLE)
Place d'Armes
Château Frontenac
Parc des Gouverneurs
Monastère des Ursulines

terrasse Dufferin

Porte St-Louis
côte de la Citadelle
Porte Durnford

Citadelle
Museum

promenade des Gouverneurs

bd. Champlain

St. Lawrence River

Parc des Champs-de-Bataille
av. Cap-Diamant

bd. de Petit-Champlain
bd. Champlain

1 **2** **3** **4** **5** **6** **7** **8** **9** **10** **15** **16** **17** **18** **19** **20** **21** **22** **23** **24** **25** **26**

0 150 mi
0 150 km

QUÉBEC

ONTARIO
Québec City
Ottawa
Montréal
Toronto
Boston
UNITED STATES
New York
PEI
NB
NS

Situated along the majestic Fleuve Saint-Laurent (St. Lawrence River), Québec City seduces from first view. Much of the oldest part of the city—Vieux-Québec, or, in English, Old Québec—resides atop Cap Diamant, a rock bluff that once provided military defense. Fortress walls still encase the upper city, and the soaring Château Frontenac, a hotel with castle-like turrets, dominates the landscape. A revitalized Lower Town, by the water, is thick with boutique hotels and cafes. The city is almost entirely French in feeling, spirit, and language: Almost everyone—95% of the population—is Francophone, or French speaking. But many of the area's 800,000 residents know at least some English, especially those who work in hotels, restaurants, and shops. START: A full day stroll can take in the sites below in the order presented. Start at Place d'Armes, the central plaza in the upper city.

❶ ★★★ Château Frontenac.

The original section of the famous edifice that defines the Québec City skyline was built as a hotel from 1892 to 1893 by the Canadian Pacific Railway Co. The architect, an American named Bruce Price (and the father of etiquette guru Emily Post), raised his creation on the site of the governor's mansion and named it after Louis de Buade, comte de Frontenac, an early governor general of New France. Guided tours of the hotel are available daily, in either English or French (C$21 adults, C$11 kids 6–16; www.cicerone.ca; ☎ 855/977-8977). The Frontenac is now a Fairmont hotel and one of the city's finest; see "Where to Stay," p 144.

❷ ★★ kids Terrasse Dufferin (and the winter toboggan run).

In warm months, the picturesque Terrasse Dufferin boardwalk promenade, with its green-and-white-topped gazebos, looks much as it did 100 years ago, when ladies with parasols and gentlemen with top hats and canes strolled it on sunny afternoons. The terrace offers vistas of river, watercraft, and distant mountains, and is particularly romantic at sunset. In winter, an old-fashioned toboggan run called Les Glissades de la Terrasse is set up on the steep wooden staircase at Terrasse Dufferin's southern end. The slide extends almost to the Château Frontenac. Hot chocolate is available to warm you up after

The stunning Château Frontenac is an icon of Québec City.

Québec City 101

Almost all of a visit can be spent on foot in the old Upper Town, atop Cap Diamant (Cape Diamond), and in the old Lower Town, which hugs the river below the bluff. High season is from June 24 (Jean-Baptiste Day) through Labor Day (the first Mon in Sept, as in the U.S.). The central tourist information center, **Centre Info-touriste de Québec** (12 rue Ste-Anne; www.quebecoriginal.com; ☎ 877/266-5687), is in Upper Town on Place d'Armes, the plaza in front of the Château Frontenac. It's open from 9am to 6pm daily from late June through August and from 9am to 5pm daily the rest of the year. (Bus tours of the city are available from several companies leaving from the tourist information center.) Information is also available at **www.quebec-cite.com.**

the quick and exhilarating ride, which can reach speeds of 70km (45 miles) an hour. *Toboggan information: www.au1884.ca.* ☎ *418/528-1884. C$3 per person.*

❸ ★★ kids **La Citadelle.** The duke of Wellington had this partially star-shaped fortress built at the south end of the city walls in anticipation of American attacks after the War of 1812 (attacks that never came). The facility has never actually exchanged fire with an invader but continues its vigil for the state. It's now a national historic site, and since 1920 has been home to Québec's Royal 22e Régiment, the only fully Francophone unit in Canada's armed forces. That makes it North America's largest fortified group of buildings still occupied by troops. Entrance is by guided tour only. If you're inclined, try to time a visit to include the 35-minute changing of the guard ceremonies (daily at 10am July 24 through the first Mon in Sept). *1 Côte de la Citadelle. www.lacitadelle.qc.ca.* ☎ *418/694-2815. Admission C$16 adults, C$14 seniors and students, C$6 children 11–17, free for children 10 and under; families C$36. May–Oct daily 9am–5pm; Nov–Apr 10am–4pm.*

The long staircase running from La Citadelle to Terrasse Dufferin is converted into a toboggan run in winter.

Aerial view of Québec City's star-shaped fortress, La Citadelle.

Changing of the guard ceremony may be canceled in the event of rain.

4 ★ kids Parc des Champs-de-Bataille. Covering 108 hectares (267 acres) of grassy hills, sunken gardens, monuments, fountains, and trees, Québec's Battlefields Park was Canada's first national urban park. A section called the Plains of Abraham is where Britain's general James Wolfe and France's Louis-Joseph, marquis de Montcalm, engaged in their short but crucial battle in 1759, which resulted in the British defeat of France. It's also where the national anthem, *O Canada,* was first performed, and where both the **winter carnival** (www.carnaval.qc.ca) and many of the summer music festivals take place. The park is a favorite place for Québécois when they want sunshine or a bit of exercise during all seasons of the year. *Parc des Champs-de-Bataille. www.ccbn-nbc.gc.ca. ☎ 855/649-6157 or 418/649-6157 888/497-4322 or 418/644-9841.*

Try Québécois home cooking at **5 ★★ Aux Anciens Canadiens,** a venerable restaurant with costumed servers in the city's oldest (1677) house. Prices are generally high, but the restaurant's basic afternoon table d'hôte, served until 5:45pm, is a bargain: soup, a main course, a dessert, and a glass of beer or wine, for C$23. *See p 147.*

6 ★★ Rue du Trésor. Artists hang their prints and paintings of Québec scenes on both sides of this narrow pedestrian street, just off Place d'Armes and adjacent to the distinctive red-roofed Auberge du Trésor. In decent weather, this "artists' alley" is busy with browsers and sellers. Artists are often happy to have a chat about their work, and it's a good spot to pick up a small souvenir painting or lithograph.

7 ★★ kids Funiculaire. To get from Upper Town to Lower Town, you can take streets, staircases, or this cliffside elevator, known as the *funiculaire.* In operation here since

A quiet stroll in the Parc des Champs-de-Bataille.

Shopping on Rue du Trésor.

1879, today's model travels along an inclined 64m (210-ft.) track and offers excellent aerial views during its short trip. The upper station is on Place d'Armes. It operates daily 7:30am until 11pm. Wheelchairs can be accommodated May through October, when there's no snow; strollers can fit, folded, year-round. The one-way fare is C$3.50, cash only; free for children under 1.1m (46 inches). *www.funiculaire.ca.*

8 ★★★ **kids Rue du Petit-Champlain.** Diminutive and maintained to an atmospheric T, pedestrian-only Petit-Champlain lays claim to the title of North America's oldest lane. In warm months, it swarms with strolling couples, cafe sitters, and gaggles of schoolchildren. In winter, it's a snowy wonderland with ice statues and twinkling white lights. There are galleries and boutiques here worth browsing, but even if you're not a shopper the 17th-century character is worth taking in. For a bite to eat, **Le Lapin Saut**é (52 rue du Petit-Champlain; www.lapin-saute.com; ☎ **418/692-5325**) is a country-cozy bistro with hearty food and a lovely terrace overlooking a small shaded garden. *www.quartier petitchamplain.com.*

9 ★★★ **kids Musée de la Civilisation.** This wonderful museum is spacious and airy, with ingeniously arranged multidimensional exhibits. If time is short, definitely take in "People of Québec… Then and Now," a permanent exhibit that is a sprawling examination of Québec history, from the province's roots as a fur-trading colony to the turbulent movement for independence that started in the 1960s. *85 rue Dalhousie. www. mcq.org.* ☎ *866/710-8031 or 418/643-2158. Admission C$17 adults 31+, C$11 adults 18–30, C$6 children 12–17, free for children 11 and under; additional fees for special exhibitions. Mid-June to early Sept daily 10am–5pm; rest of the year Tues–Sun 10am–5pm.*

10 ★ **kids River cruise.** In the warm months, 90-minute daytime cruises are offered three times a day, letting visitors see Québec City from a unique vantage point. The trip travels the short distance to the Montmorency waterfalls and the bucolic Île d'Orléans and includes commentary from a costumed guide (audioguides are also available in eight languages). Dinner cruises are another option. *Port of Québec, Quai Chouinard, 10 rue Dalhousie. www.croisieresaml.com.* ☎ *877/522-5346. Admission C$35 ages 13 and older; C$20 ages 6–12; free for kids 5 and under; dinner cruise from C$100 May–Oct.*

Québec City: **Where to Stay**

★ **kids** **Auberge Internationale de Québec**   There several sleep options in this centrally located, affordable hostel. Most beds are in dorm layouts standard to Hostelling International (HI), while others are in modest private rooms for one to five people, with either shared or private bathrooms. Linens are provided. This is a good budget option on a quiet street in the old Upper Town, just a block from the fortress walls. *19 rue. Ste-Ursule. www.auberge internationaledequebec.com.* ☎ *866/694-0950 or 418/694-0755. 277 beds, most in dorms, with private rooms available. C$66–C$147 private room for 2 with bathroom; C$22–C$38 per person for shared dorm room. Discount available for HI members. Rates for private rooms include breakfast.*

★★ **kids** **Auberge Place d'Armes**   Carefully renovated guest rooms in this high-end yet well-priced *auberge* feature exposed stone walls dating from 1640. The hotel website has 360-degree tours of each room. The hotel is located just steps from the central plaza of old Upper Town. **Note:** You need to climb stairs to reach all guest rooms. *24 rue Ste-Anne. www.aubergeplace darmes.com.* ☎ *866/333-9485 or 418/694-9485. 20 units. Doubles C$150–C$320. Rates include breakfast when booking through the hotel.*

★★★ **Auberge Saint-Antoine** This is one of the most splurge-worthy hotels in Québec City. The Saint-Antoine is a member of the prestigious Relais & Châteaux luxury group, and rooms are lavish and spacious. Artifacts unearthed during a large-scale archaeological dig are displayed throughout the hotel with curatorial care. The inventive in-house restaurant, **Chez Muffy,** is housed in a space that dates to 1822 with stone walls and wooden beams. *8 rue St-Antoine. www.saint-antoine. com.* ☎ *888/692-2211 or 418/692-2211. 95 units. Doubles C$239–C$519.*

★★ **Le Bonne Entente**   Luxuriate poolside among landscaped gardens, get a shea butter body wrap and massage at the on-site **Amerispa,** or take in a round of golf at the hotel's private **La**

The striking and elegant Auberge Saint-Antoine in winter.

The refined yet cozy lobby of Le Germain Hôtel Québec.

Tempête Golf Club. Le Bonne Entente is a Québec City resort that's only a 15-minute drive south from Vieux-Québec. *3400 Chemin Ste-Foy. www.lebonneentente.com.* ☎ *800/463-4390 or 418/653-5221. 160 units. Doubles C$169–C$523.*

★★★ kids Fairmont Le Château Frontenac Québec's magical "castle" opened in 1893 and has been wowing guests ever since. Many rooms are full-on luxurious— this is one of the premier properties of the grand Fairmont chain—and outfitted with elegant château furnishings and marble bathrooms. Prices depend on size, location, and view, with river views garnering top dollar. Lower-priced rooms overlooking the inner courtyard face gabled roofs — you might imagine Harry Potter swooping by in a Quidditch match. There are four restaurant options, including the elegant **Champlain** restaurant and the clubby **1608** wine and cheese bar. *1 rue des Carrières (at Place d'Armes). www.fairmont. com/frontenac-quebec.* ☎ *866/540-4460 or 418/692-3861. 611 units. Doubles from C$279 and way up.*

★★★ Le Germain Hôtel Québec Urban elegance is the ruling principle in one of the city's most refined boutique hotels. Built in 1912, Le Germain formerly housed Dominion Fish & Fruit Limited and became a hotel in the heart of the Old Port in 1997. Rooms are furnished with exceptionally comfortable beds and sheets that are downright heavenly. The continental breakfast is steps above most and can be taken on the leafy outdoor terrace when it's warm or near the lobby fireplace in colder months. *126 rue St-Pierre. www.legermainhotels.com/en/quebec.* ☎ *888/833-5253 or 418/692-2224. 60 units. Doubles C$239–C$445. Rates include continental breakfast.*

★★ Hôtel Château Laurier Québec A 10-minute walk from the walls of Upper Town and alongside the scenic oasis of the Plains of Abraham—the site of many city festivals—Château Laurier is many

Hôtel Château Laurier Québec is located just outside the walls of Upper Town.

Chill out at Québec's seasonal Hôtel de Glace.

different hotels in one. Its 271 units fall into seven categories that vary in age, style, and price. Check the options carefully on the website and book directly. There's an indoor pool and an on-site St-Hubert restaurant (a roast chicken casual-dining chain), both good for families. There also are nifty for-fee wine dispensers on some of the room floors—another welcome feature for parents. *1220 Place Georges-V ouest. www.hotelchateaulaurier.com.* ☎ *800/463-4453 or 418/522-8108. 271 units. Doubles C$129–C$309.*

★ **Hôtel de Glace** Meticulously crafted each winter from 500 tons of ice, Québec's *hôtel de glace* is unlike anything you've experienced, unless you've already slept in a sleeping bag on a slab of frozen water. Indoor temperatures hover around –4°C (25°F), but guests have access to (outdoor) hot tubs and a sauna as well as a bar. The larger suites are intricately detailed, and there's a glittery ice chapel. Rooms are available for sleeping from 9pm until 9am. It's about a half-hour drive from downtown, so just visiting is an option (admission C$21 adults, C$16 seniors and children, free to kids under 1m tall). The hotel is open January through March. *At the Village*

Vacances Valcartier park complex, 1860 bd. Valcartier, Valcartier. www. hoteldeglace-canada.com. ☎ *888/ 384-5524 or 418/844-2200. 42 units. Basic overnight package with cocktail, breakfast, and backup room at the Hôtel Valcartier from C$378 for 2.*

★★ **Hôtel-Musée Premières Nations** Situated on a forested section of the Wendake reservation, this is a unique property: a hotel that immerses guests in Huron-Wendat First Nations culture. It's 15 minutes from Québec City by car (in summer, there's a shuttle bus from the city). Every room features a private balcony overlooking the small Akiawenrahk River. An on-site, all-season outdoor spa has hot and cold baths and a tranquillity tent (www.nation santespa.com; C$35 per person; massages extra). The high-end **La Traite** restaurant specializes in smoked fish and wild game, including elk, venison, and bison. Wendake has a handful of shops and galleries, and local activities include canoeing the river, dog sledding, and snowshoeing. *5 Place de la Rencontre, Wendake, Québec. www.hotelpremieresnations.ca.* ☎ *866/551-9222 or 418/847-2222. 55 units. Doubles C$145–C$209.*

Québec City: **Where to Dine**

J.A. Moisan is said to be the oldest grocery store in North America.

★★ Aux Anciens Canadiens
TRADITIONAL QUEBECOIS This is one of the best places in La Belle Province to sample cooking that has roots in New France's earliest years. For one thing, the red-roofed house Aux Anciens Canadiens is based in dates from 1676. It's an admittedly tourist-heavy venue in central Upper Town, but the afternoon *table d'hôte*, which starts at C$23 for three courses and a glass

Bring Home the Flavors of Québec

The year-round indoor farmers market that was located on the Lower Town's waterfront for over 30 years shut down in 2019. It was replaced with a seasonal market in the same location and a mall-sized venture, **Le Grand Marché de Québec** (www.legrandmarche dequebec.com), 5km (3 miles) to the northwest, at 250 boulevard Wilfrid-Hamel. This glass-roofed, two-story pavilion is operated by the same group that ran the waterfront market all those years, the Coopérative des horticulteurs de Québec, and has space for 100 seasonal vendors, 20 permanent tenants, and 30 boutiques, along with terraces and a playground. Look for locally produced packaged goods such as foie gras, bee products, and wine. A free shuttle bus runs from Place d'Armes in front of Château Frontenac hourly from June to October.

In the city, gourmands should make a quick stop at **Épicerie J.A. Moisan** (695 rue St-Jean; www.jamoisan.com; ☎ 418/522-0685), said to be the oldest grocery store in North America. It's packed literally to the rafters with pâtés, terrines, jams, maple syrup treats, and more, and has a good selection of deli foods and other picnic options. It's a 10-minute walk from the gates of Upper Town.

Restaurant Aux Anciens Canadiens.

of beer or wine, offers a cost-conscious option. Consider the Québec meat pie, and the region's favorite dessert, maple syrup pie, to finish. *34 rue St-Louis. www.aux ancienscanadiens.qc.ca.* ☎ *418/692-1627. Entrees C$33–C$89; afternoon 3-course table d'hôte from C$23. Lunch and dinner daily.*

★★ **Don** *VEGAN* New in 2019, Don turns the Québec experience upside down: It's vegan in a land of meat, and a little punkish in contrast to its buttoned-up neighbors. Its inaugural menu included mushroom risotto, bibimbap, and peanut ice cream, all with vegan substitutes for the dairy ingredients. A corner location on a pedestrian-only street in the Old Port provides an ample outside terrace. *97 rue Sault-au-Matelot. www.facebook.com/don. vegan.* ☎ *418/800-9663. Entrees C$18–C$24. Lunch and dinner daily.*

★★ kids **Le Café du Monde** *TRADITIONAL FRENCH* Large (it seats 135) and jovial, this Parisian-style restaurant overlooks the waterside promenade along the St. Lawrence River and has a lovely terrace. It's a fun choice for a cheery meal of French classics—*steak frites* or salmon gravlax with blinis, with

crème brûlée to close. *84 rue Dalhousie. www.lecafedumonde.com.* ☎ *418/692-4455. Entrees C$17–C$32. Lunch and dinner daily, breakfast Sat–Sun and holidays.*

★★ **Le Clocher Penché Bistrot** *BISTRO* The trendy St-Roch neighborhood, about a 20-minute walk from Québec City's Old Port, has its own ecosystem of bistros, bars, and shops. It's less clogged with tourists and a good option for seeing another part of the city. Clocher Penché, on the main drag of rue St-Joseph, exudes a laid-back European class and a nearly reverent approach to simple, seasonal

Classic bistro dish at Le Clocher Penché Bistrot, a mainstay of Québec City's St-Roch neighborhood.

food. *203 rue St-Joseph est. www.
clocherpenche.ca.* ☎ *418/640-0597.
Entrees C$23–C$27. Lunch Tues–Fri;
brunch Sat–Sun; dinner Tues–Sat.*

★★ **L'Echaudé** *BISTRO* In a
city that specializes in the white-
tablecloth-but-still-relaxed bistro
tradition, L'Echaudé is a star. The
classic dishes are all in place, from
confit de canard to a rich fish stew
featuring lobster and saffron. Service is friendly, and the tone is
casual sophistication. For drinks
and small bites, consider its sister
wine bar, **Echo Buvette,** next door
at #67, which opened in 2019. Both
venues have terraces on the romantic, pedestrian-only street. *73 rue
Sault-au-Matelot. www.echaude.com.*
☎ *418/692-1299. Entrees C$25–
C$42. Lunch and dinner daily.*

★★★ **Laurie Raphaël** *CONTEM-
PORARY QUEBECOIS* Lots of
excellent meals are not expensive
or sophisticated. But some, like this
one, are. Laurie Raphaël was a pioneer in bringing innovative dining to
a Québec City restaurant scene that
was long dominated by the classic
French tradition. Wife-husband
team Suzanne Gagnon and chef
Daniel Vézina launched their

ultra-gourmet operation in 1991,
and the restaurant continues to
push new boundaries, now that it's
being co-managed by the founders'
children, Laurie-Alex and Raphaël.
Dinners are by tasting menu only,
7-or 11-course, and include fanciful
elements such as truffle quail ballo-
tine and maple-lacquered pork
flank, with flavor combinations such
as black garlic whipped cream and
St.Lawrence River seaweed with
strawberries and basil. Needless to
say, dinner here can be the extraor-
dinary culinary experience to add
to a Québec City vacation. *117 rue
Dalhousie. www.laurieraphael.com.*
☎ *418/692-4555. Tasting menus
C$110 and C$155. Dinner Tues–Sat.*

★★★ **kids Paillard** *LIGHT FARE*
Paillard has a high-end fast-food
feel to it, but it's one of a kind, and
thoroughly Québec. It's perfect for
an affordable lunch or dinner that
doesn't take hours, or for a coffee
break with a formidable macaron or
croissant. There are also salads and
gelati. The central location means
that you may end up stopping in
more than once. *1097 rue St-Jean.
www.paillard.ca.* ☎ *418/692-1221.
Most items under C$10. Breakfast,
lunch, and dinner daily.*

*Inventive dishes, such as eggs with lobster and sautéed chanterelles, are a signature of
Laurie Raphaël.*

The Laurentians

WHERE TO STAY

Château Beauvallon **10**

Fairmont Mont-Tremblant **8**

Hôtel Mont-Tremblant **6**

WHERE TO DINE

La Diable Microbrasserie **9**

Ocafé **5**

sEb l'artisan culinaire **7**

1 St-Sauveur

2 Val David

3 Mont-Tremblant Pedestrian Village

4 Le Scandinave Spa

The Laurentian Mountains (also known as the Laurentides) provide year-round recreational opportunities. Winter skiing and snowboarding are the most popular, but in the warmer months the mountains thaw and open up an array of other options. The highest peak, Mont-Tremblant, is 968m (3,176 ft.) high and located 129km (80 miles) northwest of Montréal. In between, and closer to the city, the terrain resembles a rumpled quilt, its hills and hollows cupping a multitude of lakes. Come for a day or stay for a week. Note that as you head north, you're more likely to find venues whose proprietors and websites are French only. START: **Drive north out of Montréal on Autoroute 15. For an orientation to the region, stop at the information center, well marked from the highway, at exit 51. Tourisme Laurentides (☎ 800/561-6673; www.laurentides.com) shares a building with a McDonald's.**

Autumn in St-Sauveur.

❶ **St-Sauveur.** Only 60km (37 miles) north of Montréal, the village of St-Sauveur is flush with outlet malls and the carloads of shoppers they attract. A few blocks farther north, the older village square bustles with less-frenzied activity. Dining on everything from crepes to poutine to bison burgers are options at the many cafes along the main street, rue Principale. Restaurants include **Crêperie Bretonne,** 396 rue Principale (www.creperiesaint sauveur.com), for rustic, country fare; **Le Saint Sau Pub Gourmand,** 236 rue Principale (www.lesaintsau. com) for pub food and atmosphere; and **Bistro Orange & Pamplemousse,** 120 rue Principale (www. orangepamplemousse.com) for vegan choices. In summer, families will want to consider **Parc Aquatique du Sommet Saint-Sauveur** (www.sommets.com/en/water-park-saint-sauveur; ☎ 800/363-2426 or 450/227-4671). The gigantic waterpark includes a wave pool, rafting in simulated rapids, and tubing down tunnels. Day tickets are C$36 for ages 13 and up, C$29 ages 6 to 12, C$18 ages 3 to 5, and free for 2 and under. For 12 days in July and August, the exciting **Festival des Arts de St-Sauveur** (www.fass.ca;

Market in Val David.

☎ 450/227-0427) presents dance, jazz and classical performances. The schedule always includes a number of free events, such as tango lessons and swing dance nights. *www.valleesaintsauveur.com.*

❷ **Val David.** Residents boast that Val David is the birthplace of rock climbing in Eastern Canada, and experienced enthusiasts flock to nearby **Dufresne Regional Park** (www.parcregional.com) to explore its 500 rated routes (climbers must bring their own equipment). The village of about 5,200 is also an access point to the bike path P'Tit Train du Nord, built on a former railroad track. Unlike the heavily visited Mont-Tremblant, where cheesy souvenir stores are plentiful, this faintly bohemian enclave is home to a handful of stylish little stores that sell well-made, authentic crafts. If you're in the area in July or August, check out the village's huge ceramic arts festival, **1001 Pots** (www.1001pots.com; ☎ **819/322-6868**). Sculptors and ceramicists, along with painters, jewelers, pewter smiths, and other craftspeople display their work. *Tourist office at 2525 rue de l'Église. www.valdavid.com.* ☎ *888/322-7030.*

Biking on the Green Trail.

Biker's Paradise: The Route Verte

The Route Verte (Green Route) is a 5,300km (3,293-mile) bike network that crisscrosses the province, linking all regions and cities (www.routeverte.com). It's similar to the Rails-to-Trails program in the U.S. and cycling routes in Denmark and Great Britain, but more thorough. *National Geographic* declared it one of the 10 best bicycle routes in the world—and that's when the network was first inaugurated and had just 4,000km (2,485 miles) of paths.

The trail is free to ride on. The Route Verte website provides maps and information on hotels and campsites that are especially focused on serving bike travelers (properties hang a sign that says *Bienvenue Cyclistes!* when they are certified accommodations). The annual official tourist guide to the Laurentians, available in print and online at **www.laurentides.com,** always has a big section on biking.

An especially popular part of the route, the **P'tit Train du Nord** linear park (www.laurentides.com/en/linearpark), is built on a former railway track and passes through Val David and Mont-Tremblant. Cyclists can get food and bike repairs at renovated railway stations along the way and hop on for a day trip or a longer tour. **Autobus le Petit Train du Nord** (www.autobuslepetittrain dunord.com; ☎ 888/893-8356 or 450/569-5596) provides baggage transport and ride planning and has 2- to 5-night packages that include lodging, dinner, and breakfast.

Mont-Tremblant village offers a bustling town and fantastic ski slopes.

❸ Mont-Tremblant Pedestrian Village. The Mont-Tremblant area is a kind of Aspen meets Disneyland. The **Mont-Tremblant ski resort** (www.tremblant.ca) draws the biggest downhill crowds in the Laurentians and is repeatedly ranked as the top resort in eastern North America by *Ski Magazine* (see "Skiing in the Laurentians," below). The ever-expanding pedestrian village at the base is a prime destination in the province in all four seasons. The village has the prefabricated look of a theme park, in the Québécois architectural style of pitched roofs in bright colors. For a sweeping view, take the panoramic gondola from the bottom of the village to the top (C$20 for 13 and older; discounts for younger

Skiing in the Laurentians

Founded in 1939 by a Philadelphia millionaire named Joe Ryan, the Mont-Tremblant ski resort pioneered the development of trails on more than one side of a mountain and was the second resort in the world to install a chairlift. Today it maintains 102 downhill trails on 4 slopes, with a south-side vertical drop of 645m (2,116 ft.). Half the runs are classified as expert, a third are intermediate, and the rest beginner.

When the snow is deep, skiers here like to follow the sun around the mountain, making the run on slopes with an eastern exposure in the morning and western exposure in the afternoon. There are higher mountains elsewhere with steeper pitches, but something about Mont-Tremblant compels people to return time and again.

Cross-country skiers have good options, too. The large **Parc National du Mont-Tremblant** (www.sepaq.com/pq/mot), north of the ski mountain, maintains groomed tracks, visitor centers, and warming huts.

kids). Throughout the village there are dozens of restaurants, bars, and shops, and most are open year-round. Well-regarded cultural offerings take place here, too, including the **Festival International du Blues de Tremblant** (https://blues.tremblant.ca), which puts on dozens of shows for 10 days in July. *www.tourismemonttremblant.com.* ☎ 877/425-2434.

❹ **Le Scandinave Spa.** Spas are big business around here. Day spas offer massages and *esthétique* services such as facials; destination spas often involve overnight stays and healthy cuisine; and Nordic spas are built around a natural water source and include outdoor and indoor spaces. If you've never experienced a European-style Nordic spa before, try to set aside 3 or more hours for a visit to Le Scandinave Spa. This tranquil complex of small buildings tucked among evergreen trees on the Diable River shore is as chic as it is beautifully

rustic. Visitors have the run of the facility. Options include outdoor hot tubs designed to look like natural pools (one is set under a man-made waterfall); a Norwegian steam bath thick with eucalyptus scent; indoor relaxation areas with low-slung chairs; and the river itself, which the heartiest of folk dip into—even on frigid winter days (a heat lamp keeps a small square of river open when it's iced over). The idea is to move from hot to cold to hot, which supposedly purges toxins and invigorates your skin. Bathing suits are required, as is silence—this is a public space that works diligently to give your mind a place to settle down. Men and women share all spaces except the changing rooms. For extra fees, massages, robe rentals, and bistro foods are available. *4280 Montée Ryan, Mont-Tremblant. www.scandinave.com.* ☎ 888/537-2263 or 891/425-5524). *Admission C$60. Guests must be 18 or older. Open daily.*

The Laurentians: Where to Stay in Mont-Tremblant

The Fairmont's heated pools are a big draw after a day on the slopes.

★★ kids Château Beauvallon
Beauvallon is a premiere property in the region for families who want to stay near—but not directly on—the ski mountain. Every unit is a one- to four-bedroom suite with either a kitchenette or full kitchen, and a living room with gas fireplace. It has year-round indoor and outdoor pools and shuttles to the Tremblant pedestrian village and to Le Scandinave Spa (p 154). The operation positions itself as an affordable retreat for seasoned travelers and delivers with tidy elegance. *6385 Montée Ryan. www.chateaubeauvallon.com.* ☎ *888/681-6611 or 819/681-6611. 70 units. 1 bedroom suite C$179–C$325.*

★★ kids Fairmont Mont-Tremblant
Directly on the ski mountain, the Fairmont stands on a crest above the pedestrian village and offers ski-in, ski-out accessibility to the chairlifts, year-round outdoor and indoor pools, and an onsite spa with massage services. It's the big name-brand resort for families who want all the conveniences for their vacation. Room renovations were in the works in 2019, so ask for an updated one when you're booking. *3045 chemin de la Chapelle. www.fairmont.com/tremblant.* ☎ *800/257-7544 or 819/681-7000. 314 units. Doubles C$237–C$589.*

★ Hôtel Mont-Tremblant
Located in the old village of Mont-Tremblant 5km (3 miles) west of the ski mountain's pedestrian village, this modest hotel is popular with skiers who want to avoid the resort village's higher prices and cyclists who appreciate the location directly on the Route Verte bike trail and across the street from the public beach of Lac Mercier. Rates include breakfast. *1900 chemin du Village (Rte. 327). www.hotel-monttremblant.com.* ☎ *819/717-1410. 19 units. Doubles C$99–C$149.*

Ice skating is a popular winter sport in Mont-Tremblant.

The Laurentians: **Where to Dine in Mont-Tremblant**

★ **La Diable Microbrasserie**
PUB Set in a free-standing chalet in the pedestrian village at the base of the Mont Tremblant ski resort, this microbrewery offers craft beer and reliable basics such as burgers, sausage with homemade sauerkraut, and a veggie sauté. It does a big *après-ski* business. *117 chemin Kandahar (in the pedestrian village). www.microladiable.com.* ☎ *819/681-4546. Entrees C$14–C$29. Lunch and dinner daily.*

★ **Ocafé** *CAFE* The region around the ski mountain is peppered with villages and parks that share the same name, and this teeny diner is in what's called the old village of Mont Tremblant. It's about 15 minutes by car from the ski resort. It offers omelettes, breakfast bowls, pastries, and what many people say is the area's best coffee, along with healthy lunch options. Find it inside the Cybercycle bike shop. *1908 chemin du village, Mont Tremblant. www.ocafe vieuxtremblant.ca.* ☎ *819/808-7725. Most items under C$10. Breakfast, lunch, and (early) dinner daily.*

★★ **sEb l'artisan culinaire**
CONTEMPORARY QUEBECOIS With appetizer options such as

Seafood Soffocato at chef Sébastien Houle's sEb.

fried smelt from Gaspê, scallop carpaccio, and venison ragù, you know you're in for inventive eating. This is a place to splurge. The four- and seven-course tasting menus encourage guests to simply give themselves over to the capable hands of chef Sébastien Houle for the elegant evening. In summer, look for the seasonal tapas and cocktail terrace menu. *444 rue Saint-Georges, Mont Tremblant (St. Jovite). www.seblartisanculinaire. com.* ☎ *819/429-6991. Entrees C$34–C$57; tasting menus C$54 and C$85. Dinner daily.*

Winter Safety in Ski Country

Winter tires are required on all vehicles registered in Québec from December 15 to March 15. The rule doesn't apply to visitor automobiles, but it demonstrates how serious the snow and ice can be. Consider equipping your own car with snow tires before driving north. Road conditions and warnings are posted by the Québec government at www.quebec511.info.

Cantons-de-l'Est

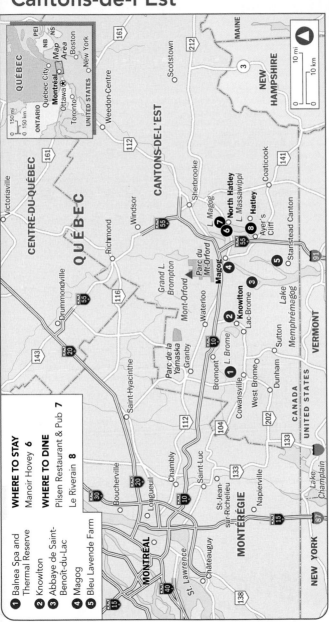

WHERE TO STAY
Manoir Hovey **6**

WHERE TO DINE
Pilsen Restaurant & Pub **7**
Le Riverain **8**

1 Balnea Spa and Thermal Reserve
2 Knowlton
3 Abbaye de Saint-Benoît-du-Lac
4 Magog
5 Bleu Lavende Farm

The countryside of Cantons-de-l'Est is largely pastoral, marked by small villages, a smattering of vineyards, and the 792m (2,598-ft.) peak of Mont-Orford, the centerpiece of a provincial park. Serene glacial lakes attract summer swimmers, boaters, and bicyclists who loop around them. In winter, skiers who don't head north to the Laurentians come this direction. It's still referred to by most Anglophones as the "Eastern Townships," and the southern edge of the region borders the U.S. states Vermont, New Hampshire, and Maine. START: Leave Montréal via the new Pont Champlain, the bridge that funnels into arrow-straight Autoroute 10, and head east toward Sherbrooke.

❶ ★★ Balnea Spa and Thermal Reserve. The Cantons conjure up images of cabin hideaways set among ponds and lakes. You can float on a lake, relax in a hot sauna, laze in a hamman steam room, stroll on a meditation path, or hike any of the 22k (13.5 miles) of marked trails. *319 chemin du Lac Gale, Bromont-sur-le-lac. www.balnea.ca. ☎ 866/734-2110 or 450/534-0604. Admission C$70. Guests must be 14 or older. Open daily.*

❷ Knowlton. For a serendipitous confluence of countryside, cafes, and antiquing, head to the town of Knowlton, at Brome Lake's southeast corner. Two main shopping streets (Lakeside and Knowlton) are thick with boutiques and antiques stores. **Novelist Louise Penny** lives here and has set her best-selling detective novels in a bucolic fictional town, Three Pines, based on Knowlton. The tourism bureau offers a map of sites in the region

that show up in the books, at www.easterntownships.org/tourist-routes/12/three-pines-inspirations-map-louise-penny. *www.eastern townships.org/towns-and-villages 46075/lac-brome-knowlton.*

❸ ★★ Abbaye de Saint-Benoît-du-Lac. Architecturally spectacular and deeply peaceful, this facility is an active monastery that's home to about 30 monks. They support themselves by making cheeses and products from their apple orchards. Visitors also can take a guided tour or attend a service in Gregorian chant. *1 rue Principale, Saint-Benoît-du-Lac. www. abbaye.ca. ☎ 819/843-4080. Guided tour C$12 adults, C$8 children 7–14, free for children 6 and under, C$30 family. Services are free to attend.*

❹ Magog. Confusingly, the town of Magog is not adjacent to Lac Magog. That lake is about 10km (6 miles) due east. Instead, the town is at the northernmost end of the long Lac

The monks at Abbaye de Saint-Benoît-du-Lac make and sell a variety of popular cheeses.

Cabanes à Sucre: Québec's Maple Sugar Shacks

Throughout Canada's history, maple syrup has been an economic and cultural boon for the Québec province. In March and April, maple trees around Montréal are tapped to harvest the sap, and *cabanes à sucre* (sugar shacks) open up in rural areas. Some just sell maple syrup and candies, while many others serve full meals and even stage entertainment. A particularly fun tradition is *tire sur la neige*, where hot maple syrup is poured onto a clean layer of snow. Guests pick up the semisoft confection before it hardens and enjoy what's known as "maple toffee." Sugar shacks in the Cantons-de-l'Est (Eastern Townships) are listed at the regional tourism website: www.easterntownships.org/tag/137sugar-shacks.

Memphrémagog. The cruise company **Escapades Memphrémagog** (www.escapadesmemphremagog. com; **888/422-8328** or 81/ 843-7000) offers tours. The town is one of the largest in the region, with 27,000 residents, lots of boutiques, and chic restaurants. *Tourist office at 2911 chemin Milletta, Magog, at the exit from Autoroute 10 onto 112. www.easterntownships.org/towns-and-villages/45075/magog.*

❺ ★★ **Bleu Lavende Farm.** It's hard to resist the allure of lavender, which is why this is one of the region's most popular destinations in July and August, when the fragrant plant blooms across the farm's rolling hills. Bleu Lavende sells products infused with *Lavandula*, including chocolate, sprays, and other goodies. *891 Narrow Rd. (Rte. 247), Stanstead. www.bleula-vande.ca. ☎ 888/876-5851. Admission C$10 late June to Sept and weekends in Oct; free the rest of the spring and fall. Closed in winter.*

Wine (& *Cidre de Glace*) Country

Canada is known more for its beers than its wines, but that hasn't stopped agriculturists from giving wine a shot. In Cantons-de-l'Est, vintners are concentrated around Dunham, about 103km (64 miles) southeast of Montréal, with several vineyards along Rte. 202. A stop for a tour makes for a pleasant afternoon. The **Route des Vins** (www. laroutedesvins.ca), offers suggestions for road trips and bike tours that travel among the 20 vintners. **Vignoble de l'Orpailleur** (1086 Rte. 202, Dunham; www.orpailleur.ca; ☎ **450/295-2763**) was the first commercial vineyard in Québec—it started its vines in 1982—and has guided tours daily year-round. Look for ice cider and ice wine, two regional products: They're made from fruit left on trees and vines after the first frost and are served ice-cold with cheese or dessert.

Cantons-de-l'Est: **Where to Stay**

Vineyards in Dunham, where local specialties include ice cider and ice wine.

The elegant Manoir Hovey is perfect for a weekend of pampering.

★★★ **Manoir Hovey** NORTH HATLEY   This manor, a member of the exclusive Relais & Châteaux luxury group, manages to maintain a magical balance: It's a little bit genteel estate for a private getaway, and a little bit grand resort for a weekend's pampering. Aristocratic touches include a carefully manicured English garden and a massive stone hearth (with crackling wood fires in winter) in a library lounge. Bedrooms are bright and airy, and amenities such as Frette towels are standard. Manoir Hovey's restaurant is consistently among the most esteemed in the region,

offering flourishes such as zucchini flower *velouté* and homemade birch tree syrup. Package deals combine experiences and meals in creative collections—consider the **Foresta Lumina** package, which includes entry to a nighttime enchanted forest experience inspired by Quebec's woodland myths and legends (read about it at www.forestalumina.com). *575 chemin Hovey. www.manoirhovey.com.* ☎ *800/661-2421 or 819/842-2421. 36 units. Doubles from C$410, which includes dinner, breakfast, and use of recreational facilities.*

Cantons-de-l'Est: **Where to Dine**

★★ **Pilsen Restaurant & Pub** NORTH HATLEY *INTERNATIONAL* Twenty minutes east of Magog and just 2.5km (1 mile) north of Manoir Hovey (p 160), Pilsen features three bucolic terraces that overlook a narrow river that feeds into the tippy-top of the formidable Lac Massawippi. The former horse-carriage manufacturing shop in the quiet town of North Hatley fills up quickly with patrons dining on warm days on mussels, onion soup, duck breast, ribs, burgers, and a signature house *boudin noir*. *55 rue Main. www. pilsen.ca.* ☎ *819/842-2971. Entrees C$18–C$39. Lunch and dinner daily.*

★★ **Le Riverain** AYER'S CLIFF *CONTEMPORARY QUÉBECOIS* Québec abounds with resort hotels that feature phenomenal food. **Le Hatley Restaurant of Manoir Hovey** at the top of Lac Massawippi in North Hatley is worth a trip even if you aren't a guest, and so, too, is Le Riverain, inside the esteemed Ripplecove hotel and spa, at the southern end of the same lake. Spectacular water views make this restaurant a special destination. *700 Ripplecove, Ayer's Cliff. www.ripple cove.com.* ☎ *800/668-4296 or 819/838-4296. Entrees C$38–C$52. Breakfast, lunch, and dinner daily.* ●

The **Savvy Traveler**

Before **You Go**

Government Tourist Offices

In Montréal: Québec's provincial tourism office runs a large **Infotouriste Centre** in the city center at 1255 rue Peel (www.quebecoriginal. com; ☎ 877/266-5687 or 514/873-2015). The city of Montréal maintains a terrific website at **www.mtl.org**.

The Best Times to Go

The summer months—late June through August—are when Montréal is at its busiest. You'll pay the most for a hotel room in this period, and it can be hot and humid, but the city is in full bloom. In May and early June it's easier to get accommodations and the weather is often more comfortable, although you'll miss out on the big festivals. September and October are less hectic and the perfect time for autumn hikes and seeing the region's beautiful fall foliage. Winter in Montréal is cold and snowy, but people still get out and play. Early spring and late fall, when the weather can get iffy and not much is happening, are quieter times in the city.

Festivals & Special Events

JANUARY. La Fête des Neiges (Snow Festival; www.fetedesneiges.com; ☎ 514/872-6120) is the city's premier winter festival and features outdoor events such as dog-sled runs, a human foosball court, and tobogganing. It's held four weekends in January and the beginning of February.

FEBRUARY. Festival Montréal en Lumière (Montréal High Lights Festival; www.montrealhighlights.com; ☎ 855/864-3737 or 514/288-9955) is a deep-winter food fest with culinary competitions and wine tastings, multimedia light shows, classical and pop concerts, and the "*Nuit*

blanche" all-night party where everyone dresses in white and heads to a free breakfast at dawn.

MAY. Montréal Museums Day (www.museesmontreal.org; ☎ 515/845-6873), usually on the last Sunday in May, is a day of free admission to most of the city's museums.

MAY–JUNE. Go Bike Montréal Festival (www.velo.qc.ca; ☎ 800/567-8356 or 514/521-8356) brings out tens of thousands of cyclists for races of varying degrees of length and difficulty over 8 days—in the Tour de l'Île de Montréal, Tour la Nuit, and Metropolitan Challenge. Some 100,000 spectators line the streets to watch.

JUNE. Les FrancoFolies de Montréal (www.francofolies.com; ☎ 855/372-6267 or 514/876-8989) is a music fest that features French-language pop, hip-hop, electronic, world beat, and *chanson*. It's based at the Quartier des Spectacles downtown, with shows both outdoors on the plaza and inside the many theater halls in the area.

JUNE–JULY. Hordes of sightseers and music fans make the **Festival International de Jazz de Montréal** (www.montrealjazzfest.com; ☎ 855/299-3378 or 514/871-1881) one of the most exciting and acclaimed music festivals in the world.

JULY. For eight evenings, **L'International des Feux Loto-Québec** (International Fireworks Competition; www.laronde.com; ☎ 514/397-2000) lights up the skies with a truly spectacular fireworks shows. (*Insider tip*: The Jacques Cartier bridge closes to traffic during the fireworks and offers an unblocked, up-close view.) Also in July, **Festival Juste pour Rire** (Just for Laughs festival;

Previous page: Ice skating and sledding are favorite winter pastimes in Montréal.

MONTREAL'S AVERAGE MONTHLY TEMPERATURES (°F/°C)

	JAN	FEB	MAR	APR	MAY	JUNE
High (°F)	21	24	35	51	65	73
(°C)	−6	−4	1	10	18	22
Low (°F)	7	10	21	35	47	56
(°C)	−13	−12	−6	1	8	13

	JULY	AUG	SEPT	OCT	NOV	DEC
High (°F)	79	76	66	54	41	27
(°C)	26	24	18	12	5	−2
Low (°F)	61	59	50	39	29	13
(°C)	16	15	10	3	−1	−10

www.hahaha.com; ☎ 888/244-3155 or 514/845-2322) brings improvisational comedy by big and lesser-known names to town. The **Montréal Complètement Cirque** (montrealcirquefest.com; ☎ 888/376-8648 or 514/376-8648) is a festival of circus arts, founded in 2010 in part by the Cirque du Soleil, that take place at the TOHU center in the north of the city and throughout Quartier des Spectacles downtown.

SEPTEMBER. Early fall is the perfect time to view the changing foliage in the city's parks and the surrounding region, especially the northern Laurentian Mountains (p 150).

DECEMBER. Celebrating the holidays *a la française* is a particular treat in Vieux-Montréal, where the streets are nearly always banked with snow and the ancient buildings sport wreaths, decorated fir trees, and glittery white lights.

The Weather

Montréal is a city of weather extremes, with two main seasons: a hot summer and a bitterly cold winter. About 3 weeks each of pleasant spring and crisp fall take place in between.

Québécois who live through half-year-long winters know how to dress for the cold. Layers are essential, and practicality trumps fashion.

A dark wool or down coat can serve both gods, but sporty ski clothes also work throughout the province. Pack a hat, gloves, scarf, thermal socks, and waterproof boots with traction in the cold months. Long underwear is probably only needed for outdoor activities. A second pair of shoes, if the primary ones get soaked, can save a vacation.

Weather forecasts from the Canadian government are at **weather.gc.ca**.

Useful Websites

- **www.mtl.org**: The slick official site of the city is info-packed with updated details about events, restaurants, and hotel deals.

- **www.lavitrine.com**: La Vitrine sells last-minute bargain tickets as well as full-price tickets for Montréal's cultural events. It's accessible both online and at the Place des Arts, at 2 rue Ste-Catherine est (☎ 866/924-5538 or 514/285-4545).

- **www.cultmtl.com**: Cult Montréal has English previews of music, nightlife, and arts events.

- **www.montrealgazette.com**: The city's English-language newspaper, the Gazette is heavy on tabloid-style reporting but still a useful source for restaurant and cultural happenings.

- **www.stm.info**: The website for Montréal's public transportation system has detailed route maps of bus and Métro lines, information on service interruptions, and a useful trip planner.

Car Rentals

If you're arriving by train or plane, you won't need a car unless you're taking day trips outside the city.

All the major car-rental companies are represented in Montréal. There are rental agencies downtown as well as at Montréal-Trudeau airport. The best deals are usually found online at rental-car-company websites, which are listed at the end of this chapter.

Québec province mandates that residents have radial snow tires on their cars in winter, from mid-December until March 15. Rental-car agencies are required to provide snow tires on car rentals during that period, and many charge an extra, nonnegotiable fee.

The minimum driving age is 16 in Québec, but some car-rental companies will not rent to people under 25. Others charge higher rates for drivers under the age of 21.

Mobile Phones

Cellphone service is good in Québec cities and sometimes spotty outside city borders. Visitors from the U.S. should be able to get roaming service or a short-term international data plan to use their cellphones in Canada. Europeans and most Australians are on the GSM (Global System for Mobile Communications) network with removable plastic SIM cards. Call your wireless provider for information about traveling.

Many people now make cross-border calls over the Web on services such as **Skype** (www.skype.com) or through social media such as **Facebook** (www.facebook.com) or **WhatsApp** (www.whatsapp.com). These services can be used from computers or apps on a smartphone.

Getting **There**

By Plane

Montréal's main airport is **Aéroport International Pierre-Elliot-Trudeau de Montréal (YUL)** (www.admtl.com; ☎ 800/465-1213 or 514/633-3333), known better as Montréal-Trudeau airport. It's 21km (13 miles) southwest of downtown Montréal.

The airport is well served by the city's **Express Bus 747** (www.stm.info; ☎ 514/786-4636), which travels between the airport and downtown. There are two route options: one makes 11 designated stops, mostly along boulevard René-Lévesque, and another makes just one stop, at Lionel-Groulx. Check as you get on to make sure you're on the right route. The bus operates 24 hours a day, 7 days a week. A

trip takes 45 to 70 minutes, depending on traffic, and buses leave every 20 to 30 minutes. One-way fares are C$10 for adults. They are sold at the airport from machines at the international arrivals level (good for 24 hours on all subways and buses) at Métro stations and the Stationnement de Montréal street parking pay stations (for use within 2 hrs.). You can also pay with cash on the bus (coins only, exact change).

A taxi trip to downtown Montréal costs a flat fare of C$41 plus tip (C$4–C$6). Call ☎ 514/633-3333 for more information.

By Car

Many visitors from the mid-Atlantic and New England regions of the United States and eastern sections of Canada drive to Montréal. All international drivers must carry a valid driver's license from their country of residence. A U.S. license is sufficient as long as you are a visitor and actually are a U.S. resident. A U.K. license is sufficient as well. If the driver's license is in a language other than French or English, an International Driver's Permit is required in conjunction with the country of residence driver's license.

The entire journey driving north to Montréal from the U.S. is on expressways. From New York City, all but the last 40 or so miles of the 603km (375-mile) journey are within New York State on I-87. I-87 links up with Canada's Autoroute 15 at the border, which goes straight to Montréal. From Boston, the trip is 518km (322 miles).

By Train

Montréal is a major terminus on Canada's **VIA Rail** network (www. viarail.ca; ☎ 888/842-7245 or 514/871-6000). Its station, **Gare Centrale** (895 rue de la Gauchetière ouest), is centrally located in a busy, safe part of downtown. The station is adjacent to the Métro subway stop **Bonaventure Station.** (The castlelike Gare Windsor is still on some city maps—it's the city's *former* train station.) VIA Rail trains are comfortable—all major routes have Wi-Fi, and some trains are equipped with dining cars and sleeping cars.

The U.S. train system, **Amtrak** (www.amtrak.com; ☎ 800/872-7245) has one train per day into Montréal from New York that makes intermediate stops. Called the *Adirondack*, it's very slow: 10 hours if all goes well, although delays aren't unusual. Its scenic route passes along the Hudson River's eastern shore and west of Lake Champlain.

The train ride between Montréal and Québec City takes about 3 hours.

By Bus

Montréal's central bus station, **Gare d'autocars de Montréal** (www.ga mtl.com; ☎ 514/842-2281), is at 1717 rue Berri. The terminal is connected to one of the city's major Métro stations, **Berri-UQAM Station.** Several Métro lines pass through the station. UQAM—pronounced "Oo-kahm"—stands for Université de Québec à Montréal, a public university that has a large urban campus here. **Taxis** usually line up outside the terminal building.

By Boat

Both Montréal and Québec City to the north are stops for cruise ships that travel along the Fleuve St-Laurent (St. Lawrence River). The Port of Montréal, where ships dock, is part of the lively Vieux-Port (Old Port) neighborhood.

Getting **Around**

By Foot, Wheelchair & Stroller

Montréal is a terrific city to experience outdoors. All the sites and neighborhoods listed in this book are compact enough to be experienced by foot. Travelers in wheelchairs or using strollers will find the city alternately accommodating and maddening. Many sidewalks have curb cuts for easy passage onto the streets, but many buildings and Métro stops are not accessible. In wintertime, sidewalks and roadways can be extremely icy.

Tap Your Own Pedal Power

Montréal is bike crazy, and it's got the goods to justify it. The city helps people indulge their passions by overseeing an ever-expanding network of about **645km (400 miles) of cycling paths** and year-round bike lanes. In warm months, car lanes in heavily biked areas are blocked off with concrete barriers, turning the passages into two-way lanes for bikers. Most Métro stations have large bike racks, and in some neighborhoods sections of the street where cars would normally park are fenced off for bike parking.

If you're serious about cycling, the nonprofit biking organization **Vélo Québec** (www.velo.qc.ca; ☎ 800/567-8356 or 514/521-8356; vélo means "bicycle" in French) has a wealth of information for cyclists and co-hosts a weeklong bike festival in late May each year (see p 160). Its main office, **La Maison des Cyclists** (1251 rue Rachel est), is located across the street from the pretty Parc La Fontaine and has a cafe, a boutique with books and bike gear, and staff to help arrange bike trips and tours.

By Public Transportation

For speed and economy, nothing beats Montréal's underground **Métro** system (www.stm.info; ☎ 514/786-4636). Stations are marked on the street by blue-and-white signs that show a circle enclosing a down-pointing arrow. The Métro is relatively clean (its first new cars in 40 years came into service in early 2016), and quiet trains whisk passengers through a decent network. It runs from about 5:30am to 12:30am Sunday through Friday, and until about 1am Sun morning.

Fares are set by the ride, not by distance. A single ride, on either the bus or Métro, costs C$3.50 (reduced fare of C$2.50 for ages 6–17 and 65 and older). Automatic vending machines take credit cards. You can purchase tickets for cash only from a booth attendant at a Métro station or at authorized retailers listed on the STM website. Tickets serve as proof of payment, so hold onto them for the duration of your trip. Transit police make periodic checks

at transfer points or upon exiting, and the fine for not having a ticket can run as high as C$500.

Single tickets can be purchased as a set of 10 tickets for C$29. If you plan to use the Métro more than twice a day, **1-day** or **3-day** passes are a good deal.

To pay, some tickets simply need to be tapped at the turnstile on the card reader. Others need to be slid through a slot in the turnstile and removed as it comes out. You can also show your pass to the booth attendant. A single paper ticket acts as its own transfer ticket; you have 2 hours from the time a ticket is first validated to transfer, and you insert the ticket into the machine of the next bus or Métro train.

Note: Métro accessibility is severely limited for wheelchairs and strollers. Just 14 Métro stations, and only along either the orange or green lines, have elevators. But even those are not always operating. Service updates can be found online. Parents with strollers often have to put strollers on escalators or have only a staircase as an entrance or exit option. Traveling by bus can be the easier option with a stroller.

Bus fares are the same as fares for Métro trains, and Métro tickets are good on buses, too. Exact change is required if you want to pay on the bus. Buses run throughout the city and give tourists the advantage of traveling aboveground, although they don't run as frequently or as swiftly as the Métro. All buses have front-door access ramps for wheelchairs and strollers.

By Bike
Montréal has an exceptionally good system of bike paths, and bicycling is as common for transportation as it is for recreation.

The self-service short-term bicycle rental program **BIXI** (www.bixi.com; ☎ 877/820-2453 or 514/789-2494) has become a defining presence of the city. A combination of the words *bicyclette* and *taxi*, BIXI allows users to pick up bikes from special BIXI stands throughout the city and drop them off at any other stand, for a small fee. Some 7,250 bikes are in operation and available at 600 stations in Montréal's central boroughs.

Visitors have three short-term options: a one-time use for C$2.95; a 24-hour access pass for C$5.25; or a 72-hour access pass for C$15. With the access passes, you can borrow bikes as many times as you want. Trips longer than 30 minutes incur additional charges. (Note that BIXI will place a security deposit of C$100 per bike on your credit card, which will stay there for a few days.)

If you'll be using a bike for a full day, it may be cheaper to rent from a shop (you'll also get a helmet and lock, which BIXI doesn't provide). One option is **Ça Roule/Montréal on**

Wheels (www.caroulemontreal.com; ☎ 877/866-0633 or 514/866-0633) at 27 rue de la Commune est, the waterfront road in Vieux-Port.

By Taxi / Ridesharing
Cabs come in a variety of colors and styles, so their principal distinguishing feature is the plastic sign on the roof. At night, the sign is illuminated when the cab is available. The initial charge is C$3.45. Each additional kilometer (½ mile) adds C$1.70, and each minute of waiting adds C63¢. A short ride downtown usually costs about C$8. Tip 10% to 20%. Not all drivers accept credit cards.

Members of hotel and restaurant staffs can call cabs. Taxis also line up outside most large hotels or can be hailed on the street.

After years of heated debate, local government has approved pilot use of ridesharing services **Uber** (www.uber.com/cities/montreal) and the homegrown alternative **Eva** (www.eva.coop) through 2019.

By Car
Montréal is an easy city to navigate by car, although traffic during morning and late-afternoon rush hour can be horrendous. All familiar rules apply, though turning right on red in the city is prohibited.

Traditional parking meters are set well back from the curb so they won't be buried by plowed snow in winter. Metered parking costs C$3.25 per hour. If there are no parking meters in sight, look for computerized Pay 'N Go stations. They're black metal kiosks about 1.8m (6 ft.) tall with a white "P" in a blue circle. Press the "English" button, enter the letter from the space where you are parked, then pay with cash or a credit card, following the on-screen instructions.

Fast **Facts**

AREA CODES Montréal area codes are **514** and **438.** Outside of Montréal, the area codes are **450, 579, 819,** and **873.** You always need to dial the three-digit area code in addition to the seven-digit number. Numbers that begin with **800, 844, 855, 866, 877,** or **888** are free to call from both Canada and the U.S.

ATMS/BANKS ATMs (*guichet automatique*) and banks are easy to find in all parts of the city. Note that some Canadian ATMs may require a four-digit pin. If your card has a longer pin, it might be declined.

AUTOMOBILE ORGANIZATIONS
Members of the American Automobile Association (AAA) are covered by the Canadian Automobile Association (CAA; www.caaquebec.com) while traveling in Canada. Bring your membership card and proof of insurance. The 24-hour hotline for emergency road service is
☎ **800/222-4357** or download the mobile phone app. The AAA card will also provide discounts at a wide variety of hotels and restaurants.

BANKS Banks are generally open from 8 or 9am to 4pm Monday to Friday. Most major Canadian banks have branches on either rue Sherbrooke or rue Ste-Catherine.

BIKE RENTALS See p 165 for details on the self-service bicycle rental program **BIXI** (www.bixi.com) and for other rental options.

BUSINESS HOURS Most stores in the province are open from 9 or 10am until 5 or 6pm daily, with longer evening hours on Thursday and Friday. That said, the city is in the middle of an experiment (running through 2020) that allows stores in much of the city to remain open 24/7. Most stores were only expected to take advantage of extended hours during major festival events.

CONSULATES & EMBASSIES Embassies are located in Ottawa, Canada's capital. Use the **U.S. Embassy** information line (☎ 613/688-5335 or 613/238-5335) for after-hours emergencies. The U.S. consulate in Montréal is at 315 Place d'Youville, Ste. 500 (☎ 514/398-9695) but visitors must first check in at 1155 Rue St-Alexandre; nonemergency American citizen services are provided here by appointment only. The **U.K. consulate** for the province is in Montréal at 2000 McGill College Ave., Ste. 1940 (☎ **514/ 866-5863**). For contact information for other embassies and consulates, search for "foreign representatives in Canada" at www.international.gc.ca.

CURRENCY EXCHANGE Commercial exchange bureaus and hotels often have the highest transaction fees. The best rates will come from withdrawing money at an ATM. There are banks and currency exchange booths all over the city, at larger train stations, and in hotels.

CUSTOMS International visitors can expect at least a probing question or two at the border or airport. Normal baggage and personal possessions should be no problem, but plants, animals, fireworks, and weapons are among the items that may be prohibited or require additional documents before they're allowed in. For specific information about Canadian rules, check with the **Canada Border Services Agency** (www.cbsa-asfc.gc.ca; ☎ 506/636-5064 from outside the country or 800/461-9999 within Canada).

Tobacco and alcoholic beverages face strict import restrictions: Individuals 18 years or older are allowed to bring in 200 cigarettes, 50 cigars, or 200 grams of tobacco; and only one of the following amounts of alcohol: 1.14 liters of liquor, 1.5 liters of wine, or 8.5 liters of beer (24 12-ounce cans or bottles). Additional amounts face hefty taxes. Visitors can temporarily bring recreational vehicles, such as snowmobiles, boats, and trailers, for personal use; however, they may be subject to inspection to prevent spread of invasive species.

If you're traveling with expensive items, such as laptops or musical equipment, consider registering them before you leave your country to avoid challenges at the border on your return.

For information on what you're allowed to bring home, contact one of the following agencies:

U.S. Citizens: U.S. Customs & Border Protection (CBP), 1300 Pennsylvania Ave., NW, Washington, DC 20229 (www.cbp.gov; ☎ 877/227-5511).

U.K. Citizens: UK Border Force and HM Revenue & Customs (www.gov. uk or ☎ 0300/200-3700).

Australian Citizens: Australian Border Force (www.abf.gov.au; ☎ 131-881 or 612/6196-0196 from outside Australia).

New Zealand Citizens: New Zealand Customs Service (www. customs.govt.nz; ☎ 0800/428-786 or 649/927-8036 from outside New Zealand).

DINING Most restaurants have menus posted outside, making it easy to do comparison shopping. Many are open all day, while some shut down between lunch and dinner. Most restaurants serve until at least 9:30pm.

To dine for less, consider **table d'hôte meals.** Many restaurants offer these fixed-price meals, often two to four courses plus a beverage, for about the price of an *à la carte* main course.

It's wise to make a reservation if you wish to dine at one of the city's top restaurants, especially on a Friday or Saturday evening. A hotel concierge can make the reservation, though nearly all restaurant hosts will switch immediately to English when they sense that a caller doesn't speak French. Except in a handful of luxury restaurants, there are no dress codes. But Montréalers are a fashionable lot and manage to look smart even in casual clothes.

DOCTORS See "Hospitals," below.

DRINKING LAWS The legal drinking age in the province is 18. All hard liquor and spirits in Québec are sold through official government stores operated by the Québec Société des Alcools (look for maroon signs with the acronym SAQ). Wine and beer are available in grocery stores and convenience stores, called *dépanneurs*. Bars can pour drinks as late as 3am, but often stay open later. Don't drive after drinking: Penalties for drunk driving in Canada are heavy.

DRUGSTORES A pharmacy is called a *pharmacie*; a drugstore is a *droguerie*. A large chain in Montréal is **Pharmaprix** (www. pharmaprix.ca).

ELECTRICITY Like the U.S., Canada uses 110 to 120 volts AC (60 cycles), compared to the 220 to 240 volts AC (50 cycles) used in most of Europe, Australia, and New Zealand. If your small appliances use 220 to 240 volts, you'll need a 110-volt transformer and a plug adapter with two flat parallel pins to operate them in Canada. They can be difficult to find in Canada, so bring one with you.

EMERGENCIES Dial ☎ 911 for police, firefighters, or an ambulance.

EVENT LISTINGS La Vitrine (www.lavitrine.com) is a ticket office for Montréal cultural events. It's accessible online and in person at the Place des Arts (see p 161).

FAMILY TRAVEL Montréal offers an abundance of family-oriented activities. Many are outdoors, even in winter. Watersports, river cruises, fort climbing, and fireworks displays are among summer's many attractions, with dog sledding and skiing top choices in snowy months. For accommodations, restaurants, and attractions that are particularly kid-friendly, look for the "Kids" icon throughout this guide. Also see "Kid-Centric Montréal" on p 42.

GASOLINE (PETROL) Gasoline in Canada is sold by the liter; 3.78 liters equals 1 gallon. In 2019, the price of a liter in Montréal was approximately C$1.19, the equivalent of about US$3.39 per gallon (on average about US$.67 more per gallon at the time of calculation).

HEALTH Canada has a state-run health system, and Québec hospitals are modern and decently equipped, with well-trained staffs. You are unlikely to get sick from Canada's food or water.

Familiar over-the-counter medicines are widely available in Canada. If there is a possibility that you will run out of prescribed medicines during your visit, take along a prescription from your doctor. Bring medications in their original containers with pharmacy labels—otherwise, they may not make it through airport security. If you're entering Canada with syringes used for medical reasons, bring a medical certificate that shows they are for medical use and be sure to declare them to Canadian Customs officials.

HOLIDAYS Canada's important public holidays are New Year's Day (Jan 1); Good Friday and Easter Monday (Mar or Apr); Victoria Day (the Mon preceding May 25); St-Jean-Baptiste Day, Québec's "national" day (June 24); Canada Day (July 1); Labor Day (first Mon in Sept); Canadian Thanksgiving Day (second Mon in Oct); and Christmas (Dec 25).

HOSPITALS Hospitals with emergency rooms include **Hôpital Général de Montréal** (1650 rue Cedar; ☎ 514/934-1934) and **McGill University Health Centre** (1001 Decarie bd.; ☎ **514/934-1934**), which includes a children's hospital. In case of emergency, dial ☎ **911.**

INSURANCE Check your existing insurance policies before you buy travel insurance to cover trip cancellation, lost luggage, medical expenses, or car rental insurance. You're likely to have partial or complete coverage. If you need some, ask your travel agent about a comprehensive package. The cost of travel insurance varies widely, depending on the cost and length of your trip, your age and overall health, and the type of trip you're taking. Insurance for extreme sports or adventure travel, for example, will cost more than coverage for a cruise. Some insurers provide packages for specialty vacations, such as skiing or backpacking. More dangerous activities may be excluded from basic policies.

Specific recommendations are at www.frommers.com/planning.

INTERNET ACCESS Nearly all hotels, as well as most cafes, offer Wi-Fi, and generally for free. Some hotels maintain business centers with computers for use by guests. Many public spaces now have free Wi-Fi.

LANGUAGE Canada is officially bilingual, but the Québec province has laws that make French mandatory in signage. About 78% of Québec's population has French as its first language. Still, most

Francophones (French speakers) speak at least some English. Hotel desk staff, sales clerks, and telephone operators nearly always greet people initially in French, but usually switch to English quickly if necessary. Outside of Montréal, visitors are more likely to encounter residents who don't speak English.

LGBTQ TRAVELERS The province of Québec is a destination for international LGBTQ travelers. Gay life here is open and accepted (gay marriage is legal throughout the province), and gay travelers are heavily marketed to. Travelers will often find the rainbow flag displayed on the doors and websites of hotels and restaurants.

Many LGBTQ travelers visit the Gay Village (also known simply as "the Village"), a neighborhood east of downtown located primarily along rue Ste-Catherine est between rue St-Hubert and rue Papineau. The Village is busy year-round, but it especially picks up during **Montréal Pride** (www.fiertemtl.com) in August and the **Black & Blue Festival** (www.bbcm.org) in October, which is one of the world's largest circuit parties. **"Fugues"** magazine (www.fugues.com) lists events and gay-friendly lodgings, clubs, and other resources. The **Montréal Gay Village** website (www.montrealgay village.com) lists LGBTQ-friendly businesses.

LEGAL AID If you are arrested, your country's embassy or consulate can provide the names of attorneys who speak English. See "Consulates & Embassies," above.

MAIL & POSTAGE **Canada Post** (www.canadapost.ca; ☎ 866/607-6301) has several locations central to tourists, including at 157 rue St-Antoine ouest in Vieux-Montréal and 800 René-Lévesque ouest in downtown. A letter or postcard to the U.S. costs C$1.46. A letter or postcard to anywhere else outside of Canada

costs C$3.04. A letter to a Canadian address costs C$1.20. **FedEx** (www.fedex.com; ☎ 800/463-3339) also offers service from Canada.

MEDICAL REQUIREMENTS Unless you're arriving from an area known to be suffering from an epidemic, inoculations or vaccinations are not required for entry into Canada. As of 2019, measles precautions are advised especially for those 12 months and younger.

MONEY Canadian money comes in graduated denominations of dollars and cents. Bills have security strips and bold colors, and start at C$5 and go up. Coins include one-dollar and two-dollar denominations, nicknamed the Loonie (for a one-dollar coin) and the Toonie (for a two-dollar coin).

Credit or debit cards are accepted at almost all shops, restaurants, and hotels, but you should always keep some cash on hand for small venues that don't take plastic.

NEWSPAPERS & MAGAZINES *The Globe and Mail* (www.theglobe andmail.com) is Canada's national English-language paper. The *Montréal Gazette* (www.montreal gazette.com) is the city's primary English-language paper.

PARKING See "By Car" in the "Getting Around" section, earlier in this chapter.

PASSES Montréal Museums Pass (www.montrealmuseums.org; ☎ 514/845-6873) is an excellent option for ambitious sightseers. It grants entry to over 40 museums and attractions. The C$80 pass is good for 3 consecutive days plus unlimited access to public transportation (including the airport shuttle, bus no. 747); the C$75 pass is good for any 3 days within a 3- week period and does not include public transport. Look for the pass at museums or the tourist office at 1255 rue Peel (downtown). **Passeport MTL**

(www.passeportmtl.com; ☎ 844/ 685-3544) offers access to 28 attractions plus public transit. Choose from a 48-hour package for C$93 or a 72-hour package for C$113. Purchase online or at the tourist office at 1255 rue Peel.

PASSPORTS For country-specific passport information, contact the following agencies:

For Residents of Australia Contact the Australian **Passport Information Service**. Visit www.passports. gov.au or call ☎ 131-232.

For Residents of Ireland Contact the **Passport Office,** Knockmaun House, 42-47, Lower Mount St., Dublin 2 (www.dfa.ie; ☎ 353/ 1-671-1633).

For Residents of New Zealand Contact the **Passports Office,** Department of Internal Affairs, Archives New Zealand, 10 Mulgrave St., Wellington 6011 (www.passports. govt.nz; ☎ 0800/22-50-50 in New Zealand or 04/463-9360).

For Residents of the United Kingdom Passport rules may change due to Brexit. Look for updates online (www.gov.uk; or call passport adviceline ☎ 0300/222-0000 or 44-0-300-222-0000 outside the UK).

For Residents of the United States To find your regional passport office, check the **U.S. State Department** website (www.travel.state. gov) or call the **National Passport Information Center** (☎ 877/487-2778) for automated information.

Make a copy of your passport's information page and keep it separate from your passport in case of loss or theft. For emergency passport replacement, contact your country's embassy or consulate (see "Consulates & Embassies," p 166).

POLICE Dial ☎ 911 for police, firefighters, or an ambulance.

SAFETY Montréal is a safe city. Still, common sense insists that visitors stay alert and observe the usual urban precautions. It's best to stay out of parks at night and to take a taxi when returning from a late dinner or nightclub.

SENIOR TRAVELERS Mention that you're a senior when you make your travel reservations; many Québec hotels offer discounts for older travelers. As well, check for reduced admission for theaters, museums, and other attractions, which are often available for visitors 60-plus.

SMOKING Smoking is banned in almost all indoor spaces and on outdoor bars, patios, and some public spaces such as sports venues and children's play areas in parks. Most inns and hotels are now entirely smoke-free as well. Check before you book if you're looking for a room in which you can smoke.

The same rules apply to cannabis, which became legal in Canada in 2018.

SPECTATOR SPORTS Montréal hockey fans are a passionate bunch, and many travelers plan their trip around attending a home game. The city's beloved NHL **Montréal Canadiens** (www.nhl. com/canadiens; ☎ 877/668-8269 or 514/790-2525) have won 24 Stanley Cups, and devoted fans pack the Centre Bell to cheer on *Les Habitants*. See "Sport Montréal" p 64 for more.

TAXES Most goods and services in Canada are taxed 5% by the federal government (the GST/TPS) and 9.975% by the province of Québec (the TVQ). In Montréal, hotel bills include an additional 3.5% accommodations tax.

TAXIS/RIDESHARING See "By Taxi/ Ridesharing" in the "Getting Around" section, p 163.

TELEPHONES In Canada, dial ☎ 0 to reach an operator.

When making a local call within the province of Québec, you must dial the area code before the seven-digit number. Phone numbers that begin with 800, 844, 855, 866, 877, and 888 are **toll-free** within Canada and from the U.S. You need to dial 1 first.

To call Montréal from the U.S.: Dial 1, then the three-digit area code, then the seven-digit number.

To call Montréal from the U.K./ Ireland/Australia/New Zealand: Dial the international access code 00 (from Australia, 0011), then the Canadian country code 1, then the area code, and then the seven-digit number.

To call the U.S. from Montréal: Dial 1, then the three-digit area code and seven-digit number.

To call the U.K./Ireland/Australia/ New Zealand from Montréal: Dial 011, then the country code (U.K. 44, Ireland 353, Australia 61, New Zealand 64), then the number.

For directory information, dial ☎ 411.

TICKETS Call venues individually for specific ticket information for concerts and other entertainment. Tickets at large stadiums are often handled by outside ticket companies and have large fees associated with them. For last-minute as well as future-event tickets, visit **La Vitrine** online or in person (see p 161).

TIPPING In restaurants, bars, and nightclubs, tip waiters 15% to 20% of the check, tip checkroom attendants C$1 per garment, and tip valet-parking attendants C$5 per vehicle. In hotels, tip bellhops C$2 per bag and tip the chamber staff C$3 to C$10 per day. Tip taxi drivers 15% of the fare, and tip skycaps at airports C$2 per bag.

TOILETS You won't find public toilets on the streets in Montréal, but they are available in tourist offices, museums, railway and bus stations, and large shopping complexes. Restaurants and bars often reserve their restrooms for patrons.

TOURIST OFFICES The **Infotouriste Centre** (1255 rue Peel; ☎ 877/266-5687 or 514/873-2015; Métro: Peel) offers help booking bilingual accomodations, dining, and attractions in Montréal and the province of Québec. It's open daily. In Vieux-Montréal, a small **tourist information office** at 174 rue Notre-Dame est (Métro: Champ-de-Mars) is open daily May through October and with limited hours the rest of the year.

TOURS A guided tour can be an efficient way to begin exploring a new city. We list some of the city's prominent **bus and boat tours** on p 163. Tours by foot and by bike are offered by **Fitz & Follwell Co.** (www.fitzandfollwell.co; ☎ 514/418-0651) and **Spade & Palacio** (www.spadeandpalacio.com; ☎ 514/806-3263). **Guidatour** (www.guidatour.qc.ca/en/; ☎ 800/363-4021 and 514/844-4021) offers professional guides for private tours of the city.

TRAVELERS WITH WHEELCHAIRS, STROLLERS, OR RESTRICTED MOBILITY Québec regulations regarding wheelchair accessibility are similar to those in the U.S. and the rest of Canada, including requirements for curb cuts, entrance ramps, designated parking spaces, and specially equipped bathrooms. That said, while the more modern parts of the cities are fully wheelchair-accessible, access to the restaurants and inns housed in 18th- and 19th-century buildings, especially in Vieux-Montréal, is often difficult or impossible. Montréal's underground Métro system has only 14 stations, just on the orange and green lines, with elevators; the rest have escalators or just stairs.

The Québec government partners with the organization **Kéroul** (www.keroul.qc.ca; ☎ 514/252-3104) to publish an online and print travel guide, *Québec for All* (www.quebecforall.com), listing accessible accommodations and tourist sites throughout the region.

Montréal: **A Brief History**

1535 A community of Iroquois establishes the village of Hochelaga in what's now called Montréal, living in 50 homes and farming the land. French explorer Jacques Cartier visits the village that year. When the French return in 1603, the village is empty. Other First Nations people, including the Algonquins and Hurons, also inhabit the region.

1608 Samuel de Champlain arrives in Québec City motivated by the burgeoning fur trade, obsessed with finding a route to China, and determined to settle "New France." Three years later, he establishes a fur trading post in Montréal where the Pointe-à-Callière now stands.

1617 Parisian apothecary Louis Hérbert and Mary Rollet become the first colonists in Québec City to live off the produce of their own farm.

1642 Ville-Marie is founded by Paul de Chomedy de Maisonneuve, who installs a wood cross at the top of Mont-Royal.

1670 Hudson Bay Company is incorporated by British royal charter, and the competition around the fur trade in the Québec province heightens tension between France and England.

1759 After over a century of conflict about who would rule the New World, the British defeat the French in Québec City and enter Montréal.

1760 Montréal falls to the British.

1763 The king of France cedes all of Canada to the king of England in the Treaty of Paris, ending the Seven Years' War.

1775 U.S. general George Washington and the U.S. Continental Congress decide to extend their rebellion north and take the Québec province and the St. Lawrence River from the British, assuming that French-Canadians would happily join their cause. They predict wrongly. American Revolutionary forces occupy Montréal and Québec City after battles in 1775 and 1776 and then withdraw after a few months.

1821 English-speaking McGill University is established.

1824 The Lachine Canal opens after 3 years of construction, helping turn Montréal into a major port.

1833 Jacques Viger, born in Montréal in 1787, becomes the first mayor of Montréal.

1844 The Parliament of Canada is established in Montréal, though it later moves to Ottawa.

1852 The most devastating fire the city has experienced, known later as the Great Montréal Fire, leaves as many as 10,000 of the city's 57,000 inhabitants homeless and thousands without jobs in the middle of a hot, dry summer.

1857 The Gradual Civilization Act helps establish the Indian residential school system, a program of forced assimilation of First Nations children.

1859 Victoria Bridge is completed.

1924 A new, illuminated cross is unveiled on Mont-Royal on Christmas Day.

1933 Marché Atwater opens.

1939 The National Film Board is established.

1962 The city begins construction of the Métro system, which opens in 1966.

1962 With the construction of Place Ville-Marie, the Underground City is born.

1967 The Montréal World Exposition (Expo 67) is held and puts the city on glorious display to the world. The event is a major benchmark in the city's modern history.

1968 Parti Québécois is founded.

1968 Canadian soldiers take to the streets of Québéc City to quell unrest by separatists.

1969 Montréal Expos, a Major League Baseball team, is established. The franchise later is relocated to Washington, D.C., in 2004, where it becomes the Washington Nationals.

1976 Montréal hosts the athletically successful but financially disastrous Summer Olympics, sending the city into years of monstrous debt.

1977 Bill 101 passes, all but banning the use of English on public signage in the Québec province.

1979 The Festival International de Jazz de Montréal is founded.

1985 Bill C-31 gives First Nations women the right to marry white men and keep their Indian status, a right long held by First Nations men.

1992 Montréal celebrates its 350th birthday.

1998 A January ice storm cripples the region, cutting off power to millions, causing massive damage to trees and property, and leaving a thick layer of ice across streets, buildings, and roofs.

1999 The definition of "spouse" is changed in 39 laws and regulations, eliminating all legal distinctions between same-sex and heterosexual couples and recognizing the legal status of same-sex civil unions.

2001 The federal and provincial government and the Cree Nation sign La Paix des Braves (The Peace of the Braves) allowing Hydro-Québec to set up hydroelectric plants on Cree land in exchange for C$3.5 billion.

2002 Construction of Palais des Congrès (Convention Center) is completed, and is an unlikely design triumph with its transparent glass exterior walls a quilt of colored rectangles.

2005 Gay marriage becomes legal in all Canadian provinces and territories.

2006 UNESCO, the United Nations Educational, Scientific and Cultural Organization, designates Montréal a UNESCO City of Design for "its ability to inspire synergy between public and private players" and reputation for design innovation.

2008 A report on provincial angst over so-called reasonable accommodation of minority religious practices declares, "Québec is at a turning point . . . The identity inherited from the French-Canadian past is perfectly legitimate and it must survive, but it can no longer occupy alone the Québec identity space."

2014 Parti Québécois is trounced in its worst defeat since 1970. The Liberal party, strongly anti-secession, takes power.

2018 The Liberal party loses to the burgeoning, right-leaning Coalition Avenir Québec led by François Legault. Marijuana becomes legal across Canada.

The Politics of **Language & Identity**

Montréal and Québec City, the twin cities of the province of Québec, have a stronger European flavor than Canada's other municipalities. Most residents' first language is French, and a strong affiliation with France continues to be a central facet of the region's personality.

Many in Québec stayed committed to the French language and culture after British rule was imposed in 1759. Even with later waves of other immigrant populations pouring in over the cities, there was still a kind of bedrock loyalty held by many to the province's Gallic roots. Many Québécois continue to look across the Atlantic for inspiration in fashion, food, and the arts. Culturally and linguistically, it is that tenacious French connection that gives the province its special character.

In 1867, the British North America Act created the federation of the provinces of Québec, Ontario, Nova Scotia, and New Brunswick. It was a kind of independence for the region from Britain, but was unsettling for many French-Canadians, who wanted full autonomy. In 1883, *Je me souviens*—an ominous "I remember"—became the province's official motto.

In 1968, the Parti Québécois (PQ) was founded by René Lévesque, and the separatist movement began in earnest. One attempt to smooth ruffled Francophones (French speakers) was made in 1969, when federal legislation stipulated that all services across Canada were henceforth to be offered in both English and French, in effect declaring the nation bilingual.

That didn't assuage militant Québécois, however. They undertook to guarantee the primacy of French in their own province. To prevent dilution by newcomers, the children of immigrants were required to enroll in French-language schools, even if English or a third language was spoken in the home. This is still the case today. In 1977, Bill 101 passed, all but banning the use of English on public signage. The bill funded the establishment of enforcement units, a virtual language police who let no nit go unpicked. The resulting backlash provoked the flight of an estimated 400,000 Anglophones to other parts of Canada.

Support for the secessionist cause burgeoned again in Québec in the early 1990s, fueled by an election that firmly placed the PQ back in control of the provincial government. A referendum held in 1995 narrowly defeated succession from the Canadian union, but the vote settled nothing. The issue continued to divide families and dominate political discourse.

In 2014, Parti Québécois lost power, in part due to its proposed "charter of values," which would have restricted headscarves worn by Muslim public employees, among other provisions, and in part for its continued advocacy for sovereignty. Even though the strongly anti-secession Liberal party took over, in 2017 the Québec legislature made national news for requiring shopkeepers to only greet customers in French.

Political change has continued: In 2018 the Liberals suffered an historic defeat by the right-leaning Coalition Avenir Québec, signaling the end of a half-century of two-party political rule. Soon after, CAQ passed a secularism law that makes it illegal for many public employees to wear religious symbols at work.

For all this back and forth, Montréal is still the most bilingual city in the world—and, due to its immigrants, Canada's most trilingual city as well. Most people are comfortable speaking French, English, and the language of their country of origin.

Two other important cultural phenomena have emerged over the past 20 years. The first is an institutional acceptance of homosexuality. By changing the definition of "spouse" in 39 laws and regulations in 1999, Québec's government eliminated all legal distinctions between same-sex and heterosexual couples and became Canada's first province to recognize the legal status of same-sex civil unions. Gay marriage became legal in all of Canada's provinces and territories in 2005. Montréal, in particular, has transformed into one of North America's most welcoming cities for gay people.

The second phenomenon is the change that immigrants have brought to the province's melting pot. Québec welcomed more than 50,000 permanent residents in 2018, and with them came dozens of different mother tongues. Together with more than 180,000 aboriginal people from 10 First Nations tribes who live in the province, immigrants help make the region as vibrant and alive as any on the continent.

Useful **Phrases & Menu Terms**

A word or two of even halting French can go a long way in encouraging a French speaker to help you out. After all, you're asking your hosts to meet you much more than halfway in communicating. At the very least, practice basic greetings and the introductory phrase, *Parlez-vous anglais?* (Do you speak English?).

Useful Words & Phrases

ENGLISH	FRENCH	PRONUNCIATION
Yes/No	Oui/Non	wee/noh
Okay	D'accord	dah-core
Please	S'il vous plaît	seel voo play
Thank you	Merci	mair-see
You're welcome	De rien	duh ree-ehn
Hello (during daylight)	Bonjour	bohn-jhoor
Hello (at night)	Bonsoir	bohn-swahr
Goodbye	Au revoir	o vwahr
What's your name?	Comment vous appellez-vous?	kuh-mahn voo za-pell-ay-voo?
My name is	Je m'appelle	jhuh ma-pell
How are you?	Comment allez-vous?	kuh-mahn tahl-ay-voo?
So-so	Comme ci, comme ça	kum-see, kum-sah
I'm sorry/Excuse me	Pardon	pahr-dohn
Do you speak English?	Parlez-vous anglais?	par-lay-voo zahn-glay?
I don't speak French	Je ne parle pas français	jhuh ne parl pah frahn-say
I don't understand	Je ne comprends pas	jhuh ne kohm-prahn pas

ENGLISH	FRENCH	PRONUNCIATION
Where is . . . ?	Où est . . . ?	ooh eh . . . ?
Why?	Pourquoi?	poor-kwah?
here/there	ici/là	ee-see/lah
left/right	à gauche/à droite	a goash/a drwaht
straight ahead	tout droit	too drwah
I want to get	Je voudrais	jhe voo-dray day-
off at . . .	descendre à . . .	son-drah ah . . .
airport	l'aéroport	lair-o-por
bridge	pont	pohn
bus station	la gare d'autobus	lah gar duh aw-toh-boos
bus stop	l'arrêt de bus	lah-ray duh boohss
cathedral	cathedral	ka-tay-dral
church	église	ay-gleez
hospital	l'hôpital	low-pee-tahl
museum	le musée	luh mew-zay
police	la police	lah po-lees
one-way ticket	aller simple	ah-lay sam-pluh
round-trip ticket	aller-retour	ah-lay re-toor
ticket	un billet	uh bee-yay
toilets	les toilettes	lay twa-lets

The Calendar

ENGLISH	FRENCH	PRONUNCIATION
Sunday	dimanche	dee-mahnsh
Monday	lundi	luhn-dee
Tuesday	mardi	mahr-dee
Wednesday	mercredi	mair-kruh-dee
Thursday	jeudi	jheu-dee
Friday	vendredi	vawn-druh-dee
Saturday	samedi	sahm-dee
yesterday	hier	ee-air
today	aujourd'hui	o-jhord-dwee
this morning/this	ce matin/cet après-midi	suh ma-tan/set ah-
afternoon	preh mee-dee	
tonight	ce soir	suh swahr
tomorrow	demain	de-man

Food, Menu & Restaurant Terms

ENGLISH	FRENCH	PRONUNCIATION
I would like	Je voudrais	jhe voo-dray
to eat	manger	mahn-jhay
Please give me	Donnez-moi, s'il	doe-nay-mwah, seel vous
		plaît voo play
a bottle of	une bouteille de	ewn boo-tay duh
a cup of	une tasse de	ewn tass duh
a glass of	un verre de	uh vair duh

ENGLISH	FRENCH	PRONUNCIATION
a cocktail	un apéritif	uh ah-pay-ree-teef
the check/bill	l'addition/la note	la-dee-see-ohn/la noat
a knife	un couteau	uh koo-toe
a napkin	une serviette	ewn sair-vee-et
a spoon	une cuillère	ewn kwee-air
a fork	une fourchette	ewn four-shet
fixed-price menu	table d'hôte	tab-lah dote
Is the tip/service included?	Est-ce que le service est compris?	ess-ke luh ser-vees eh com-pree?
Waiter!/Waitress!	Monsieur!/ Mademoiselle!	mun-syuh/mad-mwa-zel
wine list	une carte des vins	ewn cart day van
appetizer	une entrée	ewn en-tray
main course	un plat principal	uh plah pran-see-pahl
tip included	service compris	sehr-vees cohm-pree
tasting/chef's menu	menu dégustation	may-new day-gus-ta-see-on

Numbers

ENGLISH	FRENCH	PRONUNCIATION
0	zéro	zeh-roh
1	un	uhn
2	deux	duh
3	trois	twah
4	quatre	kah-truh
5	cinq	sank
6	six	seess
7	sept	set
8	huit	weet
9	neuf	nuhf
10	dix	deess
11	onze	ohnz
12	douze	dooz
13	treize	trehz
14	quatorze	kah-torz
15	quinze	kanz
16	seize	sez
17	dix-sept	deez-set
18	dix-huit	deez-weet
19	dix-neuf	deez-noof
20	vingt	vehn
30	trente	trahnt
40	quarante	kah-rahnt
50	cinquante	sang-kahnt
100	cent	sahn
1,000	mille	meel

Photo **Credits**

Shutterstock.com; p 4 top: © MTTQ, Vlan Communication; p 4 bottom: © Vincent JIANG / Shutterstock.com; p 5 top: © MONTRÉAL COMPLÈTEMENT CiRQUE, Tim Hussin; p 5 bottom: © Canadian Tourism Commission; p 6: Courtesy of Jardin Botanique/ Mathieu Rivard; p 7: © SV_Digital_Press / Shutterstock.com; p 9: © Maurizio De Mattei / Shutterstock.com; p 10 top: © A G Baxter / Shutterstock.com; p 10 bottom: © jiawangkun; p 11 top: © Susan Moss Photography; p 11 bottom: © meunierd / Shutterstock.com; p 12 top: © www.old.montreal.qc.ca, le photographe masqué; p 12 bottom: © meunierd / Shutterstock.com; p 13 top: © Adwo / Shutterstock.com; p 13 bottom: Courtesy of Pointe-à-Callière/ © MarcAntoineZoueki; p 15 left: © Eva Blue; p 15 right: © Phil Roeder; p 16 top: © Matthias Berthet; p 16 bottom: © meunierd / Shutterstock.com; p 17 left: © Pack-Shot; p 17 right: ©Patrick; p 18: © Benoit Daoust / Shutterstock.com; p 19 top: © Paul McKinnon / Shutterstock.com; p 19 bottom: Courtesy of Sir Winston Churchill Pub; p 22 top: © EQRoy / Shutterstock.com; p 22 bottom: © Tourisme Montréal, Mario Melillo; p 23: Courtesy of Jardin Botanique/ Martine Larose; p 24 top: © Espace pour la vie; p 24 bottom: © Hakat; p 25: © Jardin botanique de Montréal (Claude Lafond); p 27: © Colin Woods / Shutterstock.com; p 28: © Tourisme Montréal; p 29 left: © Place Ville Marie, Stéphan Poulin; p 29 right: © Alexi Hobbs; p 30: © Tourisme Montréal, Stéphan Poulin; p 33: © Tourisme Montréal, Pierre-Luc Dufour; p 34 top: Courtesy of Schwatrz Deli; p 34 bottom: © Matias Garabedian; p 35: © EQRoy / Shutterstock.com; p 38: © Alison Slattery; p 39 left: © Canadian Tourism Commission, Pierre St-Jacques; p 39 right: Konstantin Ryabitsev; p 40: © Andre Nantel / Shutterstock.com; p 41 left: © Sarah; p 41 right: © Tourisme Montréal; p 45: Courtesy of Montréal Science Centre/ Christian Blais; p 46: © La Ronde (Member of the Six Flags Family); p 47: © Atrium Le 1000; p 48: Courtesy of Raplapla; p 49: © Jardin botanique de Montréal (Michel Tremblay); p 52 top: © Canadian Tourism Commission; p 52 bottom: © Tourisme Montréal, Susan Moss; p 53: Courtesy of The Ritz-Carlton Montreal; p 54: © ideatrendz; p 56: © Tourisme Montréal, Stéphan Poulin; p 57: © Canadian Tourism Commission; p 60: Courtesy of Bily Kun; p 61 left: © Tourisme Montréal, Stéphan Poulin; p 61 right: © Alison Slattery; p 62: © Krista; p 67: © MTTQ / André Rider; p 69 top: Pointe-à-Callière/ Robert Baronet/ © SMQ; p 69 bottom: © Dennis Jarvis; p 71 top: © Château Ramezay – Historic Site and Museum of Montréal, Michel Pineault; p 71 bottom: © prosiaczeq / Shutterstock.com; p 72: © Jean-Pierre Dalbéra; p 73: © Philippe Du Berger; p 74: © dennizn / Shutterstock.com; p 75: © Andriy Blokhin / Shutterstock.com; p 77: © Catherine Zibo / Shutterstock.com; p 78: © Alice Gao/Commission Canadienne du Tourisme; p 79: Courtesy of Lemeac; p 81: © Tourisme Montréal; p 82 top: © La Compagnie du Cimetière du Mont-Royal, Michael Slobodian; p 82 bottom: © Tourisme Montréal, Stéphan Poulin; p 83 top: © Les amis de la montagne / S. Montigné, 2008; p 83 bottom: © Tourisme Montréal, Susan Moss; p 85: Courtesy of Patrice Patissier/ Kouign Amann; p 86: © Cagkan Sayin / Shutterstock.com; p 87: Courtesy of MBAM/ Photo: MMFA, Christine Guest; p 90: © Phil Roeder; p 92 top: Courtesy of Drawn & Quarterly; p 92 bottom: Courtesy of Raplapla; p 93: © Kiev.Victor / Shutterstock.com; p 94: Courtesy of Dubarry Furs; p 95 top: Courtesy of Harry Rosen; p 95 bottom: Courtesy of Jonathan Dorthe/ Atelier D; p 96 left: Courtesy of Grande Bibliothèque, Michel Legendre; p 96 right: Courtesy of Boutique STM; p 96 bottom: © meunierd / Shutterstock.com; p 97: Courtesy of Magpie Pizzeria/ ALEXANDRE DUCASSE; p 102: Courtesy of La Banquise/ Cyril PERROT BOTELLA; p 103 top: © Lou Stejskal; p 103 bottom: © orangemania; p 105 top: © Tourisme Montréal, Susan Moss; p 105 bottom: Courtesy of Graziella/ CarrieMacPherson; p 106: Courtesy of Magpie Pizzeria/ ALEXANDRE DUCASSE; p 107: Courtesy of Olive et Gourmando/ LAURE ILLIAN; p 108: © yawper; p 109: ©Festival International de Jazz de Montreal/ Frederique Menard Aubin; p 110: Courtesy of Dieu du Ciel/ Samuel Joubert; p 115 top: © Jardin Nelson; p 115 bottom: © Sébastien Roy; p 116 top: Courtesy of Méchant Boeuf Bar-Brasserie/ eliastouil; p 116 bottom: Courtesy of Pullman/ Bruno Braën; p 117: Courtesy of Club Unity; p 118 top: Courtesy of Montreal Jazz Festival/Benoit Rousseau; p 118 bottom: Courtesy of Upstairs Jazz Bar/ Alain Mercier; p 119: Courtesy of McGill Symphony Orchestra/ Tam Lan Truong; p 120: © Société des casinos du Québec; p 121: © Andrew Miller; p 124 top: Courtesy of Orchestre Metropolitain du Grand Montreal/ Pierre Dury; p 124 bottom: © Just For Laughs Festival; p 125: Courtesy of Comedy Nest; p 126 top: Courtesy of Montréal Science Centre/ Miguel_Legault; p 126 bottom: Courtesy of Centaur/ Vanessa Rigaux; p 127: Courtesy of Mount St Stephen Hotel/ Simon Veilleux; p 128: Courtesy of Auberge Bonaparte; p 131: Courtesy of Auberge du Vieux Port Hotel/Alexi Hobbs; p 132 top: Courtesy of HI Montreal Hostel; p 132 bottom: Courtesy of Hôtel Bonaventure Montréal; p 133 top: Courtesy of EPIK/ REVERSE PROJECT; p 133 bottom: Courtesy of Gault Montreal; p 134: Courtesy of Nelligan/ Alexi Hobbs; p 135: Courtesy of Hotel Place d'Armes; p 136 top: Courtesy of Le Saint-Sulpice; p 136 bottom: Courtesy of Square Phillips; p 137: © VBoudrias, p 140: © Rob Crandall / Shutterstock.com; p 141: Courtesy of The Fairmont; p 142 top: © Caporal David Robert; p 142 bottom: © Guillaume Cattiaux; p 143: © Andriy Blokhin / Shutterstock.com; p 144: Courtesy of Saint Antoine/ Guillaume D. Cyr; p 145 top: Courtesy of Groupe Germain Hôtels; p 145 bottom: Courtesy of Groupe Germain Hôtels; p 146: © Renaud Philippe; p 147: © Lou Stejskal; p 148 top: © _Serge_Robert_; p 148 bottom: © CATHERINE CÔTÉ; p 149: Courtesy of Laurie Raphael; p 151: © Richard Cavalleri; p 152 top: © Derek Hatfield; p 152 bottom: © Assoc. Touristique Region North Hatley; p 153: © Sean Murphy; p 155 top: Courtesy of Fairmont Tremblant; p 155 bottom: © Albert Pego / Shutterstock.com; p 156: Courtesy of sEb/ RENATA JUSZCZUK; p 158: © Sandra Cohen-Rose and Colin Rose; p 160 left: © Jean-François Renaud; p 160 right: Courtesy of Manoir Hovey; p 161: © Fitz and Follwell.